# PUBLIC SPACE
# AND DEMOCRACY

**Marcel Hénaff and Tracy B. Strong**

**Editors**

University of Minnesota Press
Minneapolis • London

The University of Minnesota Press gratefully acknowledges permission to
reprint the following articles. Chapter 2 originally appeared as "*Persona:
Reason and Representation in Hobbes's Political Philosophy,*" in *SubStance
80,* vol. 25, no. 2 (1996): 68–80; copyright 1996, reprinted by permission of
the University of Wisconsin Press. Chapter 3 originally appeared as "The
Representation of Power and the Power of Representation," in *SubStance 80,*
vol. 25, no. 2 (1996): 81–92; copyright 1996, reprinted by permission of the
University of Wisconsin Press.

Published by the University of Minnesota Press
111 Third Avenue South, Suite 290
Minneapolis, MN 55401-2520
http://www.upress.umn.edu

Library of Congress Cataloging-in-Publication Data

Public space and democracy / Marcel Hénaff and Tracy B. Strong, editors.
    p.   cm.
  ISBN 0-8166-3387-8 (alk. paper) — ISBN 0-8166-3388-6 (pbk. :
alk. paper)
    1. Democracy. 2 Public space.  I. Hénaff, Marcel. II. Strong, Tracy B.
    JC423 .P886 2001
    321.8'01—dc21

                           00-010763

Printed in the United States of America on acid-free paper

The University of Minnesota is an equal-opportunity educator and employer.

12  11  10  09  08  07  06  05  04  03  02  01      10  9  8  7  6  5  4  3  2  1

# PUBLIC SPACE
# AND DEMOCRACY

# Contents

# Acknowledgments

The essays in this volume have their origin in a conference organized by the editors at the University of California, San Diego, in early May 1996. For financial support for the conference, we should like to thank the Collège international de philosophie in Paris; the Cultural Services of the French Consulate in Los Angeles; the Dean of Social Science and the Dean of Arts and Humanities at the University of California, San Diego; the Vice Chancellor for Graduate Studies and Research at the University of California, San Diego; the Department of Political Science at the University of California, San Diego; and Dr. Marianne MacDonald.

In addition to those authors whose work is presented here, we should like to thank Professors Marianne MacDonald (Theater Department, University of California, San Diego), Waltern Donlan (Classics, University of California, Irvine), Cynthia Truant (History, University of California, San Diego), Albert Liu (Classics, Johns Hopkins), Malina Stefanovska (French Studies, University of California, Los Angeles), Harvey Goldman (Sociology, University of California, San Diego), Gerald Doppelt (Philosophy, University of California, San Diego), Ivans Evans (Sociology, University of California, San Diego), and Helene Keyssar (Communication, University of California, San Diego) for their participation in one of two roundtables that were held at the end of each day's conference sessions. In addition, the editors should like to thank Jean-Louis Morhange for organizational help.

# Introduction

# The Conditions of Public Space:
# Vision, Speech, and Theatricality

**Marcel Hénaff and Tracy B. Strong**

Res publica est res populi
**Cicero**

The common concern of the essays in this book is the nature and status of the space in which human beings encounter each other with the intention of determining how their lives in common shall be lived. Such a concern is perhaps the oldest of political questions. In Western thought it dates at least back to the second book of the *Odyssey*, where Telemachus, son of the long-absent Odysseus, calls the Achaians to assembly. It is clear that such an assembly is not a usual occurrence. The old Aigytios, mourning for the sons he lost at Troy, asks:

> Never has there been an assembly *(agora)* of us or any session
> Since great Odysseus went away in the hollow vessels.
> Now who has gathered us in this way? What need has befallen
> which of the younger men, or one of us who is older?
> Has he been hearing some message about the return of the army
> Which, having heard it first, he could now explain to us?
> Or has he some of the public matter *(agoreuei)* to set forth?[1]

Telemachus is handed the scepter that entitles him to speak and explains that his household is being scandalized and impoverished by the press of suitors for the hand of his mother, Penelope. There is, however, a tension in the situation. In classical Greece, the practice of guest-friendship required that bed and board hospitality be extended to all who came under one's roof, no matter what their status or intent.[2] Telemachus has called an assembly to deal with this matter; it is also clear that he is misusing it somewhat. On the one hand, the expectation is that such a space will be used for a public matter. In this case, however, the disruption of his household that leads Telemachus to call the assembly is a "private" matter. On the other hand, Telemachus claims that the persistence of the suitors is an infringement of the common practice of guest-friendship or, rather, a pushing of the practice to the point that it becomes destructive.

1

Next, it is significant that such an assembly or agora must be *called*. Three qualities stand out. The first is that the place of assembly has not a fixed or institutionalized character. In this it is not like the market-place in later Athens, which had a permanent existence.[3] Second, in that it is brought into existence by someone calling for it, it is *created* by the actions of human beings. It is a kind of space that human beings make for and by themselves. Third, in order to speak, one must be given the scepter: in this group, for the moment, the speaker has the authority of the ruler with him. The clear implication is that speaking to others in this manner and in this place is something special.[4]

Finally, it is noteworthy that this assembly arrives at no solution. At the assembly the Ithacan warriors deliberate the merits of Telemachus's complaint, or rather, each taking up the scepter in turn, they speak their understanding of the matter, for there is little give and take. They have, however, no way of coming to a solution. Telemachus wants a public resolution to his problems and is unable to attain one. Here we already see a limited version of public space, which, while it has particular uses, on this occasion only marginally conforms to Telemachus's problems. This is not yet the agora in the sense of an ongoing space of the kind that Marcel Detienne describes in chapter 1 and that one will find in almost all Greek cities, and not only there.

What we do see in the *Odyssey* is an early argument about what qualities space must have in order to be "public." The essays that follow explore this general problem in a variety of contexts ranging from ancient Greece through the early modern period and down to the contemporary developments of the shopping mall and the Internet. To understand better what makes the use to which a space is put *public* use, we can contrast public space with three other kinds of space. To do this let us broaden our horizon beyond Greece to other times and societies.

Generally speaking, aside from being public, space may also be *private, sacred,* or *common.* The difference among them has to do with the kinds of criteria that must be met for someone to enter that space.

A space is *private* when a given individual or set of individuals are recognized by others as having the right to establish criteria that must be met for anyone else to enter it. Thus we speak of a private room, a private meeting, private parts. Private is to be understood as distinguished from public as much by virtue of ownership as by virtue of the standards that have to be met in order to enter. Such a space is *one's own* space: the Greek word for home, *oikos,* refers to the house from which the watchman gazes out to sea at the beginning of the *Agamemnon,* as well as to where the Furies say they live, under the world (in the *Eumenides*). The significant thing about the ownership and its attendant standards here is that they are under the control of an individual (possibly corporate).

To say that a place is under the control of an individual is to say that individual is recognized as having the right to establish criteria by which access is allowed or denied. It is important to note that there is nothing necessary about any such criteria. Telemachus wants to claim his household for himself, against the claims of others. Two thousand years later, John Locke will argue that the criteria that determined access to property were the same criteria as those that applied to the access to one's person. That an individual had a right to his or her life meant that person also had a right to what that life shaped. Famously, that right extended to the plums one had picked up and to the ore one had dug. Thirty years earlier, however, Thomas Hobbes had argued that the right to life, for the preservation of which one covenanted with others to establish a sovereign, entailed no such right to possessions. The limits of privacy were those of the physical body for Hobbes, not those consequent to the extension of agency.[5] But in both cases what is private is a possession of some being or beings and cannot be entered without permission.

*Sacred* space is different and similar. At the beginning of *Oedipus at Colonus,* Antigone and her blind father arrive at Colonus, near Athens. She says: "The towers that crown the city are still far away, but where we are is surely holy ground." The word for holy is *hieros,* a space of the gods. As Vincent Scully has argued, such places were "holy and expressive of specific gods . . . embodiments of their presence."[6] The point is not that this is land reserved to the gods: it is, literally, the presence of the god. Antigone knows that this is not human space, even though it was open to those who might come to it. Here is not a question of contestable criteria: such a space is neither made by human action nor can it be owned. It *is* the god. Much the same kind of argument can be seen in the claim of sanctuary in a church during the Christian Middle Ages in Europe. In medieval England, in addition to the churches, in which a general right of sanctuary was allowed, there were at least twenty-two other sites recognized as sanctuaries; those taking refuge in them were not subject to secular legal processes, for such spaces were not under human control.[7]

At the other extreme, a space may be *common* to human beings. Common space admits of no criteria; it is open to all in the same way. It is not owned or controlled. Indeed, the so-called "Tragedy of the Commons" resulted precisely from the attempt to enclose and thereby control access to common land. What makes it common is that all can go there to extract from it what is there. Thus the sea, pastures, forests are (or can be) common space. This is not a space to which one goes to speak with others. Such a space is a location for the manifestation of the quality that the *Antigone* chorus names *deinos* (wondrous, terrible) in humans. It is not, however, a *public* realm, and its boundaries are not per se contestable. What makes it deinos is that it can be *made* human. What is often missed in the appreciation of common space is that it has the quality of being given to humans. This is as true in the *Antigone* as it is in Locke. As opposed to sacred space, however, it does not belong to or manifest anyone. Furthermore, common space is not public space, for it is not a human construct.[8]

A kind of simple matrix of the spaces in which human beings can move thus suggests itself. Spaces may be human or divine; they may be a manifestation of the being that owns them, or not.

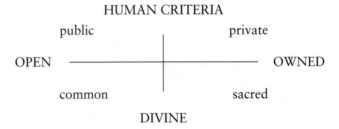

Public space, as the essays in this book show, is the space created by and for humans that is always contestable, precisely because whereas there are criteria that control admission to its purview, the right to enact and enforce those criteria is always in question. It is open to those who meet the criteria, but it is not owned in the sense of being controlled. Nor does it manifest the qualities of some being, in the way that for Locke, property was a manifestation of the agent or, for Greeks, the field around Colonus was of the god. The essays here reflect how public space is always a contestation over the legitimacy of what can be brought and what can be excluded from the life one chooses and is required to have in common with others. Different resolutions have been give to these contestations, resolutions as different as those of the Greeks, of the English seventeenth and the French eighteenth centuries, of Heidegger and Nietzsche, of Hannah Arendt and Jürgen Habermas, of John Rawls and Michael Walzer, and of a modern age in which distance has shrunk without people becoming closer together. Public space is a particular achievement of human beings. As J.-P. Vernant describes its appearance like this:

> The institutions of the city imply that there was not only a "political" sphere of action but also that there was a "political" thought/theory. . . . Thus the establishment of the polis involves a process of secularization and rationalization of social life.[9]

We may now briefly inquire as to what qualities must a space have such that it be public. The first is that of being *open* in the sense of it being clear where one is. In the second book of the *Politics,* Aristotle recounts the achievements of Hippodamus, the fifth-century BCE Ionian Greek from Miletus. Aristotle remarks that Hippodamus "invented the art of planning cities."[10] More specifically, he designed the town of Piraeus, replacing the narrow, haphazard alleys with broad straight streets that intersected at right angles, radiating out from a central agora. In our day, Saint Mark's Place in Venice is a public space; the alleys and canals are not.

Hippodamus's achievement reflects a sense that the structure of the space in which humans interact is intimately related to the nature of their interaction. He was careful to recognize three kinds of space that make up a human city: sacred, private, and public. Hippodamus's association with the public sphere, however, was particularly strong. We learn from Demosthenes that the Piraean agora was called the Hippodameia.[11] This points to a second quality: *Public space is a human construct, an artifact,* the result of the attempt by human beings to shape the place and thus the nature of their interactions.

In public space, human beings engage in a particular type of interaction. From the beginning, public space was associated with theater. In Strabo's *Geography,*[12] we find that the Piraeus has "broad straight streets, the houses of which rose one above another like the seats of a theater." There is here an indication as to a third quality of public space: it is *theatrical,* in that it is a place which is seen and shows oneself to others. Even though we clearly hear things in the theater, it is a place where the human faculty of sight is predominant. Consider this common exchange: "I went to the theater.—Oh, what did you *see?*"

The theatrical quality of public space gives us a clue as to the human faculty that has predominantly been associated with such space: it is that of *sight*. What does it mean to be associated with sight? St. Augustine found three faculties definitive of the human. In memory, he wrote, we make and retain the past; in the will, we construct and bring about the future; and in vision or sight we establish the present.[13] Presentness is thus connected with seeing and thus inevitably connected with seeing someone, something. There can be no present without an "other."

While each of these faculties are bound up with our understanding of what it means to be a person, it seems clear that sight involves us most immediately with other human beings.[14] In seeing someone or something, I create a space that is ours. The realm constituted by the interaction of humans with each other is thus necessarily a space that has been constructed by the arresting of time. The qualities that this space may have are not given; indeed, they are most often the subjects of contestation. If, for instance, I look at you through a keyhole, as it were, I am privileging myself in relation to our space, and you may take exception.

There is also little doubt, as Hans Jonas has argued, that the metaphor of sight has, in the West, "tended to serve as the model of perception in general and thus as the measure of the other senses."[15] We are not concerned here directly to challenge the priority given to sight in the West. We do hope, however, that the essays that follow achieve some exploration of the various dimensions of the space created out of time by human interaction, particularly insofar as these dimensions relate to the variety of ways in which power has been and continues to be exercised; we may call these the "regimes."

We have pointed to three criteria of the public: it is *open,* an *artifact,* and *theatrical.* From these, we have argued, the possibility of public space is centrally bound up with sight or vision. It is not surprising, therefore, that vision has been generally associated with the political in human affairs and makes central use of the human faculty of sight. However, we should note here that the idea of theater lends itself to two kinds of understandings. The first is that of Plato and seeks to reduce the importance of vision in human affairs. In this case, vision is associated with the idea of illusion and falsehood. For Plato, relying on the senses, especially on sight, was to rely on appearance. It is for this reason that the *Republic* seeks to reduce contestation (and, indeed, to reduce the saliency of politics) and to replace vision with knowledge.

The other understanding is an understanding of theater as a dramatization of that which is shared by the audience and the performance. Theater in this sense is the making available of what can be shared. If we apply this understanding to public space and politics, we find that public space will always have a double quality to it. Sheldon Wolin notes this very well:

> Vision is commonly used to mean an act of perception. Thus we say that we *see* the speaker addressing a political rally. In this sense "vision" is a descriptive report about an object or event. But "vision" is also used in another sense, as when one talks about an aesthetic vision or a religious vision.[16]

Seeing involves being seen and in this sense it entails the notion of publicness, the idea that the space of the present is offered up to examination by all those who are within it. However, it does not necessarily involve the *acknowledgment* of seeing or being seen. There are two dimensions to the space created by seeing, potentially contradictory but both necessary to it. First of all, such a space is a place where one *can be* seen. This is, we might say, consequent to the theatrical quality of public space. By theatrical here, we mean that human actions are performed in the presence of others, without the other being present to the actors. Nietzsche understood this very well. In the eighth chapter of *The Birth of Tragedy,* in a passage directly neighbor to those Samuel Weber turns to at the end of this book, he describes the kind of audience that a Greek was for his theater:

> A public of spectators as we know it was unknown to the Greeks: in their theaters, the terraced structure of the concentric arcs of the place of spectatorship *(Zuschauerraumes)* made it possible for everyone actually to overlook the whole world of culture around him and imagine in sated contemplation that he was a chorist.[17]

The word for overlook here is *übersehen,* and it permits the same double meaning of "survey" and "fail to see." The audience is in "sated contemplation," that is, nothing is missing from what it is the audience for. During this time the audience finds itself in the place of spectatorship. It knows that everything occurring before it cannot be affected by its actions. The spectator will not, therefore, as Nietzsche indicates, "run up on stage and free the god from its torments." As characters, the actors onstage are in the presence of the audience, but the audience is not in the actors' presence. There is no way in which the audience can, as audience, compel the action onstage to acknowledge its presence.[18]

What Nietzsche permits us here is an elaboration of two differing qualities that an individual may have in relation to public space. In the case Nietzsche adduces, the qualities of theatricality induce *an intransitive nonreciprocal relationship* between those involved. This is most obvious in "real" theater, but it inheres in all that in politics pertains to the realm of the ritual, the symbol, the ceremony. All these are necessary elements of the space created by vision. Some speaking does not admit of a response or only of a response in another space: a speech from the throne, for instance, or a radio or television address. Speech of this kind is intransitive, but it is not thereby not political.

The other potential relationship is that of *transitivity*. One may be not only in the presence of an other but, at the same time, also present *to* them. Most typically, this relation takes the form of speech or, more precisely, of that form of speech which is incomplete without a response. When Aristotle identified the possession of speech as characteristically human, he meant the quality that our words can have to require a response *to them* from another human being. This means that I act with the expectation that my actions will elicit a response, from you. The response can be positive or negative, but my action is undertaken with the sense that you will not be able to remain indifferent. When, for instance, African Americans and whites "sat in" at segregated lunch counters in the American South during the 1960s, they did so with the (correct) expectation that the segregationist owners could not remain indifferent to what was happening. They sought to elicit a judgment from those owners about what they were doing. They expected that the judgment would be reflective in that it would, over time, acknowledge the correctness of their actions. And they were right.[19]

That there can be a tension between the transitive and intransitive qualities of public space is clear. In a theater, were a spectator to run onstage and stop Othello from strangling Desdemona, or even to call out from his seat, something would be very wrong. And yet, in the public realm, just exactly what would be wrong in a theater will not be wrong, or at least not as wrong. It is not *as* wrong to call out during the State of the Union address as it is to try to warn Desdemona. Our point here is that political space, created by the faculty of vision, necessarily includes theatricality without being identical to it. A question to which we shall return, and which inheres in the chapters by Sylviane Agacinski, Samuel Weber, J. Peter Euben, Anne Norton, and Benjamin R. Barber, has to do with the tensions in contemporary situations (e.g., malls, newspapers, radio, television, Internet) between the transitive and the intransitive.

This claim entails another. No matter how a particular individual (or a group by means of that individual) gets into a position of power, she or he is in a position of public visibility—in the public eye, as we say. Such a person is then required—in the sense of having no choice—to speak in front of others, to make decisions concerning the community, and to justify those decisions when called upon. (Indeed, even silence becomes public and takes on the meaning of a judgment or choice for everyone to assess.) In 1586, for instance, Elizabeth I gave a speech to a delegation from both houses of her Parliament. "We Princes," she told them, "are set on stages, in the sight and view of all the world duly observed."[20] Her Majesty's not unrueful recognition of her own visibility is consequent to her understanding of herself as a person in public space. One senses that Elizabeth would have preferred not to be so set before her world but also that she knew that she had no choice.

The figure in public sight thus occupies a position, that is, embodies an image of what may be expected of him or her. The fulfillment of this requirement may sometimes be in contradiction with the private sphere, with an individual's intimate convictions or with personal preferences. The gap is unavoidable: it indicates, on the one hand, the transcendence of the position in relation to the individual and shows, on the other, the necessary difference between public choices (which involve the community) and personal preferences. It is not simply that the public and the private should be kept separate: they are unavoidable as such.

With this we raise the question of how those in public view—those with power—have determined and been determined by the field of their visibility. Risking some oversimplification, we can identify two sources. One is profane and holds that power proceeds from the human community itself. The second is sacred and holds that power derives from some nonhuman source. With some even greater oversimplification we can briefly consider two cases: that of Greek democracy and that of medieval monarchy. One conclusion will be that democracy is necessarily built into *any* conception of public space. We should note here that in the considerations that follow we are focusing on two paradigm situations of visibility, the one profane and the other sacred. Though our presentation appears to be chronological, we do not intend it as such but rather as an elaboration of two forms of visibility, two ways of dealing with and being in public space. Finally, we shall examine those developments in the modern period that have transformed the availability of public space.

## Profane Visibility: Greek Democracy

In his *Histories,* Herodotus relates the day-to-day customs and deeds of certain non-Greek peoples (Libyans, Scythians, Babylonians, Persians, and Egyptians). He continually underlines the arbitrary and uncontrollable aspect of their forms of power, an aspect that seems to him to express the essential difference between the Greeks and the "barbaric peoples."[21] Herodotus's insistence indicates those features of the transition to democratic politics that had by his time become accepted in Greece (or at least in Athens) and that confirmed the excellence and superiority of Greek power structures. They include the public quality of beliefs, debates, decisions, activities, and laws. These transformations touched jointly and simultaneously upon all aspects of religious, social, and intellectual life. In religion, worship, which in archaic Greece proceeded from the authority of royal and noble clans, had slowly become accessible to all; the priesthood itself became a public office submitted to election like other duties. Holy idols such the old Xoana, which had been talismans jealously guarded in the royal palace or in the priest's house, are now moved to the temple, a public place where, in full sight of the city, they become images made to be seen. This transition from secret to public in religious practice represents the move toward the transparency and visibility required by democracy, as if the sacred orders had submitted themselves to the categories of the profane.

This move was essential for the emergence of what then asserted itself as philosophy. "Through the spoken and written word," Vernant notes, "the philosopher addresses the whole City, all Cities. He gave his revelations complete and total publicity. By carrying the mysteries into the market place, right into the agora, he made it the subject of a public and argumentative debate, in which dialectic discussion finally assumed more importance than supernatural enlightenment."[22] In archaic Greece, the figure of the wise man merged with that of the magus, of the priest, and of the seer whose words remained ambiguous, indecipherable, and likely to mean one thing as another. Philosophy comes from the need of a noncontradictory discourse, which implies clear agreement on the subject and on the rules of the statement.[23] Truth does not originate in secrecy but in public debate. The necessity of shared knowledge is precisely the requirement of democracy. Truth is what can be verified according to discussed and acknowledged rules. Thus, there emerged a new conception—the law.

Juridical decisions no longer depend on the judgment of a particular head of clan, nor can they be entrusted to the process of the ordeal. They are now a matter for the laws known by all, promulgated after discussion and recorded in a written form. The written form puts them at the disposition of public knowledge and shields them from distortion due to oral transmission. In the meantime (as early as the eighth century BCE), the adoption of the phonetic alphabet made writing accessible to everyone (as opposed to the old graphic system mastered by a few selected scribes, employees exclusively at the service of royal houses). Much later (the first century CE), when pondering the classical city, Plutarch defined its emergence as follows: "A transformation made thanks to speech and the law *[logou kai nomou metabolé]*."

This public and visible aspect of religious, political, juridical, and intellectual life finds its direct expression in the organization of space in the city. The following are gathered at the center of the city (which is constituted both by the town and the countryside): the *hestia koiné,* "the common hearth"; the *ecclesia,* the place where the people assemble; the *agora,* the public square; and the temples.[24] This center is geographical, but it has also a symbolic meaning: it reproduces in the social and political order the sphericity of the cosmos. The equality of the citizens, *isonomia,* is reflected in the equality and the symmetry of the points of the sphere or of the circle equidistant from the center.

The center of the city has its origins in the military democracy that appeared toward the end of the archaic period with the "Hoplitic Revolution"[25] (as some historians call it), when the cavalry (reserved to noblemen) became infantry (open to everyone). The warriors, disposed in a circle, deliberate by speaking in turns and by placing themselves each time in the center, a neutral and common place.[26] It's again in the center *(méson)* that they place the booty, which is to be distributed equitably. Similarly, the agora becomes a central place in the city, which cannot be appropriated and where all become alike *(homoioi)* and equal *(isoi),* no matter what their private situation, and where everything must be said and accomplished in common and in the open.

We are perforce too brief here. However, that which constitutes itself through these elements is the very domain of politics in its democratic form. Its essential feature is the following: all that appears in public can and must be seen and heard by all. Nothing concerning the public domain may be secret. While this "publicity" is primarily the publicity of institutions and of political practices, it can also be found, just as fundamentally, in the places and in the monuments that organize its space and that allow for a public expression of passions and of bodies. What remains exemplary for us in this democratic experience (in spite of its limitations and its exclusions) is precisely that the affirmation of the institutional principles is always part of the construction of a sensed and perceived world. The words *public space* are understood *literally*. Democracy manifests itself within that space; the public expression of its being resides in its very being. In the political arena, democracy is the sensate life of the community, which shapes the institutional forms and the symbolic figures of sovereignty.

## Sacred Visibility: The Medieval Monarchy

It is somewhat risky to talk about sacred visibility in relation to the European medieval monarchy. It is important to be clear that we are not dealing with a caesaro-papist theocracy (that is, the identification of political duty with religious duty with a single ruler for both), as was the case in Byzantium at the same period. A welcome consequence of the Investiture Controversy between Gregory VII and Emperor Henry IV was precisely the *coexistence* of two types of power, the spiritual and the temporal. Both Gregory and Henry give temporal power its autonomy, its own realm. They both acknowledge that temporal power has its source in God, that is, in spiritual power. They quarrel only about the implications of this origin. Henry responds to his deposition by Gregory in 1076 with

> You have laid hands upon me also who, though unworthy among Christians, am anointed to the kingship, and who, as the tradition of the Holy Fathers teaches, am to be judged by God alone and not to be deposed for any crime, unless I should wander from the faith, which God forbid.[27]

This justification will have tremendous consequences for the development of the Western state: in the Christian era, the source of the state lies in spiritual power. Separation and complementarity both take root in the Augustinian doctrine of the two Cities, that of God and that of the Earth.

Is it possible to say that this separation allows for the affirmation of a political society as such? Is it possible to find a situation in the Christian world comparable to the one encountered in Greece? It does not seem so, and primarily for the reason that in Christian society, the political sphere is considered to be a reality that cannot represent the essential goal of life. Its goal is to form, among baptized people, a community based on faith and charity, so that each member may work toward his own salvation. The political order is an external necessity charged with the organization indispensable to existence on earth. Inasmuch as it is a Christian community, it is not a political society. Its model is not the city per se, the "public entity," as it is for the ancients, but the family (in other words, that which belonged to the nonpolitical domain for the ancients, the private realm). The Christian community constitutes a "body" whose members are all "brothers" or "sisters" symbolically forming the unique "body of Christ." This reality is "domestic" reality; its linking principle is not a public one but an interindividual one; it is not speech but charity. It exists and develops independently from and parallel to the political order.

In comparison with the ancient world, what it meant to live a life within society undergoes a considerable change. For the Greeks and the Romans, immortality was defined by glory and renown acquired through action (and mainly through public action, which is to say, political action) carried out in front of everyone and engraved in the memory of future generations (thus the importance of poems and tales perpetuating that memory).[28] Life after death could not be true life, for the community was dissolved. In the Christian perspective, these facts are completely reversed. The community is fully realized in the beyond; life on earth is no more than a foreshadowing or a preparation. Terrestrial immortality does not exist. There is nothing essential to be expected from dedication to political society whose role is at most to manage the necessities of a passing world.

With this, new questions arise: what is, now, the actual status of the political order? What is the role of the state and of sovereignty? How is the importance of the monarchic role to be understood, and more precisely, for here resides the very subject of our study, how can one explain the importance of royal decorum? Is it pertinent to talk about sacred spectacle? What is the specific organization of the visibility of such a power?

As Marc Bloch emphasizes, the ceremonies of unction and of coronation, which spread as early as the late Medieval Ages (ninth and tenth centuries), show that the monarchic role had taken on a sacred nature.[29] These ceremonies, inspired by the Bible, reproduce the consecration of David by Samuel as the war leader is consecrated by the spiritual leader: "A bishop, a new Samuel, anoints the new David, on different parts of their bodies, with a blessed oil: a gesture whose universal meaning, in Catholic liturgy, is to elevate the person or the object from a profane status to a sacred one."[30] This is not, Bloch insists, the institution of a sacerdotal royalty. Through unction, the king takes part in a spiritual power while remaining secular. He belongs to both universes while belonging to a different order: he is considered separately in terms that correspond to the very definition of the sacred.[31]

The sacred nature attached to the royal person does not, however, concern the private person but the position for which the private person is the support. Ernst Kantorowicz brought this to light in his now-classic work *The King's Two Bodies*.[32] The concept of the king's double body developed in practice (of law and of ceremonies) during the Middle Ages in England and in France, and was theoretically established in the classical age. When, in the tenth century, the bishop of Mainz crowned the German king, he did so with the understanding that "the grace of God hath this day changed thee into another man, and by the holy rite of unction hath made thee partaker in its divinity."[33] This theory distinguishes, on the one hand, the monarch as the individual whose carnal body is submitted to the same contingencies as are the bodies of other human beings and, on the other, the monarch as the depository of sovereign power, whose kingdom forms the symbolic body, in such a way that those who act "in the name of the King" are the eminent and immanent members of this symbolic body: the judge who delivers a verdict is his mouth, the headsman who executes is his hand, the intendant who watches is his eye, the captain who leads his armies is his sword, etc. The first body is mortal, the second does not die. Such is the meaning of the ritual words, "The King is dead! Long live the King!" "As if it always were the same king," comments a seventeenth-century author, "not only by representation, but also by continuation, who died only to survive in his descendants."[34]

As Kantorowicz clearly shows, the model that inspires this representation draws directly from the doctrine of the double body of Christ: the mortal body of the man Jesus, the glorious and immortal body of Christ resuscitated and now incarnate in the church as the baptized community. What the church is to Christ, the kingdom is to its king. In this sense, the king becomes the very incarnation of the public nature of the state. The king condenses it in his person. This is why the facts and deeds of this person become the deeds of the state inasmuch as he thinks, decides, and acts through it. However, the rituals and the ceremonies surrounding those facts and deeds act to demonstrate that the king does not decide and act as a private person but as the depository of an authority derived from God. This entails duties that strictly limit his power. This is why the sacred origin of this authority protects the royal duty from the vassals' rivalries and protests. (Bloch notices that cases of regicide were extremely rare in medieval Europe.) In other words, the person of the king absorbs in himself the whole public reality of the political sphere but does so as symbolic body, as expression of the kingdom, and never in a private or individual capacity. The king is entitled to honors and splendor, celebrating not his person but his duty. The "stage" on which he shines is the one where the kingdom recognizes itself and honors itself. This was accepted by all as long as the king appeared as "the king of justice" and as long as the logic of the expression of a symbolic body was understood in its religious context. But as soon as this context weakened and power became more a matter of acquired skill rather than a matter of authority conferred by tradition, the scene became blurry.

One may locate here the beginning of the transformation of the medieval monarchy into that of the Renaissance and the early modern eras. A sort of confusion of genres follows, contemporary with the birth of absolutism.[35] Progressively, all aspects of the person of the king become public; everything about him concerns all his subjects. It is this tendency that Louis XIV takes to its height when transforming the most ordinary of his private gestures (getting up, going to bed, dining, washing) into public rituals.[36] In reality, however, the public nature of the person of the king expresses itself less in the ceremony of the Middle Ages, whose highly codified religious nature erases the individual aspect, than in the spectacle that, starting with Louis XIV, becomes a personal celebration of a prince who proclaims himself to be incomparable. It is not, any longer, so much a matter of reaffirming the sacred origin of the monarchic office, whose principle remains a given, as it is to impress subjects with the splendor of the king's image.[37]

This means that the legitimacy of the monarchic power is no longer assured by religious evidence, as it was previously, but must be produced by an elaborate process of persuasion and seduction. Writers, historiographers, theologians, and jurists work at persuasion; seduction is the staging work of architects, painters, engravers, musicians, decorators, landscape gardeners,[38] and other collaborators in princely splendor.[39] The ceremonies of royal entrances into cities, such as that of Louis XIV into Paris in 1660, or the lavish entertainment of the court (as in 1668), must all contribute to that persuasion and seduction. With its ostentatious luxury and sophisticated etiquette, the Versailles court presents itself as the permanent staging of a power whose legitimacy seems to reside in the display of the signs of its greatness, as if its reality was dependent on the continuous spectacle given of itself. Between the medieval monarchy and the monarchy of the early modern age, a profound change in the nature of the theatricality of the political realm occurs: we pass from belief to make-believe. One cannot understand what becomes of public space in the modern period without understanding this. In order fully to grasp it, it is necessary to look back at Machiavelli, a precursor in whose work this mutation is already developed.

## The "Machiavellian Moment" and the Birth of Perspective

Political action is frequently referred to as an art of illusion, as a refined technique of dissimulation, in short, as a staging of power designed to "make believe," to ensure assent based upon appearances rather than upon convictions shared by citizens and leaders. It is most often so characterized with the name of Machiavelli, the thinker who, presumably, theorized this form of political conduct the most radically.

Readings of Machiavelli often moralize. Machiavellianism is referred precisely to the art of deception, to the cynical manipulation of opinion through a subtle blending of demagoguery and tyranny. And does Machiavelli not recommend that one's word may and sometimes must be broken and that means be identified with ends? Such has been the generally accepted reading and often scathing criticism of *The Prince,* and even of other texts by Machiavelli (such as the *Discourses on the First Decade of Titus-Livius*), from the sixteenth century to today.

However, a more in-depth reflection has been recently developed (for instance, in Claude Lefort's influential work[40]) that has made it possible to do away with these simplistic and moralizing interpretations. The question is no longer whether Machiavelli's analysis should be justified (in the name of realism) or condemned (in the name of right) but, rather, to understand how and why it was possible for this analysis to make its appearance at a certain point in history, in a certain place—Florence—and how it accounted for a new problem in Western political thought.

This is why one can speak, as does J. G. A. Pocock, of a "Machiavellian moment."[41] It designates the time when a break was accomplished that marked the beginning of a new political age and, at the same time, anticipated problems that would only become apparent much later. What it marked the beginning of was a conception of power as a calculation of actual forces. Such a conception was fully contemporaneous with a transformation in the representation of nature, and of the modes of action envisioned both for nature and men themselves. What that "moment" anticipated were circumstances of open competition for power already prevailing in the Republic of Florence but not yet so in states with firmly established dynastic monarchies such as, among others, France, England, and Spain (and it is precisely in those countries that Machiavelli's thought was to be the object of the most scathing rejection).

What is, then, the specific problem that Machiavelli's thought attempted to resolve? It may be defined in a way that makes it a modern question: How can political power be endowed with unquestionable authority, in a place where and at a time when neither religious faith (because of the papacy's very profane behavior) nor dynastic principle (as in monarchies maintained by "divine right"[42]) can provide it with legitimacy? Let us note that Machiavelli did not aim to establish a new foundation for sovereignty and for the state, supported on the basis of law. Machiavelli took it for granted that the state could not be done without and that the prince had to exercise sovereignty. If the state was necessary and if no transcendent reference could continue to ensure its legitimacy, the only question remaining was by what means could its existence be guaranteed. What was no longer based upon faith must now be achieved through skill (a method and a technique). This is why Machiavelli's Prince had to promote through his talent alone—his know-how and his *virtù*—what was given others by sacred authority. For a world free of that authority was a world reduced to necessity, a world of "actual reality," which is to say a world in which, as in nature, forces acted unhampered and constituted themselves as autonomous systems (in view of their means). It is likely that such a view was only possible or conceivable within a representation of the world entirely different from that that had prevailed until then. A transformation had taken place. Its sources were many and its most relevant expression was what was developed, then, as the space of perspective (and this is the object of the demonstration that is presented here).

We need therefore to grasp the precise congruence that took shape between, on the one hand, a new conception of space and concurrent new models of representation and, on the other, Machiavelli's formulation of the figure of the Prince. That may allow us to understand how the political technique of appearance, the organization of the stage of power, was for Machiavelli closely tied to a new rationality of representation.

The question of perspective, as it came to be raised in the visual arts at the beginning of the quattrocento, was not entirely novel, as Erwin Panofsky has shown in *Perspective as Symbolic Form*.[43] Vanishing-point perspective had been understood as far back as the classical age (in relation to the perception of monuments) and taken up again by geometers in the Middle Ages. What was new was that it became the ultimate question in architecture and painting. It reflects the realization that forms were no longer to be understood as offered to a divine gaze that would view equally every point in space but were, rather, understood as constructed in relation to the position of a viewer. The age of the finite world had begun. Hence the novelty of solutions in the development of constructions, such as the vanishing point in paintings, that finally made it possible to build the visual pyramid that would define the space of representation for several centuries.

The founding text in this regard was Leon Battista Alberti's *Della Pittura* (1436).[44] Alberti, who was mainly a theoretician, freely acknowledged the debt he owed a master who, in the hierarchy of trades and status, was a craftsman: the architect Brunelleschi, who had created the domes of Santa Maria dei Fiori and of Florence's baptistry. Brunelleschi had also worked out the mathematics of perspective. Alberti describes the precise device (frame, peephole, and mirror) used by Brunelleschi in order to calculate the visual pyramid and determine the lines of perspective. From that starting point, experiments and treatises were to become more and more numerous during the fifteenth century, of which we can note Filarete's *Trattato di Architettura* (1460–64), which gave a prominent place to the notion of "central perspective"; Gauricus's *De Sculptura* (1504); a Brunelleschi biography by Vasari (1550); and, above all, Vasari's treatise *Della Pittura*.

All this research led to the construction of perspective defined as a preferred locus of viewing, called the point of distance—the summit of a pyramid of which the painting appears to be the intersecting plane *("il taglio")*. It is from this privileged viewpoint that the viewer can best perceive the summit of the other pyramid, called the vanishing point, in which the lines of the painting converge and establish its depth (in other words, the representation of the third dimension on a flat surface). Without entering the debate that developed between advocates of one-eye and two-eye viewing, it remains that the point of distance was a single one ("un luogo unico," in Alberti's words). Only one place could allow optimum viewing.[45]

### How to See: The Prince as Observer

Now sight comes into its own. The development of the perspective paradigm elucidates important spatial qualities of the Machiavellian figure of the Prince. Causal relations are, of course, circular in this case. The Prince is he who knows how to place himself in the locus from which a picture made up by the whole of political interplay can best be viewed. It is through his mastery of this view that he can gain control of the field, hence the preeminence of viewing and of the optical model over others. On the other hand, the very existence of this unified picture depends on the Prince taking up this position. It could even be said that what makes him Prince is his taking up this position. The point of distance was also called the point of origin, precisely that which classical metaphysics would have called a principle (*princeps*, principle, prince).

The exercise of power was, before anything else, the ability to occupy the right locus, of which there was only one. That locus was, henceforth, the position from which it was possible to see, because seeing amounted to "controlling" action. It is now easier to understand why the paradigm of perspective was such a powerful one during the fifteenth and sixteenth centuries (first in Italy, then in Europe as a whole): it subjected political practice to the mastery of viewing. Conversely, that practice tended to be constituted as an object of viewing, as a system of appearance. This is why Machiavelli's thought is so different from its vulgar version, which we know as Machiavellianism: "deceit" *(inganno)* is but a variant of a more profound paradigm of appearance, understood as the construction of a picture.

It is as if, in an age and a place—Florence—where power was for the taking, a practice of illusion required by the interplay of rivalries had found in the new formulation of representation provided by perspective the right tool to express its legitimacy. That formulation opened, in the form of an analysis of forces (soon to be seen, from another perspective, as Hobbesian), a theory of sovereignty that political thinkers, as early as the end of the sixteenth century (such as Bodin in France) or the seventeenth century (such as Grotius in Holland or Pufendorf in Germany) would develop as an analysis of law. It is easy enough to understand why legal theoreticians radically opposed Machiavelli. However, no matter what their foundations may have been, all theories of sovereignty aimed to demonstrate the following proposition: it is necessary that one agent alone exercise power over others in order for the state to exist, for political order to be possible, and—in a very immediate way—for an end to be put to civil war.

In these circumstances, when the dynastic principle did not exist or came under threat, or the sacred origin of sovereignty could not be guaranteed (as was the case in the Florentine Republic), then forces were unleashed that spun out of control. Lacking any arbiter, a logical principle had to be found within the nature of things, which is to say within this system of forces, in order to establish the legitimacy of a balance between them, of a convergence, of an unquestionable order. That is precisely the solution the paradigm of perspective provided. Power, which is to say the mastery of forces, belonged to he who knew how and was able to act so as to take up a single and specific position: precisely that of the point of distance or point of origin. Such was the Prince's position. (It is worth noting that Machiavelli never referred explicitly to painting or architecture, or even to the question of perspective; that was the implicit element in his text, controlling its metaphors, the "blind spot" in the thought of that age.)

The sovereignty of Machiavelli's Prince was thus first a *topological* fact. By placing himself (or being placed by fate) in the right location, he was able to view the world from the center, where forces met, and to act effectively. By its unique and exclusive character, that position was analogous (but not more than analogous) to the position of the sacred in that it preexisted its holder. It was an objective locus that was part of the order of things. Hence its legitimacy was, as in the realm of art, that of Alberti's *prospettiva legitima*: it defined by its existence what legitimacy was. Whereas within the tradition of sacred sovereignty the position of power fell due to he who was designated by the dynastic rule of blood (or by any other code), in Machiavelli's conception, the game was open, the position only awarded to he who knew how to take it and therefore deserved it. (This is why democracy has been mentioned in reference to Machiavelli.) Hence the role of *virtú*, the necessity of initiative, of a combination of cunning and violence, in the Prince's behavior. The position was there; the Prince was he who knew how to hold and keep it.

## How to Be Seen: The Prince as the Observed One

For Machiavelli, therefore, the art of politics could not be separated from the ability to design the topology of proper representation—which is to say effective representation. Indeed, construction of the perspective model was called "scenography." However, between pictorial or architectural scenography on the one hand and political scenography on the other, lies a crucial difference: in the latter, the components of the picture were themselves seeing beings. The point of distance held by the Prince became, under the gaze of others, a vanishing point. The Prince was seen in the position from which he observed. This is precisely what made his position dependent upon his *appearance*. Holding power amounted first of all to offering up to the gaze of others the external signs associated with the position of power. This requirement fueled the demand for illusion expected from the Prince, a demand that reinforced the legitimacy that came with his position. This is also why the Prince always had to be kept informed of what his assistants and subjects thought so that he might construct the façade, without which, in this optical model, his power would have collapsed.

What was the meaning of that consecration of appearance? How credible was legitimization based on this new mode of spatial representation? Here lies a paradox that, regarding the system of perspective, can be applied to both the visual and the political arts.

In the case of painting, this paradox lies in the fact that to represent objects within space, relative to the position of the viewer and the distance that lies between them, which is to say the depth of field, these objects have to be distorted. Squares have to become trapezoids and circles become ellipses. In short, through precise calculations of angles and lines, descriptive geometry has to be changed into projective geometry, orthomorphosis replaced with anamorphosis. Representation no longer presents objects as they are, but as they seem. This means that for reality to be seen in its true aspect, to be accurately represented, it has to be feigned through the use of artifice. But this artifice is neither arbitrary nor misleading: it is required by reason. It is subject to precise rules (those of projective geometry).

The development of the system of perspective allows us to grasp firmly the remarkable philosophical transformation that began during the quattrocento: the pyramid of beings was no longer conceived of within an absolute space in which God is both the apex and the origin. It was now conceived of as in relation to a viewer endowed with reason and as organized in terms relative to the viewer's field of vision. Treatises on perspective developed the spatial organization of the finite.

Within that new order of spatial representation Machiavelli's political thought took its place, and that order commanded its central metaphors. The paradoxical character of his thought is striking, in that the mastery of reality *(la realità effetuale)* was exercised through the management of appearances, inasmuch as reality was only perceived through viewing, which is to say, relative to the position of a viewer. If a scenography had to be constructed to establish the proper relationship between objects, it was because this accuracy—or fairness—was submitted to a point of view and, thus, required a projective distortion in order to be accurate. An artifice was required for a true grasp of reality to be attained.

This helps us understand the purely technical and functional character power had in Machiavelli's thought. In accordance with the new ordering of the world that was developing during his time, that conception of power was a strictly topological one. That topology was the representation of actual forces and thus was a feature of nature, not of right. Power could be read in the organization of space; its place was marked there. Acquiring this power—maintaining it—necessarily implied acting upon the visible. Hence this paradox: by manipulating *appearances,* one could engineer the construction of a geometry of *reality* grounded in *truth* (which is to say "in nature"). The scenography of the political, as of painting, conformed to the new order of reason.

What is important here is the legacy of the Machiavellian moment. Machiavelli both furthers and stands for a revolution in the production of public space. It is not an exaggeration to see in the Prince a technologist of public space. His knowledge is used to produce the images that determine the *stato.* From this time on—for we inherit this world—the image of a legitimate political world is something that is produced rather than something that is simply engendered by a particular presence, such as that of the body of the king. Today, as the essays in the second part of this volume show, we must think of public space as produced.

## The Contemporary Crisis of Public Space

The above is obviously not the end of the story. The Machiavellian for-mulation of political space as a strategy of appearances meant that power could no longer be separated from the display of its legitimacy. The paradoxical consequence was that power was all the more depen-dent on those for whom its show was designed. The self-staging of power was an admission that power was subject to judgments, toward an evaluation by public opinion, the support of which was important to secure.[46] The theatrical qualities of power lead necessarily in a politi-cally democratic direction.

What has not been thought through, however, is how the transfer of sovereignty from prince to people affects the essential requirement of public space, that is to say, the right to free information. What changed or rather disintegrated was the perspectival reference point. In the past seventy years, new media (newspapers, radio, and above all, television) have transformed the way in which politicians (the holders of power) appear in public. It is from a mass of details that a positive or negative image emerges and imposes itself on public opinion.[47] There is no longer a single and privileged stage specific to the political realm. Po-litical activity, instead of being framed from a perspective point, is nothing more than another opportunity for images, which may come from any and every realm of life. While this phenomenon may be the basis of entertainment, it becomes unbearable when it is a political matter, that is, a matter of public responsibility. Hence information cancels itself through overinformation. Political public space dissolves into overexposure of the social. Public and private are mixed, as are role and individual, the essential and the anecdotal, major decisions and "news in brief." (The very word "publicity," which used to refer to debates, has been entirely taken over by the production of that which has become ultimately public—the marketable image.)

Once everything can be seen, there is no longer a domain specific to the visible. From that point on, disclosure knows no bounds: by the very logic of the obscene, political activity becomes captured and placed in blatant contradiction with the ethical intentions and claims of respon-sibility it keeps proclaiming. We must therefore either reexamine the rules of information that regulate the new media, or we must reexam-ine the nature of the political in the modern period, acknowledging that its classical forms are extinct and considering entirely new condi-tions for the exercise of democracy.

One attempt that has been made emphasizes a rationality that lies as one of the keystones of democratic legitimacy. In this mode, contemporary theorists of democracy attempt to guarantee its strength by leaving the affectual and the imaginary in limbo. Rationality alone becomes the core, and anything that would directly pertain to the imaginary is viewed with suspicion or is rejected as a dangerous ideological phenomenon.

We may look briefly at two approaches here. The first is associated with contemporary liberal theory, such as that of John Rawls. In *A Theory of Justice*,[48] Rawls sets the problem of a "well-ordered society." Justice, he writes, is about "the basic structure of society, or, more exactly, the way in which the major social institutions distribute fundamental rights and duties and determine the division of advantages from social cooperation."[49] Rawls argues that individuals choosing from behind a "veil of ignorance"[50] will choose two principles of justice. When behind the veil, individuals do not know their place in society, their class or status position, their race, sex, and religion, their natural assets, their intelligence, or their conception of the good. They *do* know that society has or will have institutions such as those familiar to us in the West, that they will need a conception of justice, that they will prefer to have more rather than less of what there may be to have, and some basic knowledge of political affairs and economic theory.

Given these conditions, Rawls argues that given shared ideas of reasonableness (themselves historically acquired), individuals will rationally choose, first, that each person have a right to an adequate scheme of basic rights and liberties that is compatible with a similar scheme for all and, second, that any inequalities must both be attached to offices and positions open to all under conditions of equal opportunity and must work to the benefit of the least advantaged members of society.

Rawls's elaboration of a well-ordered society thus rests on the delineation of conditions that must pertain to *allow* rationality to be the basis of social order. Public space is here achieved in a manner that is apparently fundamentally separate from the symbolic order. Rawls has resolved the problem of the affectual and the imaginary by confining them to a private, nonpolitical realm—all that is not susceptible to rational choice in the public realm.

A second, perhaps more complex, attempt at grounding contemporary public space in communicative rationality has been made by Jürgen Habermas. Habermas insists that when language is used for public purposes that "both ego, who raises a validity claim with his utterance, and alter, who recognizes or rejects it, base their decisions on potential grounds or reasons."[51] Rationality, Habermas argues, has a broader or deeper application than just the assessment of goal-directed actions or propositional assertions: "In the context of communicative action, we call someone rational only if he is able to put forward an assertion and, when criticized, to provide grounds for it by pointing to appropriate evidence, but also if he is following a norm and is able, when criticized, to justify his action by explicating the given situation in the light of legitimate expectations."[52] Pursuing this line of argument, Habermas argues that it is the role of the philosopher to be the "guardian of rationality."[53] Habermas seeks to eliminate all that smacks of the affectual and imaginary from at least the foundations of the public realm.

A full critique of Habermas or Rawls is beyond the scope of this introduction.[54] (Some problems in Habermas are taken up in the essays by Sylviane Agacinski and Dana R. Villa, in the second part of the book.) It is clear to us from what we have said above that the imaginary (inseparable from a stage and from imagery) cannot, as such, be *grounded* on democratic reason. Yet the latter in fact never ceases, in an unavoidable concession, to call upon its resources. One has only to start with the thought of the allegorical staging (such as that of the "Goddess Reason" standing on a float covered with flowers) and the ceremonies dedicated to the Nation that took place at the time of the French Revolution. They were meant to catch the people's imagination, to heighten their ardor and their support, which amounted to an open admission of the limits of the power of a purely demonstrative and argumentative discourse. The same could be said of nineteenth-century displays of republican pathos (fairly obvious traces of which can still be observed in present-day public ceremonies, for national holidays, military commemorations, presidential inauguration ceremonies, election celebrations).

From the point of view of reason, the value of these forms of expression remains instrumental and random, mere illustration, as if it were self-evident that any celebration requires props and symbols. Yet it may well be that these forms of expression lie at the core, as constituent elements, of the social bond, as the genesis of the symbolic order by which any community comes into being: that "us" whose identity is tied to a territory, a memory, a language, customs, symbolic figures. In fact, such processes can be observed in the forming of the smallest groups (clubs, gangs, cults, athletic teams) as well as of the largest organizations (unions, parties, companies). The social bond is, before anything else, a web of affects and symbols. Rational legitimizations always come after the fact and, most often, in order to conceal that core made of immemorial bonds, as if the acknowledgment of this uncontrollable origin of sociality constituted a threat to a state of law that claims to be based upon clear principles and upon a reason that, since the Enlightenment, has set as its task to conquer all darkness.

Indeed, this whole layer of affects, when not recognized and taken into account within the legitimate figures of sociality, is liable to return and be glorified in perverted forms. For it is very precisely the imaginary in limbo that, with great intuition, leaders of so-called populist movements address. It is precisely that resource that fascistic ideologies exploit to the point of aberration (with the drift from territory to race, from nation to nationalism, from sovereignty to the infantile cult of the leader, and so forth). In the aftermath of World War I, Freud already expressed his surprise that it would have been possible for the most cultured people in the West, those who claimed to be the heirs to a reason that was supposed to be universal, to massacre one another with such a passionate steadfastness, causing the greatest carnage in history.[55] What then should we say of its repetition, aggravated by the Nazi design of extermination, a quarter of a century later?[56] The question is not, "How could the masses allow themselves to be misled to such a degree?" but, "What was their yearning for fascination, how acute was their dissatisfaction, for them to accept being blinded to such a degree by disastrous mythologies?"

That crucial question cannot be answered by economic and sociohistorical explanations. The answer probably has to do with the destructive effects upon the understanding of the "disenchantment of the world," which Max Weber regarded as the defining feature of industrial societies. Can it be said that a reply has since been found and that the "free-floating imaginary," noncoded socially, has been mastered? One would tend to say no. However, the answer is undoubtedly yes, for the imaginary has indeed been called upon and channeled by the very authority that had cut it off from its public expression, namely by operational and market-oriented reason. From now on, it is entirely taken up by that staging of the social performed by advertising. Thus, the main public space of our time is that of consumption; hence the political is subjected to its logic and has come to be assessed by the criterion of the image.

It seems that the imaginary and the political have once again been reconciled, but under the sign of the marketplace and through active integration into its regulatory processes. Democracy thus loses its rationality. Images displace arguments. Debates are turned into games. The show never stops. All games become interchangeable; the political stage tends to be no more than one among others. So much so that its legitimate claim to be something else loses all validity. Nevertheless, the general unease generated today by that situation has one positive implication: citizens have not allowed themselves to be identified with consumers, the political has remained the specific form of expression of the community as such, and ethical choices cannot be reduced to functional regulations.

The above is, we hope, enough to establish two broad claims. The first is that public space has certain prerequisites for it to exist. The second is that the quality of public space has changed over time. Indeed, modern—meaning Anglo-European, postindustrial—society seems to call into question the possibility of such a space. No longer the place where humans appear in and as persons one to the other, what remains of the public realm is, as some of the essays here analyze, now further mediated by technologies of communication. While permitting a vastly expanded audience, these also appear to reduce the legitimacy of what is communicated. They dramatically change the role that vision plays. To the degree that the possibility of legitimate public space diminishes, it may encourage the understanding that political life is, in the end, only a matter of the matrix of the clash of private interests, "that my share in no way involves my life in common with that of an other." In this context, Raymond Williams once noted the tendency of modern societies to dramatize all human relations.[57]

Two general questions thus present themselves, and the chapters that follow address them.

First, in what ways does a life in common with others require signs, symbols, and, most fundamentally, a space in which the expression of that life can be the object of legitimate and legitimating contention? Here the question has to do with the name of what we find when we find ourselves together in a political space that we must recognize as common, as well as with the terms by which we defend it. The essays in the first part of the book focus primarily on this topic.

The second question has to do with the effect of modern technologies (film, television, telecommunications, etc.) on the qualities and possibilities of public space. As an obvious beginning point, one effect of those technologies is to diminish greatly the importance of the limitations of time and space that previously served as the boundaries of public space. This raises the possibility of what the poet Rilke once called "dummy life."[58] The essays in the second part of the volume focus primarily, though not exclusively, on this possibility. Most succinctly, all of the chapters consider the question of what has to be the case for a person coherently to claim to share a life in common with others.

## Notes

An earlier version of portions of this introduction originally appeared in *SubStance 80,* vol. 25, no. 2 (1996).

1. Book II, lines 25–32, from Homer, *Odyssey,* trans. Richard Lattimore (New York: Harper, 1967).

2. See Richard Seaford, *Reciprocity and Ritual* (Oxford: Clarendon Press, 1994), chapter 1, esp. 4, 8–10, 18–20.

3. Hannah Arendt notes that the agora was also a marketplace to which the *homo faber* came with goods to sell and asked to be recognized, thus forming an (albeit embryonic) *zoon politikon* (*The Human Condition* [Chicago: University of Chicago Press, 1958], chapter 2).

4. Thus, when Achilles throws down the *skeptron* in *Iliad,* Book I, line 245, he is both breaking the solidarity of the group and rejecting Agamemnon's authority. See the discussion in Jean-Pierre Vernant, *Myth and Thought among the Greeks* (London: Routledge and Paul, 1983), 134–35.

5. For Locke, see *Second Treatise on Civil Government,* paragraphs 25–51 in *Two Treatises on Civil Government,* ed. Peter Laslett (New York: Mentor, 1958); for Hobbes, see *Leviathan,* chapter 13 (Edwin Curley, ed. [Indianapolis: Hackett, 1995]).

6. Vincent Scully, *The Earth, the Temple and the Gods: Greek Sacred Architecture* (New York: Praeger, 1969), 3. Scully uses part of the *Colonus* citation as an epigraph.

7. See J. Charles Cox, *The Sanctuaries and Sanctuary Seekers of Medieval England* (London: G. Allen and Sons, 1911). The right of sanctuary lasted in England, despite some erosion, until the eighteenth century and in France until the Revolution.

8. For an analysis of how Rousseau seeks to turn common space into public space as a response to the challenges of the modern world, see Tracy B. Strong, *Jean Jacques Rousseau and the Politics of the Ordinary* (Thousand Oaks, Calif.: Sage Publications, 1994), especially chapter 3, and Marcel Hénaff, "The Cannibalistic City: Rousseau, Large Numbers, and the Social Bond," *SubStance,* 67 (Spring 1992); 2–23. The starting point for recent discussions of this issue is Judith Shklar, *Men and Citizens: A Study of Rousseau's Political Theory* (Cambridge: Cambridge University Press, 1985).

9. J.-P. Vernant, *Myth and Thought among the Greeks,* 181–82.

10. Aristotle, *Politics,* Book II in Book VII, he refers to this as "the modern way." *The Complete Works of Aristotle.* Jonathan Barnes, ed. (Princeton: Princeton University Press, 1984).

11. Demosthenes, *Against Timotheus* (Cambridge: Harvard University Press, 1958), 22, 49.

12. Strabo, *Geography,* 9.1.15 (n. 3).

13. See Augustine, *The Trinity,* Book XI (Edinburgh: T. and T. Clark, 1871), vol. 7.

14. See Tracy B. Strong, *The Idea of Political Theory* (Notre Dame: University of Notre Dame Press, 1990), chapter 1.

15. Hans Jonas, *The Phenomenon of Life* (New York: Harper and Row, 1966), 135. We are helped here by the considerations in Hannah Arendt, *Willing* (New York: Harcourt Brace Jovanovich, 1978), 98ff. She also cites Jonas, on 110.

16. Sheldon S. Wolin, *Politics and Vision* (Boston: Little, Brown, 1961), 18.

17. Friedrich Nietzsche, *Birth of Tragedy,* chapter 8, in *Kritische Gesammt Ausgabe* (Berlin: Gruyter, 1967ff), vol. III1, p. 55–56.

18. For a complete discussion see Tracy B. Strong, *Friedrich Nietzsche and the Politics of Transfiguration* (Champaign: University of Illinois Press, 2000), 162–66.

19. For the idea of reflective judgment and its political difference from John Rawls's notion of reflective equilibrium, see Stanley Cavell, *Conditions Handsome and Unhandsome* (Chicago: University of Chicago Press, 1990) 104ff.

20. Cited in Stephen Greenblatt, *Renaissance Self-Fashioning* (Chicago: University of Chicago Press, 1980), 167.

21. See François Hartog, *The Mirror of Herodotus: The Representation of the Other in the Writing and History* (Berkeley: University of California Press, 1988).

22. Vernant, *Myth and Thought among the Greeks,* 356.

23. Marcel Detienne, *Masters of Truth in Ancient Greece* (New York: Zone Books, 1997).

24. See the discussion in Aristotle, *Politics,* Book I, chapter 2 and Josh Ober, *Mass and Elite in Democratic Athens: Rhetoric, Ideology, and the Power of the People* (Princeton: Princeton University Press, 1989); see also Vernant, *Myth and Thought among the Greeks,* 124–70.

25. Detienne, *Masters of Truth,* Chapter 5.

26. As noted above, see *Odyssey,* Book II, where Telemachus calls the warriors into a circle, called there an agora.

27. Cited in Ewart Lewis, *Medieval Political Ideas,* volume 2, p. 511. Henry echoes the terms of Gratian's Decretum: *"Papa . . . a nemine est iudicandus, nisi deprehendatur a fide devius,"* cited from Brian Tierney, *Foundations of Conciliar Theory* (London: Cambridge University Press, 1968), 57.

28. See Hannah Arendt, *The Human Condition* (Chicago: University of Chicago Press, 1958).

29. See Marc Bloch, *Feudal Society* (Chicago: University of Chicago Press, 1968).

30. Ibid., 524.

31. Miraculous powers were attributed to the king of France until the time of

Louis XVI; see Marc Bloch, *The Royal Touch: Sacred Monarchy and Scrofula in England and France* (London: Routledge and Kegan Paul, 1973).

32. Ernst Kantorowicz, *The King's Two Bodies* (Princeton: Princeton University Press, 1957).

33. Fritz Kern, *Kingship and Law in the Middle Ages* (Oxford: Blackwells, 1956), 37.

34. Sénécé de Bauderon, *L'Apollon françois* (Mâcon: R. Piget, 1684), 139.

35. Hobbes, for instance, wanting all exercise of power to be only public, is forced to claim in chapter 24 of *Leviathan* that the hunting lands reserved to William the Conqueror were in his "natural and not his public capacity."

36. Norbert Elias, *The Court Society* (New York: Pantheon, 1983).

37. See Jean-Marie Apostolides, *Le Roi-Machine* (Paris: Editions de Minuit, 1981).

38. On gardens and sovereignty, see, inter alia, Chandra Mukerji, *Territorial Ambitions and the Garderns of Versailles* (Cambridge: Cambridge University Press, 1997).

39. Louis Marin, *Portrait du Roi* (Paris: Editions de Minuit, 1981).

40. Claude Lefort, *Le travail de l'oeuvre Machiavel* (Paris: Gallimard, 1972).

41. J. G. A. Pocock, *The Machiavellian Moment* (Princeton: Princeton University Press, 1975).

42. Cf. Machiavelli's *The Prince,* chapter 2: "I say, then, that states which are hereditary, and accustomed to the rule of those belonging to the present ruler's family, are very much less difficult to hold than new states, because it is sufficient not to change the established order, and to deal with any untoward events that may occur."

43. Erwin Panofsky, *Perspective as Symbolic Form* (New York: Zone Books, 1991).

44. Leon Battista Alberti, *On Painting* (New Haven: Yale University Press, 1966). See also a biography of Brunelleschi from the 1480s: Antonio di Tuccio Manetti, *The Life of Brunelleschi,* ed. Howard Saalman, trans. Catherine Enggass (University Park: Pennsylvania State University Press, 1970).

45. Hubert Damisch, *The Origin of Perspective* (Cambridge: MIT Press, 1994), and R. Klein, *Form and Meaning: Essay on Renaissance and Modern Art* (New York: Viking Press, 1979).

46. Cf. David Hume, "Of the First Principles of Government," *Essays Literary, Political and Moral* (Indianapolis: Liberty Classics, 1987), Book I, essay iv: "No man would have any reason to fear the fury of a tyrant, if he had no authority over any but from fear; since, as a single man, his bodily force can reach but a small way, and all the farther power he possesses must be founded either on our own opinion, or on the presumed opinion of others. And though affection to wisdom and virtue in a sovereign extends very far, and has great influence; yet he must antecedently be supposed invested with a public character, otherwise the public esteem will serve him in no stead, nor will his virtue have any influence beyond a narrow sphere."

47. For a brilliant analysis of the epistemological origins of this tendency, see Carlo Ginzburg, "Clues," in *Theory and Society* 7 (1974), 273–88.

48. John Rawls, *A Theory of Justice* (Cambridge: Harvard University Press,

1971). Rawls derives the idea of a social union from Hegel and that of equality of opportunity from Sidgwick.

49. Ibid., 7.

50. Ibid., 136ff.

51. Jürgen Habermas, *The Theory of Communicative Action* (Boston: Beacon Press, 1984), I:287.

52. Ibid., 15.

53. Jürgen Habermas, *Moral Consciousness and Communicative Action* (Cambridge: MIT Press, 1990), 211.

54. For an attempt at a critique of Habermas, see Tracy B. Strong and Frank Sposito, "Habermas's Significant Other," in *The Cambridge Companion to Habermas,* ed. S. White (Cambridge: Cambridge University Press, 1995), 263–88, and Georgia Warnke's "Communicative Rationality and Cultural Values," ibid., 120–42.

55. See Sigmund Freud, *Civilization and Its Discontents* (Garden City, N.J.: Doubleday Anchor, 1958), and *Group Psychology and the Analysis of the Ego* (Garden City, N.J.: Doubleday Anchor, 1958).

56. Cf. George Orwell in 1943: "As I write these words highly cultured people are flying over my head, trying to kill me."

57. Raymond Williams, *Drama in a Dramatized Society* (Cambridge: Cambridge University Press, 1972).

58. Rainer Maria Rilke, letter to von Hulewicz, November 13, 1935, in *Letters of Rainer Maria Rilke* (New York: Norton, 1969), 374.

**Part I**

**The World As It Has Come to Us:**

**Power, Stage, Visibility**

# The World As It Has Come to Us:
# Power, Stage, Visibility

In the tradition of Western thought, the very idea of democracy is inseparable from that of public space. We may initially understand public space as a disposition to open and contradictory debate with the aim of making possible a reasoned understanding between citizens with regard to the matter of the definition of institutions, the formulation of laws, and their enforcement. From this point of view, *public* means simultaneously: open to all, well known by all, and acknowledged by all. Public space is citizen and civic space of the common good; it stands in opposition to private space of special interests.

It is clear that in this definition the word *space* has taken on a metaphorical meaning and designates an ensemble of social connections, political institutions, and judicial practices. The literal meaning has almost been wiped out. This may be because the dimension of visibility is no longer taken into account in our democracies, paradoxically just at the moment when the image triumphs everywhere in our culture.

Public space must therefore mean something else: that which is public is offered up for examination, exposed to all. In the eyes of ancient democracies, such a visibility constituted their difference from the autocratic or tyrannical powers that were founded on secrecy or deceit. However, this visibility is not simply an ethical requirement of transparency and truth. It also includes an aesthetic dimension: sovereignty must be perceived in particular signs and externally manifested through monuments, ceremonies, gestures, symbols. The social bond in the democratic community (as in all communities) mobilizes affects around a common cause. That which unifies must be seen, felt, desired, celebrated. We might say that the requirement of visibility "puts up a front"; it exposes—and risks itself—to public scrutiny. Thus, public space necessarily becomes constituted into a *public stage*. This is the source of the ambivalence tied to the power of the stage, the place of the convergence of looks. If what we might call "staging" is a question for all regimes, it has been and remains a badly formulated question in modern democracies, which are preoccupied above all with establishing the rational foundations of their existence. It is from this uneasiness or denial that media professionals in the twentieth century have constructed their power to the point of jeopardizing the very idea of public space, the very idea of a truly *political* sovereignty. They have, in fact, aggravated our confusion over the nature of public space.

The first set of essays in this volume deal in different ways with these questions of power, visibility, theatricality, and democracy. We begin with the general question of (ancient) Greek democracy. In chapter 1, Marcel Detienne, who has written widely on the development and nature of culture in ancient Greece, offers a new approach. He takes up the practices of assembly, that is, the concrete development of a public space for debate and decision. Instead of rehearsing the generally well-known history of the development of public space in ancient Greece, Detienne brings together three different practices: those of the beginnings of Greek democracy; those of a contemporary tribe, the Ochollo of southern Ethiopia; and those of the Constituent Assembly during the French Revolution. Detienne is less interested in the theories of legitimization than in the actual organizing of space for discussion. Thus he notes, for instance, that in Greece such spaces started with the circle of warriors and the requirement that nothing be brought before the group but questions affecting the collective; he remarks on the fact that in such spaces one speaks from the center, that is, from the most common point; finally, he takes up the matter of the exclusion of women. For his second case, he turns to the Ochollo of the Gamo Mountains, where the assembly space is set out by a circle of stones that can also serve as seats. "Magistrates" preside over the assembly; women may be present but only at the outside of the circle (which is more generous than in Greece). Finally, Detienne considers the revolutionary assembly in France. From 1789 on, it had to develop, without any prior experience, the kind of space that would permit those present to exchange looks—to see each other—and it had to determine the rules that governed participation in speech and debate. Such questions of place and practical organization of democratic space are not trivial. In fact, one can go further and assume that these decisions about space and these procedures for exchange and decision are the very stuff of democracy. The visibility of power is not an accident: it is, as Hobbes knew, the very stuff of power.

One might think that in going from the sovereignty of the Greek city-state to Hobbes's idea of sovereignty we are going backward. It seems a bit as if we were returning to the archaic figure of the *basileus*, who dominated his people from the fortress that stood at the heart of the ancient city before democratic reforms imposed the *agora,* that empty space in the middle of the city *(meson)* in which all things are common, known, and shared. Hobbesian sovereignty appears to prove that evolutionary theories of institutions are problematic.

In fact, though, the Hobbesian sovereign (who, it is important to remember, may be an individual, or a group, or the entire people) is the product of a completely different history. It is in part the inheritor of the figure and the status of the medieval monarch, but most important, as a consequence of the "Machiavellian moment," its power is not given but must be constituted. Hobbes approaches the matter differently from Machiavelli: the Hobbesian sovereign has no need to seduce or solicit the passion or the approval of his subjects. Between Machiavelli and Hobbes, we might say, what had been technique becomes ontology. What has happened?

In chapter 2 Paul Dumouchel gives a clear and novel understanding of this question. He argues that the Hobbesian sovereign is defined in and by the fact that he *represents*. Representation is understood here in a double sense, both reflexively as he who wants to give expression to some one or something (as is the case in theater), and nonreflexively, that is, as having the job to be the delegate of someone else. In both cases, to represent is to be an actor.[1] Hobbes's originality comes from the fact that he completely joins both meanings. The sovereign must be seen, must hold himself on stage, must be a *persona,* not to attract votes or approval *but because that is what makes him the sovereign.* In fact, it is only by seeing him as this persona that the subjects can come to a common understanding. The public theatrical image of the sovereign brings about the political unity of the subjects. As Dumouchel argues, "This image does not represent anything other than the power of the multitude, a power it constitutes through the very act of representing it."

Thus, even in the case that appears to be the most uncongenial to democratic public space (uncongenial because, according to Hobbes, the sovereign is established by a contract to which he is not party), the question of visibility in general and of visibility as a public staging remains basic. It is at the heart of political thought after Machiavelli. Theatricality is no longer just an instrument of power, it is thought to be its very essence, the essence of political visibility. This is certainly why, from the Enlightenment on, the rediscovery of democratic political space will come as a reaction against this theatricality, to the point of trying to deny the existence of a staging power (even as this power continues to delineate the space of visibility).[2]

Subsequent thinkers learn from Hobbes (even when they denounce his program) how to push as far as possible his conception of the theatrical necessity in sovereign power. They understand, in other words, that theatricality is not an accident nor a simple tool, but the very being of power. This is the central conviction, as Jacqueline Lichtenstein shows us in chapter 3, in the work of the great French dramatist Pierre Corneille. The representation of power comes to fulfillment in the power of representation. Absolute monarchy identifies itself with its theatrical actualization, not as the production of illusion but as an expression of its own truth. If theater becomes the central literary form, it is because theater is the only form that permits an assembly of the populace (even if only a small fraction) solemnly to partake in the dramatic genesis of sovereignty, and thus allows sovereignty to achieve in theater the reality of its own being, that is, to appear in glory before the public and future generations.

What Corneille's drama also shows, however—and this is the central claim by Lichtenstein—is that it is the *author* who holds the destiny of the sovereign in his hands, or under his pen. If theater actualizes the essence of sovereignty, dramatic writing, and only dramatic writing, can bring it into being. It is as if the author not only abrogates for himself the (symmetrical) position of the sovereign but also makes it more possible. The *auctor* becomes *auctoritas*. One might then say (and this goes beyond Lichtenstein's text) that the author occupies or shows the place of an absent actor, an actor who historically will not be slow in noisily recalling his own existence to all: it is the *people*.

The various strands of Enlightenment thought always turn to this place, albeit in different ways. This claim—which seems to us correct—is not, however, self-evident. Who is the actor who speaks here? Who can make himself heard and in what spaces? What does democratic practice mean in a country with many millions of inhabitants? Can one turn without anachronistic danger to Greek democracy? Detienne reminds us that aside from Athens (which numbered up to thirty thousand citizens), Greek cities generally had no more than five hundred citizens. In concrete terms, when the scale is this large, what are the demands of democracy and what forms does public space take?

These questions are at the heart of Tominaga's essay. In chapter 4 he approaches the problem very concretely in an examination of the "popular societies" of the French Revolution—those often spontaneous groupings of citizens who had taken upon themselves the goal of thinking through in common the events of the Revolution, the decisions of the government, and the founding of the Republic.[3] These "popular societies" are first thought of as the very expression of democratic life, as kind of a necessary local relay station transmitting the actions of the representatives of the nation, as the spearhead of the Revolution. Even more, these societies, made up with that which had been greatly missing in France since the beginning of the absolute monarchy—an affirmation of civil society, composed what Tominaga calls "intermediary groups."

These societies were, without question, the expression of an emerging local public space, the very practice of democracy. The Jacobin Club was one of the most active. However, perhaps not surprisingly, starting in the fall of 1793, these popular societies were the object of systematic repression by those who had emerged from them into positions of power. Such was the famous group called the *Montagnards* (who sat on the top of the "mountain" of the semi-circle). This repression was a clear affirmation of the Jacobin tendency toward centralization, a tendency that in *The Old Regime and the Revolution,* Tocqueville shows, had deep roots in the ancien régime. Thus, the famous Le Chapelier law dissolved and forbade all corporations or professional associations on the theoretical grounds that there could be no intermediary body between the citizen and the state and that the general will could have only one legitimate expression, that of the body of representatives of the nation. Putting these local democratic groups into place—or into silence—was often ineffective or awkwardly carried out, but it does show the degree to which, in France at least, the voice of citizens was suspect when it expressed itself directly.

This points us at a central question: How can one be heard locally? Who controls the words that one hears? How may a space of and for discussion be constituted? How might one practice what Kant called "the public use of reason"? It is possible that the articulation of contemporary experience can profit by looking again at the Greeks.

This is Peter Euben's project, one that he undertakes from an unusual angle. He raises the question of the political content of *comedy* in the Greek city and in modern society. Comedy would seem to deal with nonpolitical topics, questions of private life and matters of the everyday. If one looks, however, at ancient comedy, one sees, as Euben shows us, the degree to which it was practiced in a ritual framework. Comedy undertook, in its own way, to educate citizens by an ironic look at customs and mores, at political abuses and at injustices (such as the separation of women from public life). Can one say as much of contemporary comedy, especially that on television? Euben turns here to a number of sitcoms and television series. He concludes that with some very important and significant exceptions, television has not played this role. It has refused a critical function; indeed, the very structure of television shows makes social critique difficult or impossible. Euben's verdict is severe, but he poses a fundamental question as to the status of new media in modern democracies. These are questions taken up in Part II.

### Notes

1. Cf. Hanna Pitkin, *The Concept of Representation* (Berkeley and Los Angeles: University of California Press, 1967), chapters 1–2.

2. Cf. Jonas Barish, *The Anti-Theatrical Prejudice* (Berkeley and Los Angeles: University of California Press, 1981).

3. One could also turn here to Aristides Zolberg, "Moments of Madness," in *Theory and Society* 1 (1974). All writers on this topic also owe a debt to Hannah Arendt, *On Revolution* (New York: Viking Press, 1963).

# 1

# Public Space and Political Autonomy in Early Greek Cities

**Marcel Detienne**

I must introduce these claims about early Greek cities with three disclaimers.

First, there can be no question of speaking of the Greeks as if they were directly, and by nature, the discoverers or the founders of that which was one day called—in their own language, it is true—democracy.

Second, rather than finding that Greek alterity sprang up on its own, whether in grandeur or in an empty universality (in either case, an academic and compulsive exercise), I will propose a constructive comparison between three societies or social groups. Each of these is unknown to the other, and in their observed and observable practices, each inaugurates and establishes a public space, and puts into action a sort of autonomy of the political: one, contemporary, in Africa, in southern Ethiopia; a second in Europe, the French Constituent Assembly between 1789 and 1791; and the last, some very small cities of continental Greece and southern Italy with which we become more and more familiar every day, thanks to archeological research and epigraphist historians.

One further comment: if by this comparative approach, I intend to instigate reflections on certain elements of a more complex configuration (as elaborated in the other essays in this volume and as proposed by the editors), I must also state that I reject as a starting point the stance that the political springs up, already fully equipped, as common sense silently based on the institutions of an Athenian space, a space that is itself already inhabited by Solon, if not by Cleisthenes. In saying *the political,* I allude to that which a Greek, who, when addressing himself to the Great King, called, according to the *Histories* of Herodotus, *tò politikón.* He referred to a public place where those people, which the Great King found so interesting, came together to talk while appearing to argue among themselves. Such was an exotic spectacle for the despot from Asia. My approach will be to look at practices and, more precisely, at the practices' assembly, while taking into account that these practices of assembly are constitutive both of a public space and of a certain form of the political.

First, I would like to put into perspective the three types of society, removed from one another in time and space. I will then examine the question of the birth of a public space, focusing particularly on the Greek case. Finally, with reference to that which certain anthropologists call "politico-religious," I will attempt to define what the autonomy of the political means by returning to a common consideration of these three human groups, chosen because each proposes, in its own fashion, a sudden self-awareness of the group, along with practices of debate that raise the question of the idea of the sovereignty of this group, especially as to what concerns it.

My examples regarding practices of assembly, as I have noted, are taken from Ethiopia, Greece, and revolutionary France. For me, the most exotic and surprising of these practices have been and still remain those of the first Constituents of 1789 in France. When the Third Estate begins to come together, the problem of the space in which it does so is immediately raised. They meet in the general common room at Trois Ordres, a room dominated by a platform from which the king's throne rises up and on which the court is seated. In front of this high, wide platform stands a large table at which the secretaries of state are seated; beyond this are the deputies' benches! Seats are more or less padded for the clergy and the nobility; plain wood is reserved for the Third Estate. Thus there are no rising tiers of seats, and it would appear very difficult that an assembly of eleven hundred people could confer in this space in an intelligible manner. The Third Estate, however, is going to constitute itself a National Assembly without leaving these premises and in the confusion of this space full of seats, a space designed for seeing and for listening, for audiences, not for debating. In his *Paroles de la révolution* (Words of the revolution),[1] Patrick Brasart observes that in 1989, the French had no experience of their own of parliamentary debate. The constituents are going to invent an "order of the day," choose a specific location where they can be in order, sustain public debate, and prepare the questions to be debated in commissions and committees.

Only on October 22, 1791, does a deputy, Quatremère de Quincy, ask for and succeed in getting the room laid out in a more or less circular manner or, rather, in the shape of an ellipse, such that each member of the assembly might be seen by each other. Here is a first suggestion of egalitarian space; however, the explicit request is to *hear* and to *see*, in such a way as not to be obliged to shout, for "a man who shouts is in a forced state, and, precisely because of that, he is ready to become violent, . . . he communicates the quality of where he is to those who listen to him." We have then a report, from a committee, and a decision: to give the space a semi-elliptical form, with the president of the assembly at a focus of the ellipse and, all around, semi-circular tiers of seats. The best position for the orator's tribune still remains to be chosen. It will be at the center of the ellipse. The principle of allocating the central position to the spoken word will profoundly differentiate the revolutionary French eloquence from that of the English House of Commons where, since the seventeenth century, one speaks from one's place. Two years is a short period but a very long time to reinvent the circular theatrical form that seems to us to be part of the memory of a society so sensitive to Plutarch and antiquity, to theaters and to Ecclesiai, the assemblies.

Twenty years ago, a French ethnologist who left to map kinship relations in the Gamo Mountains came back with a thesis on the organization of space that he will entitle *The Place of the Political (L'espace du politique)*.[2] This ethnologist, Marc Abélès, has since become ethnologist of the new European assemblies. In Ethiopia, he discovered the Ochollo society, which holds assemblies on a daily basis: district assemblies, subdistrict assemblies, and a general assembly of all the districts for the most important affairs. These are plenary assemblies, prepared and convoked by individuals on an ad hoc basis. And, to the great surprise of Abélès, these assemblies take place inside a circle of stones hewed into the shape of a chair. The assemblies are open to all the Ochollos, male citizens, from puberty on. The artisan castes, held to be impure, are excluded. Twenty years ago, women could speak but only if they kept themselves at the limit of the stone circle. Today—for Abélès has returned to this "field"—the women, who have profited from the progress of socialist and Maoist movements, are full members of the assembly. The person who asks the presidents—who are the "sacrificers" of the country—for permission to speak leaves his place and comes to face the assembly in the arc of the circle, in front of the seated presidents. The Constituents of 1789 could have taken inspiration from the Ethiopian agoras, assuming, that is, these agoras had already been in existence. Nothing we know at present allows us to believe that the Ochollos (considered "savages" by the Amharic

Ethiopians) might have been inspired by the *Odyssey* or the *Iliad* or, indeed, even the Constituent Assembly. One should be cautious about imputing historical influence: for instance, Italian communes between the eleventh and twelfth centuries did not borrow—from Rome, nor from anywhere else—the practices of assembly that they developed more or less at the same time, without acting in concert with one another.

The Ethiopian agora is still active today. Eight centuries before our era, about 750–730 BCE, in Asia Minor, Sicily, and the Peloponnese, groups of men speaking Greek appear to achieve self-awareness when they undertake practices of assembly, on an iterated basis, according to well-established rules. These practices deal with major goals of the collectivity of the participants in the assemblies.

Let us examine two spaces of assembly, the one monumental and archeological in one of the most ancient, if not the most ancient, Greek city founded in Sicily; the other, a space of speech and performance between the Achaians of the *Iliad* and the citizens of the *Odyssey*.

The first space: some Megarians who have left their homeland for the lands of the West trace the plan of the future city of Megara Hyblaea on the ground on the southern coast of Sicily. Somewhere in the middle of this chosen land, they set aside the location of an agora that will be designed by architects three generations later. No other site—I can point this out straightaway—was set aside in a similar manner by the founder-surveyor. This site was destined for the sanctuaries of gods, for the temples, all of which were constructed much later. Another fact suggests a social meaning and even, we might say, a sociopolitical one. The land was divided into plots, most certainly selected by lottery, more or less regular, more or less equal. The *Odyssey* evokes the figure of the founder of the Phaeacians' city: Nausithous, the father of Alcinous. He flees the neighborhood of the Cyclops—people who are both "without law" *(anomos)* and "without assemblies," brutes, violent people—and founded on territory that was nowhere, a city, a polis, with its agora, its rampart of stone, temples for the gods, and plots of land.

Let us turn to the second space of assembly: the agora in activity. It might be the fixed place chosen by Greeks in arms, as do the Achaeans of the *Iliad* when they meet at a location situated in front of the ships of Ulysses. It might even be the agora of Ithaca's citizens. The Greeks, armed and come to make war on the Trojans, sketch a site for assemblies in the space of the camp. In the vocabulary of the epic, an agora refers at one and the same time to several matters that we tend to distinguish. It is the *locality*, the place where assemblies are held; it is the *people* who make up the "deliberative" assembly, the men at arms; and, finally, it is the *speech* pronounced at the assembly. Indeed, agora, in both the singular and the plural, signifies "clash of discourse, debates that take place in the assembly."[3] It has been observed for a long time that neither in the epic nor elsewhere does agora designate an informal exchange of words; it is never a chat, a conversation that we would call private. The agora, in fact, is a place of words and of debate on the communal affairs of the assembled group. Initiating speech in this place follows a ritual described in the epic and that seems to have been the same since the agora came into existence. The ritual and symbolic dimension is marked by the divine figure of Themis, associated with deciding speech, a power that opens and closes the space and the time of the assembly.

The assembly takes the shape of a circle or a semicircle. The person who wants to speak approaches the middle, seizes the *sképtron*, the staff that confers authority to his opinions and or his counsel. His speech, his agora, must relate to what the *Odyssey* calls a "public" affair, *démion ti*, a question concerning the community, that is, concerning the agora inasmuch as it is the assembly of those who constitute the group. These individuals have the right of speech and therefore are citizens.

In the case of the French Constituent Assembly, from notes and archives we can reconstruct the proceedings that lead to the new organization of a space in which there is egalitarian and public speech. In the archaic Greece of the epic as well as that of the first cities, these practices are already in place; they are so clearly delineated that we can specify through complementary images of the agora how the assembly's space was structured. The central point of the circle or semicircle of the warriors is the locus of that which is of the most common, that which belongs to everyone. It is there, for example, that the spoils of war to be shared are deposited: it is "the pool," *xunèia keímena*. The common thing, *xunon*, at the same time as the *koínon*, defines, in the practices of sharing and of speech, this self-awareness of a group that thinks itself in an egalitarian mode, able to decide its own affairs as its own sovereign. These practices, which I believe strongly associated with the Greek warrior as a type of man, have constructed and shaped, both spatially and symbolically, a place that we can call "the place of the political."

We must now analyze, in a comparative manner, the "place of the political." On the one hand, we will look at the dimensions of public space as they relate to specific practices of publicness; on the other, we will examine the perspective of the "politico-religious," that is, of the realm of the symbolic and of its part in the grounding and autonomy of the political.

Public space, publicity, public opinion: these three categories do not have the same meaning for the Ochollo on the Gamo Mountains, nor for French society of 1789, nor for a little Greek city freshly blossomed on the shores of the Mediterranean. In the eighteenth century in France, *public opinion* takes shape as a new development when, in opposition to the state and the king, a public sphere is constituted that creates a space empowering critical and individual reasoning on public questions. Public opinion functions like a tribunal, often supreme, whose new judges are the men of letters. As for the public sphere or public space, it is the increased circulation of the printed word in the societies of the ancien régime, between the sixteenth and the eighteenth centuries, that establishes a new public space. Pamphlets and newspapers are ready to retransmit debates and decisions of the Constituents. In turn, in their search for the most propitious space in which an assembly of twelve hundred people may function, these men are very preoccupied with questions of where the public will be placed, in how many galleries, and how to keep the public of galleries from perturbing or dominating the debate of the assembly of "representatives" of a people of several million subjects who have recently been promoted to citizens.

A Greek city of the eighth or the seventh century BCE would contain between two and five hundred citizens, "united in assembly." It was a face-to-face society, without an ancien régime, and thus resembles Ethiopia's Ochollo society, with its general assemblies of two or three hundred people. Here public opinion does not have to function like a tribunal, for these are assemblies that directly administer the communal business.

Indeed, in the Ochollo society there are different categories of public places. Those of the subdistricts serve to prepare the plenary assembly that takes place on the eldest of spaces. This plenary assembly is the true place of political speech: the decisions of the plenary assembly, taken by consensus, engage all of the Ochollo, from different districts. Therefore, the greatest publicity is sited in the place of the plenary assembly. This fact does not erase the public character from places of the debate that is dispersed within the subdistricts. In order to grasp how interesting is the Ethiopian configuration (known as "southern mountainous"), it is necessary to remember that in a great part of "tradition-al" West Africa there are no "public places," delineated and circum-scribed as such. What is more, there is generally no space between the power of the king or the royal chief and a society organized by clans. The king brings together in his person all the powers disseminated in the clans or the lineages. His power is very often made sacred. There is no chink left between his person, covered with prohibitions, and the society of clans or of lineages, which only becomes self-aware in recog-nizing that the king has the privilege of ensuring the union of the so-ciety with the totality of visible and invisible forces of nature. Such so-cieties quite unconsciously show that the foundations of authority are inconceivable and unintelligible without having recourse to rituals re-lated to power. Such rituals, complexes, and niches mobilize more strength and energy than does the participation in assemblies in Ochollo country.

My hurried evocation of the landscape of these African kingships allows me to insist upon a central quality of the beginnings of the Greek city: this takes place on a horizon from which sovereignty, so visible with the Mycenean palaces, has disappeared and been erased. This absence, of course, facilitates many experiments in the field of the "governing of the people by the people." Public space, publicity, and public opinion: Are any of these present in the early Greek cities? Public opinion, in the eighteenth-century sense of the term, is not the concern here. By strengthening itself and, above all, by its own means of publicity, public space renders public opinion useless. By its practice of assembly, the agora signifies the direct participation of citizens with full rights. From archaic texts, which are pragmatic but neither politi-cal nor juridical, we will conclude that the agora is the place of decid-ing and deliberating. It is also to the agora and before the assembled citizens that in Crete, for example, one comes to declare that one adopts a certain person or accepts such and such goods in the case of a contested heritage; it is where one files a proclamation to begin pro-ceedings in the case of a homicide, much in the way that Draco an-nounced in Athens around 620 BCE.

Public space and "the political" will be considerably reinforced by the institution of the tribunal of blood and the appearance of a penal right in the case of homicide. More important, the first cities passed legislation and statutes concerning the murder of a member of the com-munity in terms that evoked "we the citizens." Between 620 and 530 BCE, the laws or decisions made concerning a murder were written in large letters and in color on steles, both in the young cities in Sicily and Magna Graecia as in the continental cities, like Argo or Athens. If an individual were killed in the space of a city, from that moment on, the city is the one affected. It is the city that sets the compensation due to the parents and to the collectivity. The extension of public and civic space, on the one hand and, on the other, the subjection of the murderer to law, either committed voluntarily, involuntarily, with premeditation, or legitimately, according to the casuistry put into place by Draco or Zaleucos. In the same way, the city will soon institute a space for judgment, a public space with citizens' participation in juries; there, the confrontation between the accusation and the subject presumed guilty takes place. The Greek city assembled at the agora and debated in public, that is to say, it faced itself. Thus, the affairs of the city and of the citizens could have prolonged these practices of speech and assembly, as they do for the people of Ochollo.

In effect, a culture of the spoken word makes itself evident in these small cities. It happens that the Greeks have an alphabetic form of writing. This is a very human and completely new invention, an important instrument of publicity. Around 650 BCE, Dreros, a small city on Crete, engraved on a block of gray limestone *(sideropétra)* the following decision: "The city has decided: when a person is appointed to *cosme* [the highest magistrate], for ten years, that same person can no longer be the *cosme,*" and so forth. What can this practice of engraving practical regulations on stones, on steles sometimes as high as one meter, mean? Such surfaces are entirely reserved to writing. We find a particular law about homicide engraved on an object usually reserved for the practical regulations, such as one found in Chios, where we read "that the Assembly may come together twelve days after the festival of Apollo." Or that found in San Mauro di Caltaglione, in bronze this time, with the inscription that the murderer, according to culpability, will be subject to certain compensation. What does this mean? We can perhaps quickly disregard the hypothesis that these public inscriptions were written for the intention of the future epigraphist. It is more convincing to believe that this writing of the city is a political writing destined to make public in time—the time to come—that which the citizens, united in assembly, have decided to put into practice, "to meet at that moment."

The council *(boulé)* introduces a position, and the majority of the assembly decides what it wants. These engravings record practical decisions and more or less important rules. Indeed, one of the essential rules of the magistrate function is to provide accounts. They complete and redesign the project of the assembly or, let us call it more precisely, its will. The regime of the first Greek cities thus follows a volitional model: all the rules are conceived as established at a given moment, and all the decrees said to be *thesmoi,* "firmly established words," are sanctioned by the civic group to the degree that it has a consciousness of itself. (Thus we find "we, the city," or "it pleased the council and the assembly.") What is affirmed through the many decisions posted, published, and exposed in visible and symbolic places is the idea of the sovereignty of the group itself. This sovereignty extends to all of social life; it encompasses that which a city of Crete calls in order to distinguish them "the affairs of the gods, and the affairs of men." We can say that there is no true constitution in Greece, nothing more than a code of laws, in the strict sense of the term. We are at times tempted to translate *politeia* as "constitution"; however, the word implies *a certain way of reacting* in the political domain. Thus, every city proposes its own way. Retrospectively, however, certain common traits stand out, most particularly, the double register of the affairs of men and those of the gods.

Now I take on the last question: that of the politico-religious sphere and, inseparably, the question of autonomy of the political. Here, the comparison should focus on the two configurations, Ethiopian and Greek, that are the most directly marked by the mixture that can be called politico-ritual or politico-religious. Revolutionary France invented a new revolutionary praxis that, in the debates of 1789–91, questioned the status of religion in the new regime. Religion in this case, however, coincides with the discourse that connects it firmly to Catholicism and thereby with the great weight of the church that wants to think of all as *katholon,* as "in general," including society, education, and knowledge. The major questions of this long debate are, "Should the state have a religion?" Is the only skill that cannot fundamentally define the field of action of the citizen the discussion of the form of a religion? Therefore, one should argue for a possible plurality of religions, along with a guarantee of a supreme being? These questions are more comparable in the first instance to what the American Revolution encountered, posed, and reformulated in its own way from a plural tradition formed by Protestantisms. In the Ethiopian or, rather, the Ochollo arena (which, incidentally, was not the only African society to have chosen this method), the politico-religious is rather legible even at the level of organization of the first assembly. It takes place in relation to two positions, those of the *magistrate* and of the *sacrificer*. The magistrates or dignitaries are persons chosen for their capacity to react and to decide on common affairs; they are elected and designated "messengers of the assembly," the decisions of which they execute. As for the sacrificers, they control all the ritual and sacrificial activities of a space completely controlled and crisscrossed by altars and the ceremonial. The role is hereditary and is linked to the assembly by the religious authority of their status. They sit at the place of honor in the semicircle of the amphitheater. The sacrificer and magistrate are the two essential characters of the assembly and the two poles of the space of the political. The magistrates have the privilege of ritually delineating the space of the assembly as well as opening the debates by benedictions. The sacrificers, on the other hand, are experts in all forms of ritual; they represent a religious authority in the circle of the assembly and are held to silence during the debates conducted by the magistrates, who, nonetheless, must in turn respect the equality of individual speech, under the penalty of being thrown out and banned from the assembly. In a very concrete manner, the religious and the political are respectively held in equilibrium, in a space of assembly that proposes a political figure. In the political, one sees that autonomy and experience continue; indeed, it is carried on under the eyes of the returning visitor, twenty years later, at the moment where the assembly, prohibited by Maoist diktat from the capital (as "a remnant of the past"), was reborn under the impulsion of young Ochollos engaged in the new political life. The book by Abélès is in the course of being translated into the language of the Ochollo, and it seems to play an nonnegligible role in the understanding of a "place of the political," modern and very out of keeping with other contemporary African societies.

In what forms did the politico-religious appear within the first Greek cities? When the Greeks established a place of assembly, in the middle of their camp, they installed an altar for their gods, those to whom they offered sacrifices, to the gods who were, without doubt, "of all the Greeks." The matter is made very precisely in the *Iliad* (11, 807): "Where there is agora, the assembly and Themis/themis, the power that opens and closes the agora, that which represents speech firmly established in the common decision, that is where the altars of the gods have been built"—altars and not temples (that perhaps were made of wood, anticipating a siege that might endure). At Megara Hyblaea, circa 730 BCE, near the agora, the founders did not forget to plan spaces both for altars and emplacements for the temples.

The Greek temple soon come to function as a public space, a property of the city, the care of which is confided each year by the assembly to the elected magistrates. The Greek gods are in the world, in the midst of humans, implicated in all the sectors of human activity, including the then most recent: when the people, as is told, invent a new way to live together, that is to say in the *city*, the gods soon quarrel over the honor of presiding over the pantheon foreseen in each political establishment. They jostle with one another for the position of being the divinity with the most important territories. No Greek god was ever upset at not having invented the agora or the political. It is thus that writing is a question concerning only the mortals.

The Greek city is an object of contradictory interpretations. Some see in it a sort of church, with its festivals and temples. Others celebrate the coming into being of the secular. If it is proper to insist on the specificity for the invention of politics in the early Greek cities, one should not neglect to mention that the public space encompassed the gods and the men, and that the domain of the political takes in its charge the affairs of both men and gods. Therefore, gods are thought of as distinct and separated from man but without any transcendence and whose impact is scattered and fragmented in all of the social practices, thus constituting polytheism and its cultural network. Two traits seem to me to characterize the politico-religious regime in Greece. First, the assemblies, opened by the sacrifices that define the public space and formed by other sacrificial activities, are sovereign for a majority decision as to not only the material details of the religious calendar (festivals and sacrifices) but also the modification of that which we call the structures of the pantheon: the calendar, the order of the festivals, the choice of one god or hero or goddess of another power. Second, there are thus assemblies that deliberate for the affairs of the gods, without denying the right to deliberate also for the affairs of the people. In which order does this occur? The affairs of the gods would take precedence over the proceedings to admit a newly introduced citizen into the assembly and, above all, over the claim that only the citizens of first rank have the right to examine them. A newly appointed citizen is excluded; he enters into the assembly *after* the "affairs of the gods," *metà ta hiera*. Only well-born citizens, with three generations of citizenship, are qualified to decide by a majority the price of sacrificial victims and of the hierarchy of the god candidates in the sanctuaries of the city. The temporal order—first the gods, then human affairs—expresses therefore a discrete and well-established hierarchy. Independently of the philosophers and the sophists who are going to theorize the models of the political, the practice of the assembly in the Greek city is going to shape this style of the political in its abstract autonomy, an autonomy that gives itself symbolic support. The gods of the city are in the background of the self-government plan of men for the sake of men. This is how the magistrates who have the most authority hold on to their dignity *(timè)* from the half-religious, half-political power that in many cities is called the common hearth, Hestia, a sister to the Roman Vesta. The common hearth—insofar as it becomes the very idea of the city, one and many—is abstract as a center that implies an equal sharing, and it is as real as the flame on the first altar inaugurating a new city. This common hearth thereby opens the procession with a series of concepts (decision, persuasion, agreement, consensus) and of half-religious powers like Aphrodite, Hermes, or Artemis, and also of half-political categories. All these prove useful for thinking through an important question for any group—how does it give itself rules?—and, at the same time, thinking through the inherent reasons for acknowledging them according to what Solon calls vigor and force (*ischus* and *krato*), always with the zest of "violence."

Be this in Sicily, or on Mont Gamo, or in the hotel "Menus Plaisirs du Roi" along old Saint-Martin Street in Paris, we find that practices of assembly, at three different moments in human history, have paths both near and far to explore, at the limits of social life, the symbolic realm that is for us, I believe, *the secret part of politics* (as Claude Lefort says), where and when the political is realized in its autonomy, an autonomy that is neither one nor "catholic."

### Notes

1. Patrick Brasart, *Paroles de le révolution: Les assemblées parlementaires, 1789–1794* (Paris: Minerve, 1988).

2. Marc Abélès, *Le lieu du politique* (Paris: Société d'éthnographie, 1983).

3. See here Françoise Ruzé, *Délibération et pouvoir dans la cité grecque: De Nestor à Socrates* (Paris: Publications de la Sorbonne, 1997).

# 2

## *Persona*: Reason and Representation in Hobbes

### Paul Dumouchel

Representation is usually considered one of the key concepts of modern political theory. As such, representation is viewed as a mechanism of legitimization that defines a form of government, and it is generally linked to modern democracy. A representative government is a type of political organization where power is held through the accord, agreement, or authorization of those governed. From this point of view, "representation" is seen as a characteristic of the government or political power—as something political power does: it represents, or is taken as a condition that government satisfies (or should satisfy), as in the expression, "No taxation without representation." There is another way in which the term *representation* is used in the context of politics; for example, in such expressions as "the representation of power," or when we say that "Versailles was constructed to *represent* the power of Louis XIV both to French nobility and to all of Europe." In cases like this, representation is taken as something exterior to political power itself, something added to it. Though in many instances this representing is done by government itself, it is not an intrinsic characteristic of a certain form of political power but something that can be added to any type of power.

Conceptually, these two meanings of representation are clearly distinct and logically independent. A nonrepresentative government can represent itself, for example, through a personality cult. *A contrario,* a representative government can fail to represent itself (properly), as, for example, in Canada, in a recent referendum campaign. At the conceptual level, two major characteristics seem to distinguish these two meaning of representation: first, as hinted before, reflexivity in the case of *representing* power and nonreflexivity in the case of *representative* power. On the one hand, a government is representative only if what it represents is not government itself, but the people, the nation, interest groups, major social agents, etc. It is only through them that it finds its legitimacy and meaning as being a representative government. On the other hand, representing power is reflexive. It is power representing itself. Though others such as artists, historians, or journalists may be doing the actual representing, we speak of the representation of power only if the end result of such representing is the very power represented. If, from making manifest political power, what follows is not the enhancement or at least the stability of that power, we usually do not speak of representing power but of criticism, of analysis, or even of sedition.

The second characteristic is that nonreflexive political representation tends to be all or nothing, at least in the following sense: we may disagree as to which regime is actually representative, or we may consider that one form of political representation is preferable to another, or even that members of some groups are represented while others are not. But in each case, representation either takes place or it does not. The reason is that, conceptually, political representation is procedural, and in real life, either the procedure is respected or it is not.[1] There is no in-between. If transgression of the election law has been too frequent, if it took place in half of the documented cases, then the result is not half representation but that the election is void.

On the contrary, reflexive political representation, like theatrical representation (which, in a way, is also reflexive), can be more or less successful or efficient.[2] It can be good or bad, better or worse, but generally the alternatives are not simply existence or nonexistence. A bad play is still a play. Reflexive representation is continuous rather than discrete, by degree rather than all or nothing. The representation of political power, unlike political representation (which can be absent but not more or less), is always present but often unsuccessful. Power does not always succeed in making itself manifest as it wants. The image it gives of itself is not always the one it desires.

My goal here is to inquire into the relationship between these two types of representation in Hobbes's political philosophy. I want to show that in Hobbes's case, contrary to what pure conceptual analysis suggests, the relationship between the two meanings of the word *representation* is not simply exterior and accidental. I will argue that within Hobbes's political construction, the fact that power should be represented is not a contingent fact but derives necessarily from its structure as representative power: more precisely, it is indistinguishable from it. Further, the representative dimension of power imposes constraints on the way in which it can be represented if that representation is to be successful. Not only is an adequate representation of himself part of the sovereign's duty toward his subjects (being a necessary condition of political stability), but all of Hobbes's political philosophy can be seen as an effort to supply such a satisfactory form of representation to existing powers. Finally, I wish to argue that Hobbes's method of demonstration is determined by the way in which, according to him, political power should represent itself.

Some may want to argue that Hobbes confuses the two meanings of representation. It is true, as we will see, that the central concept of Hobbes's theory of political representation (what I will refer to as his theory of representative power), that of *persona* or actor, is taken from theater and that Hobbes may be suspected of having failed to distinguish reflexive from procedural political representation.[3] But we should, I believe, at least at first, refrain from judgments about Hobbes's consistency or his analytical abilities. Hobbes's conflation of the two meanings of representation did not stem from a conceptual confusion but from what he believed was empirical evidence. Contrary to us, Hobbes thought that representative power constitutes not one form of government among others but the very essence of political organization. This is what allowed him to intertwine so closely the two concepts of representation, in what I will argue is a coherent theory. The question, I believe, still remains open as to whether Hobbes was right in considering that determining the essence of political power is an empirical question, rather than a conceptual one.

### La Boétie and Hobbes: "Voluntary Servitude" or Consenting Subjects?

Approximately eighty years before Hobbes began publishing, Etienne de La Boétie asserted, in *Le discours de la servitude volontaire* (1574),[4] that tyrants could rule only with the help of those they oppress:

> He who thus domineers over you has only two eyes, only two hands, only one body, no more than is possessed by the least man among the infinite numbers dwelling in your cities; he has indeed nothing more than the power that you confer upon him to destroy you. Where has he acquired enough eyes to spy upon you, if you do not provide them yourselves? How can he have so many arms to beat you with, if he does not borrow them from you? The feet that trample down your cities, where does he get them if they are not your own? How does he have any power over you except through you? (11–12)

What shocked La Boétie was not simply that in an oppressive regime subjects could be seen as accessories to the crime of which they were victims but that essentially, without them, the crime could not have been perpetrated. The *Anti-Dictator or Discourse on Voluntary Servitude* was intended as a charge against repressive political powers, but seen from a Hobbesian point of view, it does not constitute a delegitimization of tyranny so much as the ultimate proof that all political power is representative. Hobbes agrees with La Boétie's observation, but he draws a different conclusion. Were it not for the hands, the eyes, and the feet we supply to it, no power could rule over us, and this clearly means that there can be no power over us without our consent. The reason this conclusion is inescapable, according to Hobbes, is because there is no natural way out of the state of nature. There is no end to the war of all against all that, in spite of Hobbes's improperly named "natural dominion," does not rest on the contract, a social artifact whose essence is representation. Given that no one, according to Hobbes, is strong enough to subjugate all others by his mere power,[5] all political organizations, no matter how unpleasant or oppressive, exist only through the consent of those subjected to them. This consent constitutes the sovereign as representative of his subjects.

Hence, Hobbes's claim concerning the representative dimension of political power should not be seen as normative (as ours usually are when we speak of representative government) but as descriptive. According to Hobbes, representation is a fact obscured in the institutions of his time, but no power can exist without the consent of those subjected to it. That is why no political power is illegitimate, and why Hobbes wrote that tyranny is only the name given to monarchy by those who dislike it, and not a different form of political organization. For Hobbes, representation is revealed in the mere existence of relatively peaceful, stable political regimes, since such peace can result only from a power so great that it could not exist without the consent of its subjects.

This is why the question of the existence of representative power is first and foremost empirical. If existing political powers were not to some extent authorized, we would find all around us the war of all against all. But since this is not what we see, representation is a fact—a social fact rather than a fact of nature.[6] It is not a goal to be attained but an indisputable characteristic of any sufficiently pacified polity. What scandalized la Boétie, and condemned (or so he thought) arbitrary power to absurdity, appeared to Hobbes to be the fundamental problem of political theory. What to La Boétie was a contradiction, proof of the illegitimacy of a particular form of government, to Hobbes was the indication that all forms of political power are legitimate, if only they can guarantee the security of their subjects, for no power able to do so can exist without their consent.

But it was also the proof that all forms of political power are excessively fragile, for they are dependent on the changing opinions of the subjects. One of Hobbes's major goals was to solve that difficulty. How could political power rest on the consent of the subjects and, at the same time, not be hostage to their moods or fashions? That difficulty led to a series of paradoxes: how can political power be coercive? How can one agree to his own death or punishment? How can subjects be said to consent to a power whose decision they reject?

### *Persona*: Unity and Unlimited Trust

Hobbes's means of approaching these difficulties is through his concept of representation, which, as we will see, rests on an idea originating in Roman theatre: that of *person* or *persona*. As Hobbes tells us in *Leviathan*, "A person is he *whose words or actions are considered either as his own or as representing the words or actions of another man, or of any other thing to whom they are attributed, whether truly or by fiction*" (101, italics in original).

A person, then, is he or she who can act. That person is called a "natural person" if his words and actions are attributed to him, or an "artificial person" if they are attributed to someone or to something else, whether that attribution is true or fictional. Thus, a person is a "representer," representing himself, another, or some thing. *Representing,* as the quote indicates, is first and foremost a question of attribution. The legitimacy of representing is then the question of the legitimacy of certain attributions of words and actions. A *represents* B, if A's action can be attributed legitimately to B. Nonetheless, it does not follow that attribution is legitimate, that A's action is in consequence necessarily B's action. A university, a church, or a bridge, Hobbes tells us, can be represented, though this can only take place in the state of society, for such inanimate objects cannot be the authors of any action (102–3). The authors of the action in such cases are those who own or govern the represented object—a deacon, dean, or caretaker—and who are authorized or have authorized others to represent the given institution.

The attribution of action in such cases is fictional but not so the representation. A spokesperson, if he or she is duly authorized, actually speaks for the university, the church, or the bridge. Attribution is successful if the representation was authorized. The authority is the author's permission, by which the actor or person (here, let us assume it is a "he") impersonates what or whom he represents—which may or may not be the author. But in all cases, the actor's action can be attributed to what he represents only inasmuch as the actor is authorized. The author recognizes the representer's act as his own only to the extent that the actor has not gone beyond his commission.

Finally, an actor or an "artificial person" can create unity among a multitude. The *persona* will do this if he is authorized by each particular person to represent him. Through that process, Hobbes tells us, the multitude is made one, "For it is the *unity* of the representer, not the *unity* of the represented, that maketh the person *one*" (104).[7] Representation is, then, a question of attribution, and attribution is successful only if the person is authorized.

Representation, as we saw, is also a question of action, for the essential characteristic of a person, whether natural or artificial, is action.[8] In representing, it is the representer's actions that are *attributed* to the author (or to something else under his care), and not the author's actions that are *represented* by the artificial person. This is fundamental, and it marks the main difference between Hobbes's notion of political representation and our concept of representative government. The goal or essence of representation, according to Hobbes, is not for the representer to manifest, reproduce, or render public the actions, desires, or intentions of he whom he represents but that the *represented* should *own* the actions, words, and deeds of the representer. Though it may happen that the representer is merely a mouthpiece for he whom he represents, in *essence* the representer is a plenipotentiary minister whose decision binds their author—the authority he represents.

This is clear from the fact that political representation is essentially the artifact through which one person represents a multitude of individuals and thus reduces them to unity. This representation cannot mean that the actor or persona reenacts the various actions of all the members of the unity but that they have all agreed to recognize the representer's actions as their own. We tend to understand political representation (representative government) in the context of something like a correspondence theory of truth. We think representation is true or successful if the representer presents an exact or faithful image of what or whom he represents. To the contrary, Hobbes understands representation as a theory of unlimited trust. We are true to representation when we recognize as ours the representer's actions, whatever they may be. In the first case, in its modern sense, representation imposes a duty upon he who represents. In Hobbes's sense, it imposes a duty upon those who are represented.

As Hobbes's reminds us at the beginning of chapter 16 of *Leviathan,* "Of Persons, Authors, and Things Personated," the word *persona* also means the mask the comedian wore in ancient tragedy (101). One can argue that for Hobbes, the actor or representer is essentially that: a mask that hides as much as it reveals of the character impersonated. For it is not only the individual who plays the role who is dissimulated behind the laughing or crying mask but all characters who are thus reduced to a unity of expression. So is it with the sovereign: he conceals the diversity and reveals only the unity of those he represents.

## A Trade-Off in Rights

In the social contract or covenant, each member of the multitude lays down his absolute right to everything, under the condition that everyone does the same, and all transfer their right to one who is not a party to the contract, and who is then said to bear their person and to represent them. In transferring their absolute right to that artificial person, Hobbes tells us, they do not add anything to his right, which was already absolute, but they free its exercise from all the impediments that, until then, were constituted of everyone's competing right (181, 109). This does not mean that the sovereign obtains no new power though he receives no new right. In the state of nature, everyone's absolute right to everything came from the fact that each one was the absolute judge of what was and was not necessary for his protection and survival. By abandoning their right to everything, all have transferred that absolute judgment to the sovereign, and because that judgment is absolute, they have abandoned it absolutely. This does not mean that subjects will never again judge on anything concerning their protection or survival, for that would be impossible, but that they have agreed neither to challenge nor to oppose the sovereign's decisions concerning what is necessary for their security. So, when he orders them to do this or that, they are obliged to obey, for they have agreed that the sovereign is the sole judge of what is necessary for their peace. Of course, it may be wondered why they have agreed to such a complete translation of rights, why they consented to such perfect subjection.

Hobbes's answer is well known. It is that if everyone retained his absolute right to everything, a state of permanent insecurity and ever-lurking violence would follow. Each one's right to everything is void as long as it is claimed by everyone. It is only by relinquishing their right to everything that men can come to have the right to some things. Given this, according to Hobbes, if in the world as we know it, some have a right to more than others and if they can secure their possessions, it is only because, though men may not know it or may not remember it, all have abandoned and transferred to the sovereign their absolute right to everything.[9] It is only because they have chosen one, or some, to represent and act for them, that there is anything men may call their own. The artificial person is not there to be their image, or to resemble those he represents, but to act in their stead and, in this way, to give to the multitude a unity and a cohesion it does not have naturally.

Therefore it is not surprising, nor an accident, nor does it constitute a contradiction, if the will of the sovereign often goes against the will of various citizens. The act by which he is instituted is the act by which everyone agrees to recognize the sovereign's judgment as having priority over his own, or at least to not oppose the sovereign's decisions. That some should have a different opinion than the sovereign's then is not surprising and does not indicate a failure of representation but the very reason a sovereign was instituted. If each were to follow his own opinion, none would obtain what he desires. The representer is not there to express the diverging intentions, aspirations, or desires of those he represents but to silence the discordant multitude, whose divided opinions can lead only to chaos. Political representation, according to Hobbes, is not an image: it does not mirror the diversity of goals and aspirations of particular individuals. It is a mask that imposes the seal of an artificial unity upon what is, naturally, chaos, confusion, and division.

That is why political representation, according to Hobbes, can be seen as reflexive. It does not represent anything other than the power of the multitude, a power it constitutes through the very act of representing it. For as Hobbes reminds us many times, before it is united through its representer, a multitude neither acts nor has any power. What is represented in representative power, according to Hobbes, are not the various groups, classes, or interests that make up the nation, nor the people, but political power itself, an artifact that only exists as a result of representation. For Hobbes, there is no sense in talking of a people or a nation before it is united in a political institution. A people does not precede the existence of civil society; it follows it (111–12,

125). Through representation, the will of the people is not expressed but united, inasmuch as the actions of one representer can be attributed legitimately to all members of society. The will of the people, according to Hobbes, is neither that of the majority nor the average opinion but the will and deeds of the sovereign whom all recognize as theirs.

## The Sovereign: Inspiring Awe and Self-Recognition

Self-representation is therefore of the essence of political power, of the essence of political representation as Hobbes conceives it, and not just a contingent addition to it. Political power is the power of the multitude united through being represented. How should that representation take place for the institution to be stable? The short answer is that the sovereign should appear such that he strikes terror in the hearts of his subjects. Such that he seems powerful enough to deal out punishments to anyone who might try to forgo his oath of obedience. As Hobbes states in *Man and Citizen,* "For all men, by necessity of nature, choose that which to them appears to be the less evil."[10] The sovereign should represent himself as one who is able and willing to make anyone, no matter how powerful, regret his transgression more than he may profit by it. But that is only the short answer. For if, as Hobbes said in *Leviathan,* "Covenants without the sword are but words, and of no strength to secure a man at all" (106), one could add: the sword without words is but war and has no ability to secure peace. Fear is not enough, and unqualified terror clearly goes against the office of the sovereign, which is *"the safety of the people."* By safety, Hobbes continues, "is not meant bare preservation, but also all other contentments of life, which every man by lawful industry, without danger or hurt to the commonwealth, shall acquire to himself" (218). Men must not simply fear their sovereign as an enemy. They must also recognize themselves in him, in his decisions, in his decrees. They must see that he represents them. Otherwise they will view his punishments as signs of hostility rather than as the expression of justice, and in consequence, they will consider him as simply one of them, one enemy among others, and the whole multitude will return to the original chaos of war. The problem of representing political power then is precisely that the sovereign must both appear as a power different from the people, as holding an irresistible power, and yet, if that power is to exist, men must be able to recognize themselves in the sovereign.

That recognition nonetheless cannot be complete or perfect. For if one could see his visage in the face of the sovereign, others either would do likewise and discover the sovereign as merely one of them, or, each seeing himself, the sovereign (whose sole being is the unity of those he represents) would disappear, and men would be left alone among themselves, condemned to unending opposition. To put it in slightly different language, either political power is monopolized by one group or party, or it becomes itself a prize for which various factions vie. But in either case, it fails to supply the multitude with the unity necessary for the establishment of peace. Men must recognize themselves in the sovereign, but this representation of themselves must at the same time hide them from themselves.

## The Leviathan

The most famous image associated with *Leviathan* comes from the title page of the 1651 edition, best known as the Head Edition. On the bottom half of the page the title is surrounded by civil and religious symbols of power, but on the top half there is a somewhat fantastic engraving, which has struck the imagination of many generations. In the foreground we see a city whose main building is a church; beyond the city walls the ground rises to form a small hill. Villages are scattered along its slope, and from behind the hill springs the giant head and torso of a man. From his majestic height this imposing character, facing the viewer, overlooks the city and countryside. A crown rests on his head; in his right hand he holds a sword, symbol of justice, and in his left, a scepter, symbol of sovereignty. From a distance he appears to be wearing a coat of chain mail, but as we come closer, what appeared to be the links of mail are recognized as hundreds of small images of persons, like a crowd seen from behind: together they make up the giant king. These persons are looking toward the face of the power that they constitute; all we see are their backs. Only the face of the king, Lord and Protector of the land, is turned toward us. At the top of the page is a quote from the Book of Job, about the Leviathan: "There is nothing on earth which compares to him."

Such is the Leviathan, a fictional being made of innumerable persons who gaze upon the power that they constitute, as do the readers of the book by that name. This power, Hobbes will say, is so great that men cannot be imagined to make any greater. But if we look carefully, the transparent body reveals that it is nothing but all of us united. Yet in him, not one of us in particular is visible, nor is any one recognizable. We are present in the sovereign power but faceless, our expressions hidden. He represents each one of us but only inasmuch as each is similar to the other. As Hobbes notes toward the end of the introduction to *Leviathan*:

> He that is to govern a whole nation must read in himself, not this or that particular man, but mankind, which though it be hard to do, harder than to learn any language or science, yet when I shall have set down my own reading orderly and perspicuously, the pains left another will be only to consider if he also finds not the same in himself. For this kind of doctrine admitteth of no other demonstration. (4–5)

This image's success does not come from its aesthetic value, which is rather limited, but from the fact that in many ways it is conceptually adequate to Hobbes's theory of political representation, to his conception of sovereign power, and to his method of demonstration. Taken as a key to Hobbes's political philosophy, this fantastic engraving reveals the conceptual tension in Hobbes's notion of representation and the subsequent problem of stability that continuously threatens Leviathan. It reveals the fundamental difficulty of representing (in the sense of staging, or giving an image of) a rational political power, and it suggests that such an enterprise is impossible.

The image that represents political power to us in a conceptually adequate way is more like the rendering of a fantastic apparition than a portrait. At first sight this may seem like an advantage, for if the sovereign must present himself to his subjects, if they must see him and feel his presence, if political power needs to be made manifest, it is because subjects must be awed and, through fear, made to keep their promises and fulfill their obligations. This the sovereign does by the sheer size of his power. An irresistible strength that reaches to the sky. A power so great, Hobbes tells us, that men can imagine none greater. Yet for all the theological resonance of that last formula, this godlike power must remain transparent and reveal its purely earthly origin.[11] For all its height and might, the sovereign is denied transcendence. Leviathan, whom Hobbes dubs "the mortal god," is made of mortals, and he must ensure that at all times this is seen and known, otherwise he will disappear into thin air, like a ghostly apparition that terrorizes only those who believe in him. If men cannot recognize themselves in the power that rules over them, it will cease to exist, and they will return to a state of unending conflict. Political power is a rational fiction that exists solely through the consent of the subjects. It has no natural image, no gross and material body that can be represented. Ultimately, political power, according to Hobbes, can be staged only in the theater of the mind, and that is why we are sent back to ourselves to see if we "read there not the same."

## Notes

1. The idea of "conceptually procedural" may seem bizarre at first sight. It is not the case that an ideal or conceptual procedure is nothing at all, and that in order to bind a procedure must be real? This is true, but in this case the expression simply means that the concept of representation (in the sense of representative government) is procedural, that the only requirement for a form of government to be representative is that a certain agreed-upon procedure has been followed.

2. Theatrical representation is, in a sense, not reflexive, for an actor represents someone other than himself: he impersonates a real or fictional character. But it is reflexive in the sense that theatrical representation represents or produces theater itself. Outside of the art and practice of the stage play, written dialogues do not constitute theater, while improvisations can lead to a theater that has no existence outside its performance, its representation.

3. From now on, I will refrain from using the expression "representative government" to refer to representative political power in Hobbes's sense. For representation in the sense of "representative government," as we understand it, is not an essential characteristic of all political power, but a contingent requirement that power may or may not satisfy, and that is precisely the alternative that Hobbes's political theory rejects.

4. Etienne de La Boétie, *Anti-Dictator: The "Discours sur la servitude volontaire,* trans. A. Kurz (New York: Columbia University Press, 1942). The first complete publication of La Boétie's essay is in a Huguenot collection of pamphlets assembled by Simon Goulard, *Mémoire de l'Estat de France,* which came out in 1574, ten years after La Boétie's death. But, according to Montaigne, La Boétie's *Discours* was finished before the author had reached eighteen years of age, which means that it would have been composed before 1548. Hobbes's first publication, his translation of Thucydides, was originally published in 1628.

5. Thomas Hobbes, *Leviathan,* ed. E. Curley (Indianapolis: Hackett, 1994). It can be argued that Hobbes goes even further. God himself, who, according to Hobbes, is the only one strong enough to conquer all others in the state of nature, cannot rule men without their consent. That is why, though God's power extends over all of nature, Hobbes tells us it cannot properly be called a kingdom, for "he only is properly said to reign that governs his subject by his word, and by promise of reward to those who obey it, and by threatening them with punishment that obey it not" (234).

6. The case for political representation is somewhat ambiguous. In one sense, it is not a natural fact, because it does not exist when man is taken in isolation. In that sense, it is artificial, which in Hobbes usually means social. But artificial representation can and must exist before all civil society, for society very clearly rests on it, and without the prior existence of artificial representation, society could not

come into being. In that sense, artificial representation is then natural. The conclusion, I think, is that we should accept that Hobbes's vocabulary is deficient in this matter and conflates three clearly distinct situations into two.

7. This is probably why Hobbes always expressed a preference for monarchy over other forms of government. In a monarchy, the personal unity of the representer is greater or more assured (or so Hobbes thought) than in an assembly, where it is only realized through the rule of the majority.

8. Hobbes, unlike us, always associates actions and words. It's not that he was unaware of the difference between them, but clearly he was more sensitive to the performance aspect of language than to its logical or semantic dimensions.

9. That is why, according to Hobbes, private property, contrary to what Locke thinks, is not original and does not antedate the institution of civil government. In consequence, the sovereign has a right to everything that is more fundamental than any private claims, for it is only through the action of government that anyone can have property. The sovereign is the source of all honors and possessions.

10. Thomas Hobbes, *Man and Citizen* (De Homine and De Cive), trans. C. T. Wood, T. S. K. Scott-Craig, B. Gert, and T. Hobbes (Indianapolis: Hackett, 1991), 176.

11. Some authors, Pierre Manent (1977), have made much of the resemblance between Hobbes's conception of political power, as being so great that man cannot be imagined to make any greater, and the conception of God in the ontological argument, a power so great that none greater can be conceived. A resemblance, they argue, that cannot be a mere accident. Hobbes was too well versed in the scholastic tradition to be unaware of the proximity between the two formulas. From this they conclude, following Leo Strauss (1936), that Hobbes was writing for both the wise and the untutored, reserving his atheism for the first with formulas like that one, and hiding it from all others. A double play at which he was so successful that even today he deceives many! Be that as it may, one should remember that God, according to Hobbes, is not so great that nothing greater can be conceived, but so great that He *cannot* be conceived. Hence, political power, which is such that none greater can be imagined, is precisely as great as it can possibly be while still failing to be transcendent (see P. Manent, *Naissance de la politique moderne: Machiavel, Hobbes, Rousseau* [Paris: Payot, 1977]; Leo Strauss, *The Political Philosophy of Hobbes: Its Basis and Genesis*, trans. E. M. Sinclair [Oxford: Clarendon Press, 1936]).

# 3

# Representation of Power, Power of Representation

**Jacqueline Lichtenstein**

Translated by Paul Joseph Young

Corneille's Theater is a Political Theater, or rather, it is a theater of the political. By this I mean that his theater is not so much in the service of politics, not the expression of political ideas, as much as it is the staging of a thinking about the political.

Corneille is a political thinker, no doubt the most important political thinker of the seventeenth century. He is constantly raising questions about the nature of power, the foundations of its legitimacy, about the relationships between ethics and politics, about the legitimacy of force, or about state interests *(raison d'état)*, in short, taking up all of Machiavelli's questions. From the point of view of political thought, Corneille's theater articulates an often critical dialogue with Machiavelli's writings. But what is interesting is that this political thought, this response to Machiavelli, is not enunciated in the form of a theoretical treatise but rather in a theatrical form. For if there is unquestionably a political theory in Corneille's writings, a reflection on the state of power, Corneille himself is not a political theoretician, nor a philosopher, but rather a poet, a dramatic author. His thought is expressed through theater, within a genre that imposes its own demands and whose first rule, to which all others are subordinate, is to please the spectator. Corneille states as much in the beginning of his first *Discours sur le poème dramatique*. For not only is Corneille a masterful political thinker, he also developed important reflections about the theater in his prefaces, his examinations *(examens)*, and especially in his three *Discours sur le poème dramatique* published in 1644 with his examens, in the beginning of the first complete edition of his works. Whereas Corneille's political theory is expressed in a theatrical form, Corneille's reflections on the dramatic arts, in contrast, take a theoretical form. Together, these prefaces, examens, and discourses constitute what could truly be called a poetics, where Corneille takes up all of the questions raised by Aristotle, in order to discuss them point by point. If

Corneille's theater is a response to Machiavelli within the political realm, Corneille's poetics is a response to Aristotle. But, as Corneille himself states, contrary to all of the previous commentators on Aristotle, he bases his reflections on fifty years of experience working within the theater. His is a theory of a practitioner, a man of the theater.

In analyzing the ties that link Corneille's politics with his poetics, I argue that this theater of the political is articulated by a poetics and, as I will try to show, a politics of the theater.

The fact that what could be considered the most important political thought of the seventeenth century is to be found in the writings of a man of the theater, and expressed in the form of plays rather than in political treatises, is in itself indicative of the relationship between theatricality and politics in seventeenth-century France.

The seventeenth century, as we are all aware, marks a fundamental rupture in the history of the theater. Beginning in the 1630s, theater achieved a new theoretical and social legitimacy, brought about by changes too complex to discuss here. Theater reclaimed a status that it had not enjoyed since Greek or Latin antiquity, praised by learned men and fully recognized as a legitimate literary genre, if not the greatest of all the genres. Corneille played a major role in this process of recognition of the dramatic author as a "writer," notably through the control he exercised over the publishing of his plays. But the seventeenth century is not only a century in which theater rises to new heights in the minds of both the public and of scholars, it is also the century during which views of the world, of politics and of society, are dominated by the theatrical model. As Louis Marin has shown, the power of the seventeenth century, that of the absolute monarch, cannot be separated from the representation of power. It is constituted in and through its staging. The importance of Corneille's theater stems from this, because it stages the establishing of this power and reflects it in both senses of the word *reflect*—that of thinking about it and of presenting it to be seen in a representation. That is, representing it, but while presenting it.

That Corneille's theater is a political theater, a theater of politics, is dependent on Corneille's definition of tragedy. (In this essay I speak only about tragedy, although one could show that what is at stake in Corneille's comedies, or at least in some of them, also has a relationship with political stakes.) For there to be tragedy, Corneille states, there has to be the "risk of death," and this risk has to be linked to "something of great interest to the State." Both of these elements are necessary. "When one stages a simple love story between kings, who run no risk of death, nor of losing their States, I don't believe, even though these people are illustrious, that the action is illustrious enough to make this a true tragedy," Corneille writes in the *First Discourse*. "Even though there are great State interests in a poem . . . if there is no risk of death, or of the loss of the State, or banishing, I don't think it has the right to be called anything greater than a comedy."[1]

This means that every tragedy is, by its very nature, political. First of all, because what is at stake in a tragedy is always political. (And it is in this sense, and only in this sense, that love has a place in tragedy. The stakes of love need to be political; they must concern interests of the state, not only private interests.) But also because what is represented by the theater is the tragedy of the political, and this cannot be reduced to the Corneillian all-too-famous dilemma, the dilemma concerning the competing demands of passion and duty. This tragedy of the political staged within political tragedy must be thought about in Hegelian terms, such as the conflict of moral life—this conflict between a subjective and an objective morality—which defines the individuality of the hero. In the opening remarks of the chapter in *The Philosophy of History* devoted to the Roman world, Hegel writes:

> Napoleon, in a conversation which he once had with Goethe on the nature of tragedy, expressed the opinion that its modern phase differed from the ancient, through our no longer recognizing a Destiny to which men are absolutely subject, and that policy occupies the place of the ancient Fate. This therefore he thought must be used as the modern form of destiny in Tragedy—the irresistible power of circumstances to which individuality must bend. (278)

Yet, what is interesting is that Corneille's tragedy represents the tragedy of the political under two different guises, and that this difference corresponds to a chronological distinction in Corneille's works that one could make, and that, indeed, has often been made.

In the first period, which would extend up to *Cinna*, Corneille stages the genesis of the political according to two essential axes: the birth of the city (thematized in *Horace*) and the constitution of the monarch, dramatized in *Cinna*. Rather than analyze these plays in detail, here I will simply emphasize that in both cases, what is at stake is the question of foundation and its legitimacy: the foundation of the city and the foundation of power.

## *Horace*: From Myth to History

The subject of *Horace* is the political foundation of Rome stemming from a double event that constitutes the two "actions" of the play. On the one hand, there is the fighting of the three Horaces and the three Curiaces that secures the Roman victory over the Albans and, on the other hand, Camille's murder by her brother, Horace. Corneille was criticized for this lack of unity of action, a fault he recognized. However, he was wrong to admit to this, because in fact, these two actions really constitute a sole action, or rather, each action is subordinate to the other. This is most notably the case because each of these actions is an act of parricide, in the generic sense that seventeenth-century France gave to this term. (*Parricide* designated fratricide or matricide as well.) Horace's crime, it goes without saying, is a true parricide: a brother kills his sister. The war between Rome and Alba, on the other hand, is a parricidal war, at least in a symbolic sense. Rome is the daughter of Alba. It is a "more than civil war," as Augustine wrote in *The City of God,* a war in which "the daughter-city (Rome) fought against the mother-city (Alba)." As Sabine exclaims to the Romans in the beginning of the play, "Ingrate, you sprang from Alba: stop, remember/you thrust the knife in your mother's breast." (*"Albe est ton origine, arrête et considère/que tu plonges le fer dans le sein de ta mère"* [I, ii, 55–56]). Horace is in this way doubly parricidal: he thrusts the sword into his mother's breast (Alba's), as well as into his sister's (Camille). In this sense, the brother's real crime finishes what the son's symbolic murder had started, putting an end to the time of origins by a gesture that returns to origins, by a crime that itself belongs to an originary gesture— the founding of Rome by an also parricidal crime, that of Romulus murdering his brother.

*Horace* stages the passage from myth to history, from origin to beginning, the birth of a history whose beginning necessarily marks the end of an origin, the advent of a history that can only truly begin on the condition of doing away with its origin once and for all. This is precisely what the monarch's speech accomplishes. Tulle, around whom the play ends, closes the time of origins by presenting himself as a new origin, by claiming to be the sole source and foundation for all legitimacy. It is up to the strongest to transform force into right; in fact, this is the first effect of his strength—to render, as Pascal will write, what is strong into what is just, for lack of being able to make what is just, strong:

(This crime) though great, though monstrous, though unpardonable
springs from the same sword, from the same arm
that makes me master of two states today.
Two scepters in my hand, Alba subjected
Speak forcibly in favor of his life:
But for him I should bow where I command
And should subject where I'm twofold king.
. . . Such servants are the very sap of kings,
And therefore such are held above the law.
Let law be silent then, and Rome be blind
To what she saw in Romulus at her birth. . . .

Ce crime, quoi que grand, énorme, inexcusable
vient de la même épée et part du même bras
qui me fait aujourd'hui maître de deux Etats.
Deux sceptres en ma main, Albe à Rome asservie,
Parlent bien hautement en faveur de sa vie:
Sans lui j'obéirais où je donne la loi,
Et je serais sujet où je suis deux fois roi.
. . . De pareils serviteurs sont les forces des rois,
Et de pareils aussi sont au-dessus des lois.
Qu'elles se taisent donc; que Rome dissimule
Ce que dès sa naissance elle vit en Romule . . . (V, iii, 1740–46, 1753–56)

This first figure of the monarch is incomplete and still a little dim.
He owes his victory to Horace, not to himself. He takes the place of the
monarch and truly takes it once he has it; his first gesture is a true
monarch's gesture. But it cannot be said that he earned his position. He
has achieved glory but not yet merit, and as Corneille will demonstrate, these two ideas are inseparable. (Bossuet will repeat this to
powerful men, most particularly to Louis XIV. The synthesis of merit
and glory is one of the central themes of the seventeenth century).
Tulle's legitimacy is not full and complete. His power is legitimate from
a political point of view, but it isn't yet legitimate from an ethical or
philosophical point of view, as Augustus's will be in *Cinna*.

## *Cinna*: From History to Myth

If the subject of *Horace* is the political birth of Rome, the subject of
*Cinna* is the political birth of the monarch. As in *Horace,* the question

raised by Corneille in this play is that of foundation: What is the foundation of the power of the monarch? And, as in *Horace,* this foundation is conceived of as an act of self-foundation, an originary act by which the monarch comes into being for himself and for others by severing the ties that bound him to the past. Here, however, the past is not a mythical past but rather a real past, which refers back to a real history: the city exists; it has already been created. By a process that is similar, yet to some extent the reverse of the one exposed in *Horace,* the monarch becomes monarch by presenting himself as an origin, but this act consists here of leaving behind history in order to enter the realm of myth.

*Cinna* stages the genesis of the absolute, how man achieves mastery, which is to say, freedom, or how Octavian becomes Augustus. When the play begins, Augustus is weary of his power and dreams of abdicating, until he discovers the plot and Cinna's betrayal. In a long monologue, he reflects upon himself, what he has done in order to gain power, and upon his crimes: "Octavian, search your heart, eschew self-pity" (IV, ii, 1130–31). (Notice that he refers to himself as Octavian. He will only finally call himself Augustus in the final lines of the play: "Augustus, learning all, would forget.") This remembrance of the past forms a profound meditation on the question of the legitimacy of power, on the relationship between force and right, which corrects any Machiavellian elements Tulle's speech might have had and anticipates what Rousseau will write in chapter 4 of his *Social Contract* about the right of the strongest. Augustus realizes that he deserves what happens to him because of his own previous actions: "You who have spared none wish yourself to be spared" (IV, ii, 1131–32). Augustus is tempted to commit suicide and then learns that Emilie, whom he has loved like a daughter, is at the head of the conspiracy. The question of parricide is again raised in these moments. Finally, he learns of the betrayal by his faithful friend, Maxime. It is at this moment, when he is at his lowest, destroyed by the past, crumbling under the weight of history (for the conspiracy is the consequence of crimes he had committed: Emilie wants to avenge her father's death) that Augustus will be born, shrugging off the skin of Octavian. He is born as an absolute master of the world, by being born as the absolute master of himself. He becomes sovereign because he becomes a "subject" in the Cartesian sense of the word—sovereign subject. The sovereignty of the monarch is the sovereignty of the subject. And this is what distinguishes the monarch from the tyrant. For the tyrant it is enough to say, "I am the master of the universe." Only he who can say, "I am master of myself as I am of the universe," philosophically deserves the political title of king. This is why Augustus becomes a true monarch only after having triumphed over himself. Then he is both a philosophical and political subject, master in every sense of the word, of himself, and of others. Augustus's character is the most complete expression of Corneille's conception of the subject as king, and the king as subject. For the first (and, as we shall see, last) time, the royal place of the subject is identified with the place of the royal subject. And this birth to one's self and to others, as sudden as it is dazzling, is brought about within forgiveness.

> Gods! is this not enough? has harsh fate yet
> Some intimate of mine it would subvert?
> To aid it, let hell's banners be unfurled:
> I'm master of myself as of the world;
> I am, I will be. O posterity,
> Preserve forever my last victory!
> Today, the holiest anger I subdue
> Whose memory might reach right down to you!
> Let us be friends, Cinna, I wish it so.

> En est-ce assez, ô ciel! et le sort, pour me nuire,
> A-t-il quelqu'un des miens qu'il veuille encore séduire?
> Qu'il joigne à ses efforts le secours des enfers.
> Je suis maître de moi comme de l'Univers.
> Je le suis; je veux l'être. O siècles, ô mémoire,
> Conservez à jamais ma dernière victoire!
> Je triomphe aujourd'hui du plus juste courroux
> De qui le souvenir puisse aller jusqu'à vous.
> Soyons amis, Cinna, c'est moi qui t'en convie. (V, iii, 1693–1701)

Augustus's birth is an act of generosity; Augustus forgives. What does it mean to forgive? It is a pure gift, which is to say a sovereign act that consists of erasing away all prior debts—an inaugural act that liberates the present from the past, from the weight of memory and history. Let us recall the last line of the play: "Augustus, learning all, would all forget" ("Qu'Auguste a tout appris, et veut tout oublier"). The crimes of the past are those of Octavian, not of Augustus. As Livie says to Emilie, "His death, whose memory ignites fury, was the crime of Octavian, not of the emperor." Augustus is no longer the character of a story made up of crimes and atrocities, as Octavian was; he becomes the author of a new history. He is no longer an actor, he has become an author. He no longer inscribes himself in history, he writes it. No longer speaking in the name of the past, he now addresses posterity. When he says, *"O siècles, ô mémoire, conservez à jamais ma dernière victoire"* ("O posterity, preserve forever my last victory!" [V, iii, 1697–98]), he is speaking to a memory yet to come, to posterity. As Livie will say to Augustus at the end of the play, he now has a place among the immortals, he has become an example for posterity. He has entered into the sphere of representation. Now monuments will be raised to his glory.

With *Cinna,* the cycle of the "Roman" plays ends. Augustus is a Roman in Rome, a master in his city, master of a city that is mistress of the world, that "rules over land and sea." The cycle of what I will call the "colonial" plays begins next. These no longer take place in Rome, but in the Roman empire. Rome is no longer in Rome, to paraphrase the famous line from Sertorius. Yet, all of these plays stage the despair of power denied a master, of an absolute monarch exiled from his place, which is to say deprived of his real and symbolic center, with the hero's weaknesses and the strength of conspiracies by ministers and counselors. Small, private interests have taken the place of important state interests; heroic struggles to achieve control of power, inseparable from the power of control, have given way to minor power struggles. It is the triumph of the politics of politicians, the reign of what Corneille (and La Fontaine) call *"les pestes du cour."* What tragedy represents now is no longer the tragedy of the political; it is the tragicomedy of politics.

### *Pompée*: A Defense of Absolutism

As we have seen, the idea that power must necessarily fall apart once it is deprived of a master who ensures and founds its legitimacy, rests on a philosophico-political conception of the subject. The absolute power belongs to the subject and therefore dissipates once the subject is missing. This idea has been staged by Corneille in *La Mort de Pompée,* a play that situates itself, in the chronology of Corneille's work, between the Roman plays and what I have called the colonial plays. The last of the Roman plays or the first of the colonial plays, *La Mort de Pompée* therefore marks a turning point. This tragedy, which takes place in Alexandria, is built entirely around an absent hero or, rather, around the absence of a hero. In his examen of the play, Corneille wrote: "There is something extraordinary in the title of this poem, which bears the name of a hero who does not speak in it; but he never ceases in some way to be the principal actor, because his death is the sole cause of everything that happens." For the first time we can see, in *Pompée,* what politics becomes in the absence of the master, after the death of the hero, after the assassination of the greatest of all Romans. Power has been decapitated, both literally and figuratively, since the head of Pompée has been cut off, and his body is being tossed about in the waves. Philippe, the faithful freed slave, will find the cadaver on the shore but not his head, which is being held by the conspirators. At the end of the play, Cornélie, Pompée's widow, shows Caesar the urn and tells him: "See the urn of Pompey, his head is missing;/Do not deny me it, it is the sole favor/Which I can still beg of you with honor." To which Caesar replies: "It is just, and Caesar is all ready to give back to you/This remain to which you have a rightful claim." The body of power is in pieces from now on; unity is in ashes.

## The Artist as Absolute Monarch

Yet Corneille dedicated this play to Cardinal Mazarin, and its dedication letter is truly fascinating, notably because it illuminates the strange role that Rome plays for Corneille:

> I present you, Eminence, with the great Pompey; the greatest figure of ancient Rome for the most illustrious person of the new Rome. I am placing under the protection of the Prime Minister of our young King a hero, who in his good fortune was the protector of many kings, and who in his bad fortune still had kings for his ministers. He hopes for generosity from your Eminence, that you will not disdain protecting this second life which I have tried to give him, and that conveying this justice, which you convey throughout the kingdom, you will revenge that evil politics of the Egyptian court.

*Rome*: one signifier for three signifieds. Rome refers to Roman history; Rome is also the Italian Rome, the fatherland of the Renaissance of arts and letters; Rome is also Paris wanting to be the new Rome (a new antique Rome, and a new, modern, Italian Rome). The dedication to Mazarin is constantly playing with this ambiguity of the signifier *Rome,* since Mazarin is an Italian who left the old Rome for the new one. Corneille is also playing admirably with another ambiguity, between Pompée and the author of the play ("He hopes . . ."). If Pompée is the hero of ancient Rome, Corneille imagines himself as the hero of the new Rome.

If Corneille thought about and represented absolutism before it even existed as such (*Cinna* dates from 1640, and *Pompée,* as a defense of absolutism [showing the despair of the political once it no longer has a master], dates from 1642–43), he also thought about the corruption of politics submitted to court intrigues, anticipating descriptions that the writers of the following generation, like La Fontaine or La Bruyère, will make. If Corneille is effectively a theoretician of absolute monarchy, he is the theoretician of the greatness and the decadence of absolutism, of its weakness as much as of its power. In this sense, the *representation* that Corneille's theater gives of power is really a *presentation*; it is the historical *real,* which re-presents what theater has presented and presents it a second time. To speak in the style of Borges, one could say that Corneille didn't represent the reign of Louis XIV; rather, it is the reign of Louis XIV that illustrates the theater of Corneille.

Thus, when Corneille wrote in 1663 a *Remerciement au roi* to thank Louis XIV for the pension of two thousand pounds granted him as "the greatest dramatic poet in the world," he starts by reminding the king of the past, evoking the successes of the young Louis:

> You, the only worthy comparison of yourself
> Was seen then demonstrating your praiseworthy actions,
> Filling good men with love, and evil men with fear.

To which he soon added:

> Until then, however, everything was not yours:
> And whatever pleasant effects your victory produced,
> The advice of the great Jules shared your glory.
> Now that we see you as worthy potentate
> Unite in your hands the reins of the Nation . . .

Corneille thus opposes a "now" to this "before," the very mention of which, to an absolute monarch, is not devoid of a certain audacity. Mazarin having died in 1661, Louis has "now" become a master; he is finally entirely self-sufficient, an absolute monarch, who owes his glory to himself. He is no longer Louis XIV, the fourteenth of that name, which would mean there were thirteen Louis before him to whom he could be compared; now he is "Louis le grand," the sole of this name, absolute and without comparison, a monarch who inscribes himself in history not following all those who have preceded him but rather as a starting point, a founding subject of a history of which he is the author. We have seen this question of the changing of one's name already in *Cinna,* where Octavian becomes Augustus. But it was also already present in *Le Cid.* After Rodrigue's victory over the Moors, the king says to him: you will no longer be called Rodrigue, but The Cid, el Cid campeador. He is no longer his father's son but rather his own son. In contrast to important men who are always the sons of someone (*hidalgo,* as they say in Spanish—*hijo de algo*), and to the common people, who are the sons of no one, the hero is the sole person to carry a name that is truly his own, because he breaks historical continuity; he breaks tradition.

However, three lines later, in the *Remerciement au roi,* we discover that this "now" also has meaning.

> Now . . .
> It is time for me, to paint
> in a more dignified manner
> an accomplished monarch in you;
> To make you a model for kings yet to be born
> And to present you as master so they may learn how to reign.

What is Corneille saying to the king? Now that everything is yours, you need me to represent you and to pass your image on to posterity. In fact, it comes down to Corneille to write the king's history. With an impressive assurance, Corneille says to the king: if you want people to know, today, and in the centuries to come, that you are an absolute monarch, that you are making history, you must give me the means to write your history; therefore you must become the character, the actor of a story of which I am the author. (In the seventeenth century, *acteur* meant both the character and the actor playing this character). To use a Borgesian formula again, I would say that by a paradoxical movement, the very movement of representation, Corneille becomes the author of Louis XIV. You exist, but you will really exist because I represent you.

> "I will make your name universally adored
> But this masterpiece needs a great theater!"

The real absolute monarch, the real subject, the sole true author, is the artist. Corneille never stops saying this, loudly and clearly, and making it manifest by demanding, for example, that his name figure on the bottom of the posters for his plays (which had never been done before, the author usually being considered as someone appointed by the troupe) and by supervising the publication of his plays. He was the first to lead what is called today in France a *politique d'auteur,* demanding complete authority over his works. The name of the artist is really a proper name, belonging only to him; it incarnates the "union of merit with glory"; the artist gave it to himself and it shines brightly, throwing a prodigious brilliance upon everything he touches. Corneille is perfectly aware of this power. He says this to the king but also to the women that he wants to seduce, like the "belle marquise" to whom he wrote:

> Because you love glory, and you know that a king
> Cannot assure you of as much as I,
> It is more in my hand than in a monarch's
> To make you rival Petrarch's lover,
> And more than any king I can make one ask
> Whether you or Laura deserve more glory.

The political ideal of the absolute monarch is also incarnate in the artist-king. Unique, without compare, self-sufficient, without predecessors nor successors, the artist is an absolute subject, who engenders himself in a process of continual self-creation, which is not without certain links to both the Cartesian *cogito* and to divine creation, as Descartes defines it—a continuous creation. An author—someone about whom it may be said that his entire race is made up only of him, as La Bruyère says about those rare men who appear from time to time on the face of the earth: "Similar to those extraordinary stars whose causes are unknown, and about which one knows even less when they have disappeared, they have neither forefathers nor descendants. Their entire race is composed of them alone" (97).

## Notes

I dedicate this essay to the memory of Louis Marin, who taught at the University of California, San Diego, for many years, and who was particularly fond of the work of Pierre Corneille.

1. Unless otherwise noted, translations are those of this essay's translator.

## Works Cited

La Bruyère, Jean de. "Du mérite personnel." From *Les Caractères,* in *Oeuvres complètes.* Paris: Gallimard, 1951.

Corneille, Pierre. *Théâtre Complet.* Ed. Maurice Rat. 3 vols. Paris: Garnier, 1962.
————. *Pierre Corneille: Seven Plays.* Trans. Samuel Solomon. New York: Random House, 1969.
Hegel, Georg Wilhelm Friedrich. *The Philosophy of History.* Trans. J. Sibree. New York: Dover, 1956.

# 4

# Voice and Silence of Public Space:
# Popular Societies in the French Revolution

### Shigeki Tominaga

In 1791 the successive debates in the Assembly began in March with a proposal by Pierre-Gibert Allarde for the abolition of guilds. In June, Isaac-René-Guy Le Chapelier argued for the prohibition of labor unions, and in September, debate focused on the limitation of the activities of political associations, in particular those of the popular societies *(les sociétés populaires),* a representative example of which was the Jacobin Club. These debates seem to have run fairly smoothly, a fact that stands in rather sharp contrast to their grave influence on French social organization throughout the nineteenth century. While the reports made by Le Chapelier and others are generally short and sweet, and say little about the important issues that these debates raised, the discourse on the side of the counterattack was even weaker and lacked any insight into the principles of social organization. Secondary or intermediary groups, which had the potential of serving as important public spaces at the beginning of the modern era, were thereby totally ruled out, at least in the perspective of the revolutionaries, before they could play their role in the newly constructed social organization. Voluntary association was silenced, and with it was silenced the very sociability of citizens whose rights had been acknowledged.[1]

Just a few days after the adoption of the last decree aiming at the restriction of the activities of the popular societies, Robespierre read a text about this decree at the public meeting of the Jacobin Club: "What kind of change does [the recently adopted decree] bring about in the existence of the patriotic societies? We say with confidence that it will bring nothing that realizes the intentions of the enemy of these societies."[2] Such a statement shows how little the Jacobin leaders understood the possible result of a series of decrees proposed by the Constituants. The following two years fulfilled Robespierre's prophecy: nothing happened to the popular societies, which, instead of decreasing or disappearing, continued to proliferate in Paris and throughout France.

Some contemporary historians, including specialists in eighteenth-century French social movements, seem to have been so influenced by this Jacobin tradition that they overlook the fatal effects of the decision made in 1791. Instead, they emphasize the proliferation of the popular societies and their place in the so-called development of French democracy in the following years.[3] These historians believe that in spite of the silence imposed by the Constituants, they can still clearly hear some distinct voices, or perhaps noises, in the clamor of social communication during the Revolution. Sometimes they even take these sounds to be proof of Habermas's famous argument about the historical emergence of the public sphere in eighteenth-century Europe.

There would seem to be a contradiction here between political philosophy and social history, between ideas or discourse, and the facts that historians never stop describing. Although we are more concerned here with ideas of social organization than with gathering historical facts, it is important not to deny the fact of the proliferation of the popular societies after the year 1791. What is most persuasive in this regard are the historians' statistics concerning the number of popular societies established in revolutionary France. Yet even if we must admit that these statistics are accurate, we still require an explanation of "the paradox of the second year." How do we explain the fact that, with the advent of the revolutionary government in October 1793, the movement of popular societies was suddenly restrained, precisely at the moment when "its networking was at the peak and its dynamism was to be revealed as one of the essential factors for the victory of the Montagnards?"[4] To understand this paradox, we shall have to re-examine some situations in these years, paying special attention to both the silence and the voices (and perhaps, at times, the noises) that could be heard in the popular societies. This is, I think, the only way we can clarify the problem concerning the fate of secondary groups as one of the public spaces that was imagined at the beginning of modern political culture in France.

### Silence

As Marcel Gauchet once put it, sometimes "the way we think of freedom prevents us from realizing it."[5] Oddly enough, this phrase aptly characterizes the 1791 revolutionary decrees and measures concerning various kinds of voluntary association. While aiming to fulfill the rights of man and to transform a mere man into a citizen (from "nothing" to "something," to employ Abbé Sieyes's expression[6]), the revolutionaries almost totally closed off the most important space where this transformation could be realized.

The authors of the Constitution of 1791 conceived of a social system that would only consist, on the one hand, of individuals and, on the other, of the total society, which is nothing other than the nation. Such a system would function without any secondary or intermediary groups. "There exist only the particular interest of every individual and the general interest. It is not allowed for anyone to inspire some intermediary interest in the citizens and to separate them from the state [la chose publique] by a corporative spirit," said Le Chapelier, when he argued that labor unions should be banned.[7] This point of view underwrote all the other relevant decrees of the time, reflecting a "distrust of the grouping of citizens" prevalent during the revolutionary period as a whole.[8] Since the law, which is the expression of the general will, is framed at the National Assembly that represents the nation, there is no need for citizens to communicate with one another and, consequently, no need for a space where they might do so, with the sole exception of the occasions when deputies are elected. Any other form of association represents a danger, both to the maintenance of the integrated nation and to those free individuals of which it is composed. For these two reasons, secondary groups had to be eliminated from the new society.

It is clear that these ideas were derived in part (and with a certain amount of misunderstanding) from Rousseau's claims about the priority of the general will over the particular will found in the "partial associations," which are not necessarily harmless to that great association which is the state.[9] But they were also derived from Turgot, a *physiocrate* who, as head of the royal finance before the Revolution (1776), had tried to abolish the corporative system of workers and communities of merchants because he considered them an obstacle to industry and to the free movement of labor. Although this attempt failed, Turgot's name was mentioned in Allarde's report.[10] In this sense, a series of actions proposed in the year 1791 did not contradict the Enlightenment ideal of man's total freedom from the constraints of social groups, especially those which had come down from feudal times. To form an analogy concerning this revolutionary ideal, we may say that the abolition of guilds and the prohibition of new workers' unions was to economics what the limitation of the action of popular societies was to politics.

These actions, however, did not go uncontested. Jean-Paul Marat, for example, often criticized both measures concerning workers and was an obstinate adversary of such privileged corporations as the Academy of Science. In his famous newspaper, *L'Ami du peuple,* he wrote that "an unlimited freedom, granted to all citizens, to exercise any profession that pleases them will infallibly cause the ruin of the arts, workshops, factories, and the State." According to Marat, an arbitrary, uncontrolled freedom to choose one's job or profession would arouse a kind of uncontrolled selfishness in workers and merchants. How, he wonders, could young men receive any training in the absence of a corporative system? Marat contends that "for the arts to flourish, one must subject boys to a rigorous apprenticeship lasting six or seven years."[11]

To express Marat's claims about the function of labor unions in contemporary sociological terms, we can say that he feared that the absence of any kind of socialization would lead to the isolation and atomization of the individual. The question of socialization could not be neglected in the revolutionary context. The education and formation of workers was indispensable given that labor was a necessary condition of citizenship and especially of the status of active citizen enjoying the right to vote. The well-known distinction between active and passive citizens was not permanent, if we are to believe Rabaud Saint-Etienne, one of the Constituants, who declared that "it is not difficult to obtain the title of active citizen. You have wisely wanted to make it an object of emulation for all the Frenchmen, a motive to work, and a stimulus to industry."[12] Although learning a profession was a necessary condition of becoming a citizen, revolutionary legislation prohibited the social space where this form of socialization was to take place.

Just as the new type of labor union should have played an important role, according to Marat, in the formation of skilled young workers, political associations were also supposed to have a significant role in the more general socialization of citizens. "A patriotic club is a school where one is taught the science of free government," reads the motto of a review published by the Parisian popular societies. This motto is quite eloquent with regard to the anticipated role of these societies, which is nothing other than that of facilitating communication among those who congregated in them.[13] Even though, as we stated earlier, the Constituent Assembly was largely oblivious to the profound implications of its decrees concerning secondary groups, the question of socialization was not totally neglected. For example, François-Nicolas-Léonard Buzot raised a question when, in May 1791, Le

Chapelier proposed another decree prohibiting petitions by the societies or Parisian sections. Where, he asked, can citizens who are not
yet ready to get involved in public matters learn about laws and about
civil norms more generally? The deputy, who was to be banished as
one of the Girondins two years later, insisted, "So that citizens can
communicate their motives and errors to each other, it is necessary to
give them the means to gather so that they can deliberate peacefully."[14]
But precisely this very deliberation was banned by the decrees proposed by the camp of the Constituants, for in their opinion the National Assembly was the only establishment allowed to deliberate about
public matters. And so Buzot's argument in favor of political association as a public space reserved for free citizens found no support and
was dismissed.

For the majority of the national representatives at this moment,
popular societies simply should not have played their role as a public
place where citizens could meet and communicate their political opinions. To a large extent, the very idea of public space was entirely absent from the minds of the Constituants. Sieyes, their leader in political
thought, was so indifferent toward the issue of communication and sociability that he was capable of uttering the following chilling phrases:
"It is good that the members of the same primary assembly can see
each other, get to know each other, and form relations without having
to travel very far; what is above all necessary is that they be able to get
together on Sundays to practice the military drills that the National
Assembly authorizes."[15] This may very well have been the sum total of
his statements about sociability in the newly reconstructed social organization. Le Chapelier denied the very existence of the public space
and its raison d'être as a place where citizens meet and exchange information: "As the streets and the parks [les places publiques] are common property, they therefore belong to no one, but belong to all [the
members of the Nation]." This was why putting up posters on the
streets or in the parks had to be prevented at the same time that groups
were forbidden to make petitions by the decree of May. In the same
context, Le Chapelier went on to say that he could not recommend
these public spaces or political associations as places for communication and sociability: "It is not on the street corner that education is acquired. Education occurs in quiet gatherings where people discuss
without deliberating and enlighten each other without passion and
without a partisan spirit; education is achieved through books, and
lastly by laws dictated by a healthy philosophy."[16] His mention of

books as a means of communication cannot help but arouse our interest, for in a way it harmonizes with the model of "the public use of reason" set forth by Kant in his "An Answer to the Question: 'What Is Enlightenment?'" (1784), where the philosopher discusses the action of intellectuals who speak before the entire reading public by means of their writings.[17] Even so, silence and perhaps even solitude were made to prevail in the public space exactly at the moment when that space should have been seen as the most necessary site for the creation of citizens.

## Voice

The attentive reader may notice a slight but significant difference between the views of Le Chapelier and Buzot in the passages we have cited: while the former talked about "the quiet gatherings where people discuss without deliberating," the latter mentioned gatherings where people "deliberate peacefully." The difference here cannot be overemphasized, because deliberation *(la délibération),* which the Constituants assigned only to the National Assembly, was one of the actions the popular societies were not allowed to engage in. It is crucial here to take note of the distinction between discussion and deliberation, the latter of which aims at reaching a certain resolution and, from the standpoint of the Constituants, therefore has a close connection with the very formation of the general will. It is in this sense that Sieyes, for example, defined the task of the National Assembly: "When men get together, it is in order to deliberate; it is in order to know each other's opinions . . . , to bring their particular wills together, to adjust them to each other, and finally to produce a result which is common to them all."[18] One sees why it was deemed important to prevent the popular societies from taking part in such a deliberative process.

Just one day before Le Chapelier proposed his decree, Jacques-Pierre Brissot spoke at the Jacobin Club in defense of the existence of political associations, beginning with an argument dealing with this very topic: "They exclaim that, in the representative regime, only the representative organization can deliberate over the laws—Yes, if we understand this word to refer to the making of the law. . . . But is it in this sense that the patriotic societies intend to deliberate? These societies limit themselves to emitting, not a law, but their own opinion on the law; and certainly it is their right to do so."[19] The man who would in a few months become the head of the Girondins tries here, by re-

defining the word, to allow popular societies to have the right to deliberate. Instead of denying the existence of the National Assembly and
its mission, he establishes two different kinds of deliberation: the first
has a preparatory or intermediary character in relation to the second,
which has the task of actually establishing the general will. Even so,
the preparatory kind of deliberation is important because voluntary
political association builds a bridge between citizens and their representatives, transmitting opinion from the former to the latter. "How
will the legislative body know the general opinion, the general will, unless it consults it?" asks Brissot. "And can it consult it better, and obtain it more surely anywhere other than in our patriotic societies?"[20]

In addition to this intermediary role of political associations, Brissot
argues for another social function of deliberation, which is nothing
other than the socialization of citizens. In his view of the situation, his
countrymen have not yet entirely become citizens and are still "little
accustomed to the exercise of the rights of freedom." If Enlightenment
is such an imperative for the French Revolution that the instruction of
children should be undertaken by the government, men and women
above the age of schooling also need a certain civil education. Newspapers provide useful instruction, but the people cannot afford them;
information can also be had at cafés, but some unfortunate events
occur there as well; and so popular societies are, he thinks, the very
best school for adults. Deliberation has many virtues, for it is by means
of deliberating over political matters (which is not the same thing as
idle discussion) that one can learn "the art of listening . . . and talking
fairly." After they have received such training, citizens will know "how
not to judge precipitously, how not to believe thoughtlessly, . . . how to
despise and to unmask wicked men courageously." In short, popular
societies and the deliberations they make possible are "the means to
improve human reason and to extend it to all social classes."[21]

That reason and deliberation are connected is what makes it possible for Sieyes to claim that the formation of the general will is the result of the deliberation of the national representatives. Although it is
difficult to decide whether deliberation really brings rationality to the
world and, consequently, whether the general will or public opinion is
rational as the result of deliberation, it was nonetheless believed in the
second half of the eighteenth century that this connection was not
simply possible but was an actual potentiality capable of being realized.
The idea can be found, for example, in Montesquieu, who had penned
these lines: "In a free nation, it is very often a matter of indifference

whether individuals reason well or ill; it is sufficient that they reason: hence springs that freedom that serves as a guarantee against the effects of these very reasonings."[22] Whether Brissot had read Montesquieu and been influenced by him does not matter; what is more important is that this defender of political association acknowledges the rationality of popular societies and of the deliberations they made possible, a rationality that Sieyes finds only in the National Assembly. For Brissot, political association must be rational, which is why it can be a school for citizenship.

From this rationality follows another trait of popular societies, at least as they were imagined by Brissot. In the perspective held by Sieyes, Le Chapelier, and others, traditional guilds and the newly born political associations belonged to a single type of social group, namely, the *corporation*. One reason why some activities of popular societies had to be forbidden was that they limited their members' freedom, just as the guilds controlled the economic activities of artisans and merchants, excluding anyone who disobeyed the established rules. Prior to the Revolution, Brissot often criticized such privileged and exclusive corporations as the Academy of Science, sometimes even more severely than Marat had done.[23] He never identifies popular societies with the closed and privileged corporations that had survived since the Middle Ages, and he clearly distinguishes between closed and open associations. Brissot attacked the Feuillants Club, formed in July by deputies who left the Jacobins after a political struggle, calling it "a particular club." Brissot proclaimed that "any society that is open to only one class of public men is soon contaminated by the corporative spirit."[24] In order to play a role as a school of citizenship, a political association must be open to all and exclude no one from its deliberations.

While Brissot's discourse of September 1791 suggests some "theories" about the social significance of popular societies as a new type of voluntary association, that of François Lanthenas, published six months later, gives us a concrete image of the activities taking place within the space constituted by such associations. He too begins his argument by asserting the necessity of a form of public instruction in citizenship, proposing that "another branch of public instruction" be reserved for adults: "It is desirable that large, convenient and salubrious places, where one can hold readings and lectures [*des lectures et des conférences*], be constructed."[25] The pamphleteer who provides here a single, salient image of the social system once proposed that the Hôtel-Dieu Hospital should be torn down so as to create a wide-open public place in the very center of the capital.[26] It should be instructive to see what the author of such a concrete image of public space has to say about the activities he has in mind for the popular societies.

When Lathenas refers to *lectures,* he is thinking of public readings from books and newspapers—or, in his words, "works on morality and politics which public opinion has appraised." And when he refers to *conférences,* he has in mind public explications of texts previously read. These activities may be contrasted with Le Chapelier's previously quoted proposal for the socialization of citizens. In the same breath that he ruled out street-corner sociability, Le Chapelier recommended reading as a way of learning about laws and public opinion, but the reading he favored was the action of an isolated individual. It may be useful here to recall that Condorcet, while designing the public school system, was eager to recommend education by means of books. This Enlightenment *philosophe* compared the latter to the educational practices of classical antiquity, which had consisted mainly of teaching the art of eloquence, favored because of its appeal to the passions. Printed books were to be preferred because they nourish reason through the cool and attentive act of reading. Gathering people together is unnecessary, for a reading public requires no face-to-face communication and, hence, no natural voice.[27] In sharp contrast with Condorcet's idea, Lanthenas seeks to give voice to the rationality of political association by means of oral readings.

The voice of sociability heard in Lanthenas's discourse has nothing to do with noise. After describing the readings and lectures to be held at the popular societies, he adds a few words emphasizing the necessity of "carefully avoiding those denunciations and discussions, the object and form of which awaken interests, appeal to the passions and chase away reason."[28] It is obvious that the Girondin pamphleteer did not favor the denunciation or accusation of members holding opinions diverging from one's own, which was always one of the grounds for attacking popular societies. From the viewpoint of the history of communication, Lanthenas's image of popular societies corresponds to an intermediary step between oral and print communication. He invites us to listen to a voice that makes an utterance in a public place, a voice that cannot be found in the isolated and silent communicative schemes endorsed by Condorcet and Le Chapelier. This voice incarnates what Brissot or Lanthenas had in mind for the new type of voluntary association, an association that differs fundamentally from such archaic and closed social groups as guilds.

## Noise

The voice that is faintly heard in the years 1791 and 1792 would, however, confront not only the silence but also the noise of the following months, disappearing totally from the revolutionary scene. In spite of the decree adopted at the end of September 1791, and contrary to the intention of Le Chapelier, popular societies proliferated, gaining more and more influence in Paris and throughout France. This is what the historical statistics show, but it is crucial to observe that this proliferation also involved a change in the societies' character. Both the multiplication and metamorphosis of these societies is made manifest in an opinion expressed by a deputy in June 1792, who again called for their repression: "If these assemblies, which have no public character, no political existence, suddenly become a powerful body or dangerous association, then you lawmakers are there to put them down."[29]

It is Brissot himself who, in the autumn of 1792, reveals the change that has occurred in the Jacobin Club, a violent replacement of the voice by noise. With the intensification of the conflict between the Montagnards and the Girondins after the fall of the royalty and the proclamation of the Republic, Brissot, who is finally accused and excluded from the Jacobin Club in September 1792, must speak about the transformation or degradation of the society that he had enthusiastically defended a year earlier. According to his own response to the accusation, the Club of Paris had become "a perpetual theater of deceptive denunciation, a center of fermentation, an arena where gladiators wearing the mask of patriotism tear each other apart," a place "where freedom of speech is proscribed" and where "a small but boisterous minority enchains a sound but weak majority."[30] Setting aside the fact that this text is itself a result of and an accusatory contribution to the very political dispute it decries, Brissot's text allows us to hear the silencing of the moderate voice that Lanthenas thought he could hear in the modern rational association. In Brissot we hear the infinitely various noises that took its place: the sound of the gladiators' sword-rattling, the boisterous and drunken tones of the noisy accusers and persecutors, the bubbling of the crowd's angry passions.

Although Brissot had to confront these noisy denunciations, he still kept in mind the possibility and necessity of the ideal clubs he had presented only a year earlier. For this "theoretician" of rational popular societies, these groups had to become "the center of instruction for their members." Any failure in the realization of this ideal was simply due to circumstances. As far as Brissot is concerned, it is only the Jacobin Club of Paris that is corrupt, having succumbed to the perverse influence of a minority, while the societies in the provinces remain untouched. For this reason what was happening in the Parisian group could not warrant the destruction of popular societies as a whole; instead, they could justify their continuation "by purifying themselves." Brissot claims that "the Parisian society of equality and liberty must subsist: the public good demands it; but the public good also demands that this society become useful and at last fulfill the objective of its institution."[31] The Parisian society has fallen into error, he thinks, because it considers itself to have a great influence over its own members and over the other societies as well. As all of the societies and their members in fact have an equal status, the situation can be improved, he holds, when the Parisian group recognizes its error.

As the destiny awaiting Brissot and his colleagues shows, the error in question was not to be rectified. On the contrary, for this error in fact derived not only from an increasingly radical revolutionary situation but also from the very heart of the popular societies. It was none other than Le Chapelier, as we have seen, who deemed denunciation or accusation to be one of the most dangerous elements of the popular societies he attacked. Robespierre would in turn have to defend his own club when it was threatened by the Constituants. In so doing, he could not help but reveal his real motives, finally recognizing the accusatory character of the societies when he responded to Le Chapelier with the following words: "Is it then such a great misfortune that, in our current situation, public opinion and the public spirit develop at the expense of the reputation of some men who, after having seemed to serve their country, went on to betray it all the more audaciously!"[32] Here, Le Chapelier and Robespierre, strangely enough, coincide concerning the fundamental character of the political association; they only disagree over the value of the accusatory process. For the future Jacobin leader, the denunciation and exclusion of members was a normal activity, something necessary to the worthwhile growth of the society's influence.

During the same year, Jean-Nicolas Pache, who has been characterized as "one of the most enigmatic figures of the French Revolution,"[33] discussed the activities of the popular societies. At the time he was still close to the camp of Girondins, and it is not too difficult to find some subtle differences between his views and those of Brissot and Lanthenas. Pache spoke, as had Lanthenas, of the virtue of deliberation in the popular societies, considering "the free oral communication of thoughts" to be one of man's natural rights. But it is particularly "a moral and political sensibility," instead of rationality, that these social groups teach the citizens, and there is no mention of the voice of reason in Pache's discourse. Pache insists on the necessity of having the people maintain surveillance over the servants of the state (or the national representatives, according to the usage of the time), thereby preventing the popular societies from becoming corrupt. Although it must be said that the supervision of the deputies was designated as one of the important activities of the popular societies in Brissot's discourse as well, Pache's use of the word *people* forces us to imagine something noisy in this context, for we know that the recall of the deputies by the people was admitted officially in the Constitution of the year II.[34] Or do we read Pache differently in part because we know that in the following months he left the Girondin group in order to join the Hébertists, the most radical and populist revolutionary group?

If the popular societies increased throughout 1792 in both number and influence, as has been observed by well-informed historians, what also increased was their aggressiveness and the substitution of the voice by noise. The modernized type of association that Brissot, Lanthenas, or Buzot had dreamed of became impossible as the popular movement grew, especially in the capital. The movement's participants, mainly the sans-culottes, fully inherited the corporative spirit from the traditional type of secondary group.[35] The noise reached its crescendo in the summer of 1793, with the victory of the Montagnards over the Girondins; this victory was followed by the institution of the dictatorship of the Committee of Public Safety, bringing in turn the end of the political associations' very existence. In December 1793 it was decreed that "any congress or central assemblies, established by the representatives or by the people or by the popular societies, whichever denomination they can have, . . . are revoked and expressly forbidden by this decree as subversive of the unity of governmental action." For Billaud-Varennes, who proposed this decree, it was indispensable "to leave no distance between the legislator and the people."[36] The Montagnards, who had gained power by relying on the support of the popular societies, excluded them from the political process, without concealing their idea of the popular society as a simple instrument to increase their influence and giving the same reasons as the Constituants had done.

Although the Jacobin leaders, such as Robespierre, may have initially had little insight into the significance of the voluntary associations for which Brissot and his colleagues pleaded, their ideas on the subject eventually took shape: "Do the people always exist in the popular societies?," asks Robespierre just after setting up the dictatorship.

"No. . . . the people are not present when only lazy or malicious persons deliberate in these societies."[37] Saint-Just also has bitter words for these associations: "The popular societies *were in the past* temples of equality. . . . In those societies the people *were seen,* united with their representatives, enlightening and judging them. But ever since the popular societies were filled with deceitful persons calling loudly for their promotion to the legislature, to the ministry, to the generalship . . . , the people are no longer there."[38] Perhaps this bitterness should be heard as a lamentation over the noise and loud cries that had proliferated in the popular societies, taking the place of the rational voices that Saint-Just had hoped to hear in them. In any case, he and his comrades no longer thought of restoring the ideal political association.

The public space, which had been expected to play an important role in the process of making citizens, thus disappeared from the revolutionary scene. The situation remained the same even after the fall of the Jacobins: the Constitution of year III included several articles prohibiting the activity of the societies, and just a day after the proclamation of the Constitution, the National Convention admitted, according to a deputy who was still preoccupied by aggressive images of the Jacobin Club, that "any assembly known under the name of club or popular society is dissolved."[39] The voice of a possible modern sociability founded on reason was silenced, on the one hand, by the silence imposed by the Constituants and, on the other hand, by the noise produced by the group's own dynamics. Here we cannot agree with Habermas's account of the public sphere at this epoch: "The French Revolution created overnight, freely but also less permanently, what in England required a progressive, century-long development: the institutions that the politically reasoning public *[das politisch räsonierende Publikum]* had previously lacked."[40] At least one type of modern public place for sociability could not easily appear because of the revolutionaries' own vision of the social system; and when it did manage to appear, its survival was endangered by its growth parallel to the radicalization of the Revolution.

The fact of the extinction of intermediary groups by the French Revolution is well enough known, even in the history of sociological thought, to be often designated as one of the origins of sociology. Robert Nisbet, among others, saw the rise of Auguste Comte's sociology in the disruption of primary social ties and in the atomization of modern man caused by the French Revolution.[41] Yet our examination of the relevant discourses suggests that this thesis should be modified. What was really lost in the Revolution was not only the community bond represented by the traditional guilds, which was to weaken necessarily in the transition from *Gemeinschaft* to *Gesellschaft*, but also the possibility of the new type of sociability recognized in the popular societies, a sociability that could have played an important role, particularly in the process of creating citizens. This public place for the socialization and communication of citizens was silenced, on the one hand, by the idea that society consists only of individuals and the nation-state and, on the other hand, by the noisy radicalization and aggression of the groups that had taken the place of the old form of solidarity. A faint voice, heard between this silence and noise, is the emblem of the misfortune that the intermediary group in France could only face with resignation.

And so a possible public space disappeared from the social life of the French. What is even more remarkable is that this disappearance of voluntary political association may have added some negative characteristics to the very notion of the modern subject and to the conception of rationality that is linked to it (at least in France). Although citizenship is by nature abstract, the abstraction and isolation of the modern subject may have been augmented by the nature of the process of citizen-making that was proposed, for the process envisioned was not a matter of face-to-face communication but a form of solitary reading to be practiced by a widely dispersed public. This fact can lead in turn to a reconsideration of the Enlightenment itself as a process of citizen-making. What is more, the outburst of noise in the midst of popular societies meant to promote rational and moderate voices suggests that the rational social process that had been envisioned contained the very seeds of irrationality within itself. Does this mean, then, that the perversion or corruption of the group's rationality must not be attributed solely to the development of the political circumstances of the Revolution but to the dynamics of the group? Is this, then, another twist of the dialectic of Enlightenment? In order to answer these questions, we must further study the ways in which rationality and socialization were imagined in the second half of the eighteenth century. At any rate, the French Revolution could not bring the full growth of public space, as was expected at its starting point.

## Notes

1. For a sociological account of the legislative process involved in these decrees, see Shigeki Tominaga, "L'impossible groupement intermédiaire: Été-

automne 1791," *Zinbun: Annals of the Institute for Research in Humanities*, 28 (1993): 1–22.

2. F. A. Aulard, *La Société des Jacobins: Recueil de documents pour l'histoire du Club des Jacobins de Paris* (Paris: 1892), 3: 165. All translations are my own.

3. For example, Raymonde Monnier, *L'Espace public démocratique: Essai sur l'opinion à Paris de la Révolution au Directoire* (Paris: Kimé, 1994); and on the activities of the Parisian sections, Maurice Genty, *L'Apprentissage de la citoyenneté* (Paris: Editions sociales, 1987).

4. J. Boutier and P. Boutry, "Les sociétés politiques en France de 1789 à l'an III: 'Une machine'?," *Revue de l'histoire moderne et contemporaine*, 36, no. 1 (1989): 50.

5. Marcel Gauchet, "Droits de l'homme," in *Dictionnaire critique de la Révolution française*, ed. F. Furet and M. Ozouf (Paris: Flammarion, 1988), 695.

6. *Qu'est-ce que le Tiers Etat?*, ed. E. Champion (Paris: Presses Universitaires de France, 1982), 26.

7. *Archives parlementaires*, 27: 211.

8. Lucien Jaume, *Le Discours jacobin et la démocratie* (Paris: Fayard, 1989), 222.

9. Jean-Jacques Rousseau, *Du contrat social,* in *Oeuvres complètes* (Paris: Gallimard, 1664), 2: 371.

10. *Archives parlementaires*, 23: 200. For the influence of Turgot on Allarde, see W. H. Sewell, *Work and Revolution in France* (Cambridge: Cambridge University Press, 1980), 86–89.

11. *L'Ami du peuple* (March 16, 1791 and June 18, 1791), in *Oeuvres complètes* (Brussels: Pôle Nord, 1993), 4: 2523, 5: 3049.

12. *Archives parlementaires,* 21: 252. This respect for labor will be later reconfirmed as article 16 of the Constitution of 1795: "Young people cannot be inscribed on the civil register unless they can prove that they can write, read and exercise a profession."

13. *Journal des clubs ou sociétés patriotiques,* no. 1 (November 20, 1790): 4. According to I. Bourdin, *Les Sociétés populaires à Paris pendant la Révolution* (Paris, 1937), the same expression can be found in the charter of a society created in a section of Paris.

14. *Archives parlementaires*, 25: 695.

15. "Observations sur le rapport du comité de Constitution, concernant la nouvelle organisation de la France," in *Ecrits politiques,* ed. R. Zapperi (Paris: Edition des Archives Contemporaines, 1985), 250–51.

16. *Archives parlementaires*, 25: 680–81.

17. "An Answer to the Question: 'What is Enlightenment?'," in *Kant's Political Writings,* ed. Hans Reiss, trans. H. B. Nisbet (Cambridge: Cambridge University Press, 1970), 55.

18. "Dire sur le veto royal," in *Ecrits politiques,* ed. Zapperi, 238.

19. Jacques-Pierre Brissot, *Discours sur l'utilité des sociétés patriotiques et populaires, sur la nécessité de les maintenir et de les multiplier par-tout* (Paris, 1791), 4.

20. Ibid., 5.

21. Ibid., 11, 12, 16.

22. Montesquieu, *De l'esprit des lois,* in *Oeuvres complètes* (Paris: Gallimard, 1951), 2: 582.

23. Jacques-Pierre Brissot, *De la vérité* (Neuchatel, 1782), 165–66.

24. Brissot, *Discours,* 21.

25. François Lanthenas, *Des sociétés populaires considérées comme une branche essentielle de l'instruction publique* (Paris, 1792), 2.

26. François Lanthenas, *De l'influence de la liberté sur la santé, la morale et le bonheur* (Paris, 1792), 4–6.

27. *Cinq mémoires sur l'instruction publique,* ed. C. Coutel and C. Kintzler (Paris: Flammarion, 1994), 139–40. On the social impact of printing and solitary reading, see A. J. La Vopa, "Conceiving a public: Ideas and society in eighteenth-century Europe," *Journal of Modern History,* 64 (1992): 80.

28. Lanthenas, *Des sociétés populaires,* 3.

29. G. Delfau, *Opinion sur les sociétés populaires,* reproduced in *Archives parlementaires,* 45: 566.

30. Jacques-Pierre Brissot, *Sur la société des Jacobins à Paris* (Paris, 1792), 30, 34.

31. Ibid., 33–34.

32. *Oeuvres de Maximilien Robespierre* (Paris: Presses Universitaires de France, 1952), 7: 748.

33. Patrice Gueniffey, "Commune de Paris," in *Dictionnaire critique,* ed. Furet and Ozouf, 530.

34. Jean-Nicolas Pache, *Observations sur les sociétés patriotiques* (Paris, n.d.), 1, 5, 6. Judging from the pagination of this pamphlet inserted in the bound document at the Historical Library of the City of Paris (B.H.V.P.), the date of publication seems to fall between that of Lanthenas's text (April 1792) and Brissot's second discourse (October 1792), consequently during the summer of the same year when the author was possibly beginning to change his political position.

35. Comparing popular movements in France and America during this period, Patrice Higonnet remarks a salient contrast, according to which "no traditionalist corporate bedrock" existed in the newly born people; see his *Sister Republic* (Cambridge: Harvard University Press, 1988), 237.

36. Jaques-Nicolas Billaud-Varennes, "Rapport sur un mode de gouvernement provisoire et révolutionnaire," reproduced in *Moniteur,* 18: 475. For the article of the decree quoted earlier, see ibid., 612.

37. Maximilian Robespierre, "Intervention à la Société des amis de la liberté et de l'égalité," in *Oeuvres* (Paris: Presses Universitaires de France, 1967), 10: 287.

38. Louis-Antoine Saint-Just, "Rapport sur les factions de l'étranger," in *Oeuvres complètes* (Paris: Gérard Lebovici, 1984), 728, my italics.

39. J.-B. Mailhe, *Rapport sur les clubs et sociétés populaires* (Paris, year III), 8.

40. Jürgen Habermas, *Strukturwandel der Öffentlichkeit: Untersuchungen zu einer Kategorie der bürgerlichen Gesellschaft* (Frankfurt: Surhkamp, 1990), 137, translated as *The Structural Transformation of the Public Sphere* (Cambridge: MIT Press, 1989). For a critical assessment of Habermas's argument concerning eighteenth-century France, see Keith M. Baker, "Defining the Public Sphere in Eighteenth-Century France: Variations on a Theme by Habermas," in *Habermas and the Public Sphere,* ed. Craig Calhoun (Cambridge: MIT Press, 1992), 181–211.

41. "The French Revolution and the Rise of Sociology in France," *American Journal of Sociology,* 49 (1943): 156–64.

# 5

# Aristophanes in America

### J. Peter Euben

This essay is animated by a question whose answer seems perfectly obvious. The question is, can television, particularly television comedy,[1] play a role in contemporary American democracy that drama, particularly Old Comedy, played in ancient Athenian democracy? And the perfectly obvious answer is "no." Ancient drama was a highly specific, if not unique, historical occurrence. When we examine its context of performance, which we must to understand its "content"—its place within a designated time and space as part of a vast conglomerate of religious ritual and civic festival, the claims dramatists made to be the political educators of their audience, and at the way in which that audience coincided with the civic order of citizens who originated, regulated, and judged dramatic competitions—the juxtaposition my question poses seems far-fetched at best. The same conclusion presents itself if we begin with the historical specificity of television. Think of how different our world is from that of the ancient Athenian, politically, religiously, socially, economically, and culturally, or of those huge transformations of sensibility and scale that establish the context for "television." Just imagine putting a classical Athenian down in New York or Los Angeles. It is itself a pretty promising comedic premise.

One can hardly ignore the significance of such disparities, which means that insofar as I do, I can only ask the reader for a certain suspension of disbelief and willingness to play along as Aristophanes did his audience. And though I will make something of an argument, my purpose, like his and the TV comedies I examine, is more interrogatory than constitutive. It is true that Aristophanes thought ridicule, parody, and mockery had ethical import and that the comic poet was the true political educator of his fellow citizens. But even he never claimed that humor constituted a politics or ethics. The point, rather, was to laugh at those who confidently assumed they knew what morality was, at those political leaders who were sure of their wisdom and power, and at those social conventions and cultural practices that were assumed or claimed to be "natural." Of course, for Plato this lack of respect for authority was part of the problem, which is one reason why he is so unrelenting in his criticisms of comedy in *The Republic* (which is not to deny that there are comic elements in that text).

There is a delicious irony in the fact that what Plato regarded as the height (or depth) of popular culture, namely Aristophanic comedy, we now regard as "classic" and so part of high culture. Clearly, works of art move up and down the cultural ladder. So do genres, as is evident in the case of movies which have become "film" and "cinema" with baroque theories of their very own. All this suggests two questions which I can only raise here: how do such transformations take place, and is there any reason to suppose that television comedies such as *Seinfeld, In Living Color, Roseanne, The Honeymooners,* or *The Simpsons* will climb a similar cultural ladder?

In the case of comedy there is a danger in achieving cultural respectability. Tragedy invites and can easily bear the weight of serious analysis. But comedy is highly susceptible to the disease of didacticism because it seems to evaporate under the scalpel of academic attention. E. B. White called this the "frog" problem, which seems particularly appropriate in the case of Aristophanes who wrote a play by that name. Analyzing comedy, White suggested, was like dissecting a frog; both die in the process of displaying their innards.[2] On the other hand, there is something comical about academics scurrying to make Aristophanes into a philosopher in drag (which is not so different from what I am about to do), or insisting that he offers a double message, one for the refined and sophisticated (i.e., us) and one for the unwashed masses.

In what follows I want first to say something about the cultural climate in which Aristophanic comedy was produced, the performance conditions of that production, and the content of the plays which can only be understood in terms of that climate and those conditions. More specifically, I will be concerned about the relationship between democracy and comedy and the role of the comic poet as political educator of his fellow citizens. Second, I will turn to the critics of television and their charge that it is a form of anti-political education that corrupts democracy, and then criticize the critics, not because I think them wrong, but because I think their attitude toward television (which some are quick to say they seldom watch) is self-fulfilling and therefore politically suspect. My critique of the critics is intended to provide some space for thinking about the ways in which television might become something other and better than it seems necessarily to be and for reintroducing the juxtaposition between Aristophanic and TV comedy present in my initial question. Finally, I will elaborate this juxtaposition by suggesting that if Aristophanes were to find himself in New York or Los Angeles he might well have been a writer for *The Honeymooners* or *The Simpsons*.

## I

The relationship between theater and politics in Athens was quite different than it is for us. A playwright did not create a drama and seek to have it produced for an audience that would exist only at the moment of performance. Nor was the play a piece of writing destined for individual consumption by private readers. The audience, which in this respect largely coincided with the civic order of citizens, was already constituted and the poet applied for permission to appear before it.[3] There was a preliminary selection of which text would become a play and a subsequent judgment that awarded prizes by a jury chosen from the general public according to procedures analogous to those used for deciding membership in the *boulè*. This meant that theater was a communal time and place even when representative aspects of that community were being subject to ridicule and critique. It also meant what contemporary critics find so hard to accept—that ordinary citizens voted first prizes to plays that were highly critical of their own leaders' policies, foibles, and cultural accommodations such as those concerning gender and class.

But to speak of theater as a whole elides the differences between tragedy and comedy and begs the question of whether comedy did indeed have practical consequences outside the prescribed festive celebration of which it was a part.

Theater provided a place and time in which the assembled citizenry saw itself represented onstage confronting issues such as leadership and authority, democracy and empire, generational and sexual conflict, the relationship between *oikos* and *polis,* gods and humankind, wisdom and madness, power and freedom, ingenuity and transgression, nature and convention, as well as the place of drama in public life. But the form of representation and so the way those issues were considered were different in comedy and tragedy. Tragedy relied on stories from heroic myth, emphasizing dire personal and social events that had befallen heroines and heroes, families and dynasties in the distant past, mostly at places other than Athens, mostly in highly stylized language. Comedy, by contrast, was firmly anchored in the present and Athens was openly topical about its objects of ridicule—militarism, greed, litigiousness, Socrates, the sophists, war with Sparta, Cleon, Pericles, education, the gullibility of the *demos,* patriotism, and the glory of the past. Except when parodying the conventions of tragedy, its language was colloquial and its choice of linguistic and musical registers as well as subjects much wider. While a tragic hero was likely to meet a horrific fate as the result of an equally horrific transgression, the comic "hero" was likely to be a farmer or artisan who was merely trying to "make ends meet." And while tragedy encouraged its audience to reflect in the most general way on issues of agency and fate, reason and passion, comedy's satirical depiction of Athenian democracy was designed "both to arouse laughter and to encourage reflection." Like a modern topical cartoon, it humorously distorted reality in order to draw attention to gaps between truth and lies, principle and practice.[4]

Though a tragedy might speak about an otherwise unspeakable act (such as incest) or a character in it might question the gods, it was comedy that was free to engage in types of ridicule audiences regarded as illicit in public life. Because comedy was allowed or even encouraged to indulge in forms of personal ridicule and flaunt otherwise common standards of propriety, it was the quintessential expression of parrhesia, frank and honest speech unintimidated by power. To a degree impossible in tragedy, comedy ridiculed gods and politicians, generals and intellectuals, mocked the *demos*'s favorites and its critics, all the while exulting in verbal abuse, uninhibited sexuality, and repeated references to excrement and flatulence.

Third, comedy, unlike tragedy, broke "the fourth wall" between stage and audience and called attention to the staged character of the dramatic action. It is true that the audience for both could be boisterous (there are stories of food being thrown at incompetent actors) and that in this regard the sedateness of modern audiences is closer to Plato's ideal audience than anything that existed in Athens. But it was in comedy that actors spoke of themselves as performers, referred to stage and scenery instead of the dramatic setting, and made the audience aware of itself as a group of spectators and as a spectacle being seen by others.

James Redfield has argued that tragedy is "a partial art" that calls forth its antitype, "Old Comedy."[5] While tragedy brings home the limiting conditions of human freedom, comedy mocks these constraints.

The cultural forms that tether human possibilities to the earthly realities of everyday life are ridiculed in a way that reminds us that culture
is something invented and can be renewed and recast. In *The Wasps,*
the judicial process is likened to a game that could just as easily be
played with cooking utensils; in *The Birds,* the hero decides to conquer
the air rather than other cities; in *The Akharnians,* he opts for making
a separate peace with Sparta and then makes fun of his compatriots
who self-destructively keep fighting; In *Lysistrata,* the women take
over the city; in *The Ecclesiazusa,* the question is raised about whether
the Athenian assembly could make women men if they so desired.
After all, why should nature be a limit? If the Athenians have the
power to make every sea and land a highway of their daring and conceive of themselves as an island and then act in the world as if they
were one—proposals made by Thucydides' Pericles—then what is to
stop them from voting to make women men?[6]

In one instance comedy goes so far as to claim superiority over
tragedy. In *The Frogs,* Aristophanes presents an agon between Euripides
and Aeschylus over who is best at making the people better citizens.
Dionysus, the judge, decides for Aeschylus. But since it is the play that
renders final judgment, the implicit claim is that the comic poet, not
any tragedian, is the city's true political educator.

But in what sense was Aristophanes the political educator of
Athenian democracy? There are two questions here. The first concerns
whether the audience brought its theatrical experience (whatever that
might be) to their participation in other political venues or, more
broadly, whether comedy had any substantial political consequences.
The second concerns the ways in which its possible consequences
could properly be termed "democratic."

Many commentators believe that Old Comedy was necessarily conservative since whatever anarchic, transgressive, and liberatory impulses
might be present in the plays were domesticated by the "controlled environment" of state-sponsored religious rituals. "The deliberate transgression of social norms" and the "consistently outrageous humor we find
in Aristophanes," one critic writes, was "permissible" only in a carefully marked-off, tightly controlled festive space. In these terms comedy
seems more carnival than a prelude to an action, more a letting off
steam "than a challenge to conventional hierarchies." Because of this,
whatever visions of renewal comedy might offer remained a mere vision
since it "lacked any programmatic" dimension. Add to this a nostalgia

for a "simpler time" and comedy could not pose a viable alternative to the inequalities embedded in city-state life.[7]

Part of this skepticism about comedy having radical consequences outside the carefully patrolled context of festival and theater may stem from skepticism about democracy and the capacity of the *hoi polloi* to make intelligent judgments. (It is a skepticism mirrored by leftist critics of television who see it as a vehicle of the capitalist class controlling the unwitting masses and by conservative critics who see the medium as further debasing an already contemptible popular culture.) While it is true that the playwright had to please the judges and audience, it does not follow that pleasing them meant flattering them or that they could not appreciate mockery of their own foibles and excesses. Nor is re-affirming traditional values quite so conservative if those values are democratic and if, as I shall argue, they include a tradition of collective self-critique.

Nonetheless, the argument is a useful corrective to my presumptions about what an Athenian audience took away from a dramatic performance (though the argument has its own presumptions about this.) No one can be sure whether Aristophanic comedy had any effect on Euripides' reputation or the fate of Cleon, for example. Indeed, Cleon was voted the generalship soon after the judges awarded first prize to *The Knights* in which he is viciously lampooned. Nor, given the bivalent meaning of *skoptein* and its cognates—to joke with reference to play, fun, and humor, and to mock or deride in ways that dishonor—can we be certain that ridicule did not exacerbate rather than heal divisions within Athens (presuming what is not obvious, that such healing is always positive). In a culture as shame-oriented as ancient Greece, the derisive dimensions of laughter were volatile indeed.[8] It also sharpens the distinction between an immanent critique of Athenian democracy as found in Aristophanes and a transformative one present in *The Republic,* and reminds us that Aristophanes' plays meant something very different to their original audience than they do to all subsequent audiences and readers.[9]

But it is not obvious that Aristophanes is nostalgic for some simpler time. Old Education, Aeschylus, and the rustic Strepsiades are subject to as much ridicule as New Education, Euripides, or Socrates. More importantly, there is evidence that comedy was expected to and did have substantial impact on Athenian democracy. There is, to begin with, Plato's harsh and persistent criticism of what comedy does to the citizenry. And of course Plato and Xenophon thought Aristophanes' caricature of Socrates helped shape the animus against him.[10] Then there is the fact that Aristophanes was awarded a crown by the city after the performance of *The Frogs* in 405 B.C.E. for having given it good advice. In addition, Cleon's lawsuit against Aristophanes makes little sense if comedy had no political consequences outside the frame of theater and play. Moreover, the fact that the liberty of comic ridicule was suspended by law (from 440/39 to 437/6) suggests that it was regarded as something more than lighthearted entertainment.[11] Penultimately, there is the sheer implausibility of the idea that theatrical experience could be tightly compartmentalized, both because laughter is uncontrollable and contagious, and because other posited compartmentalizations in Athens surrounding gender and public and private are far more permeable than official designations indicate.

Finally, there is the poet's claim, acknowledged by the city, that he was its political educator, not in the sense that Plato's Guardians were or Plato himself perhaps hoped to be, though Old Comedy, like *The Republic,* exposed the *demos*'s tendency toward self-deception and confronted the artifices of a political system that tended, as all political systems do, to naturalize its practices. Rather, Aristophanes offered advice by way of parodying the city's favorite leaders, giving some issues more salience than others, articulating shared resentments or a general malaise, pressuring for reconsideration of policies already adopted or minority views previously rejected, and in general providing a stage in which the tensions, instabilities, and transformations of democratic life could be dramatized, mediated, and explored.[12]

One could say that comedy was aporetic in the sense that it "transferred the last word to the audience who were left to enact [their] own part but a little more reflectively than before."[13] In this sense comedic political education could help its citizen audience think about what they were doing and what others were doing to them, sometimes in their name, always for their supposed benefit.

All this sounds like Socrates' project as he describes and exemplifies it in Plato's *Apology.* He, too, engaged in political education without normative blueprints or practical solutions. And this suggests what I can only assert here,[14] that comedy helped constitute a tradition of democratic self-critique upon which Socrates could build even when he criticized democracy's shortcomings. In these terms his oft-quoted claim that "the unexamined life is not worth living" is less radical and Socratic political philosophy is less discontinuous an activity than they appear to be. Without for a moment denying that comedy and philosophy are and do very different things, or that philosophers have almost always rejected with disgust the idea that irreverence, ridicule, parody, scatology, and vulgarity could be a ground for "serious" ethical and political critique, one way to understand Socratic political theory as portrayed in *The Apology* is as an extrapolation of comedic political education.

Still, none of this directly addresses the question of how much and whether comedy extended and deepened democratic practices and culture. Suppose we think of democracy as an ethos[15] that includes a form of governance of, by, and for the people, and an egalitarian constitution of cultural and political life. A democratic ethos encourages the sharing of power and responsibility, presuming both that the former can enhance the latter (but without the naive expectation that it necessarily does), and that the sharing of power is a prerequisite for dignity as well as self- and mutual respect. A democratic ethos is suspicious of hierarchies, especially but not only political ones, and is prejudiced against claims to authority by actual or potential elites. Similarly, democrats may treat political leaders with respect, but ultimately the people are the government, and leaders are more advisors and competitors for public stature than august representatives of the state.[16] A democratic ethos presumes that political knowledge is constituted discursively rather than deductively, that at the very least it requires the contributions of high and low, and involves sometimes heated debates among people who may differ intensely about what they should do and who rightly constitutes the "they." A democratic ethos can tolerate some economic inequality as long as it does not compromise political equality or legitimate moral or significant social inequalities. Penultimately, a democratic ethos is a social process through which fixed identities and naturalized conventions periodically confront their conventional status. This does not mean that people can shed such conventions easily or that simply naming them as conventional could or should be liberating. It does mean that social and cultural conventions are modes of performance, instantiated in thousands of small and large actions in ways that elude full cognitive disclosure. Finally, a democratic ethos assumes that democracy is as much a politics of disturbance as a form of government and order.

In what ways does Old Comedy exemplify and define such an ethos? We know that conservatives disliked it, that it was exceptionally inclusive in subject matter and audience, and that comic fantasies and inversions of the norms provided a vision of things as they used to be or should and could still be against the weight of the status quo.[17] Then there is the additional fact that while tragedy at its origins was patronized by tyrants, comic drama was officially accepted into the Dionysia only in 486 and into the Lenaea about 45 years later, suggesting that it was the product of "democratic patronage."[18]

In addition, comedy was a cultural form of political accountability. Here is Jeffrey Henderson:

> The precise effects of comic ridicule and comic abuse are impossible to gauge. But surely no prominent Athenian imagined that the laughter of the *demos* at his expense could possibly do him any good, and the better the joke the less comfortable he would be thereafter. For this very reason the *demos* institutionalized the comic competitions. In return for accepting the guidance of the "rich, the well-born, and the powerful" it provided that they be subject to a yearly unofficial review of their conduct at the hands of the *demos'* organic intellectuals and critics, the comic poets.[19]

Moreover, comedy helped sustain the egalitarian constitution of political and cultural life. In *The Clouds,* for example, everyone becomes a spectacle for everyone else: the chorus and characters onstage; the characters who, stepping out of their roles, talk directly to the audience about themselves as actors and refer to the theater in Athens; "Aristophanes" when he comes forward to address the audience in the parabasis and the audience when he looks out at them. No one escapes being part of the spectacle; each is in turn seer and seen. Each moment of superiority, of laughing at others, and ridiculing their foibles is reversed as if Aristophanes was, in the context of theater, imitating rotation in office that was distinctive to Athenian democracy.[20]

When we first meet Socrates in *The Clouds,* he is on high in a basket (or baskette) mingling his rare thought with the ethereal air, contemptuous of anything that would ground the delicate essence of his thought in gross mundanity. While he is all intellect, mind, and philosophy, Strepsiades is all body, or more precisely, all anus, phallus, and stomach. With his nose to the ground (which gives him a distinctive perspective on the heavens), he is dogmatically literal-minded, bringing every idea and thought to earth with a resounding thud.

Both are ridiculous figures. Yet both have something necessary and admirable about them despite *The Clouds'* absurd characterization of them. But the play does more than present the tension between them; it mediates it in the sense of itself employing a language that is tied to but not wholly weighed down by physical desire and bodily needs, being a mode of thought that is sensuous and relying on "concepts" grounded in place and the body. Doing so it suggests, against Plato's *Republic*, that high and low are complements to each other and absurd alone.

Penultimately, and as I have suggested, Old Comedy helped constitute a tradition of self-critique in which various practices and cultural accommodations basic to Athenian public and private life were called into question. An example of such self-critique is present when Thucydides' Pericles criticizes the convention of giving Funeral Orations that required and entitled him to do what he is about to do, thereby dislodging the practice from the tradition that legitimized it. Such problematizing of what is also enacted (which is also present in Socratic philosophizing) is an aspect of the restless daring the Corinthians tell us (in Thucydides I 70, Crawley trans.) typifies their Athenian enemies. "To describe their character in a word, one might truly say that they were born into the world to take no rest themselves and to give none to others." A few pages later, the Athenians echo those words in the course of boasting about their daring patriotism at Salamis. (The restlessness is brilliantly parodied by the twitching of the flea-infested Strepsiades in the opening scene of *The Clouds*.)

Finally, Aristophanic comedy does not simply endorse such daring and self-critique but provides a stage on which "conservative" and "postmodernist" excesses are both ridiculed. Thus, *The Clouds* dramatizes the costs of the displacements democratic politics may demand and which it otherwise celebrates. Consider, for example, the way the play treats the opposition between town and country, upper and lower classes. Strepsiades comes from a lower-class farming background while his wife comes from an aristocratic family linked to Pericles. The birth of their son exacerbates these differences as they fight over his name. They finally compromise on "Pheidippides," meaning "cheap aristocrat." But this solves nothing when the son is instructed to honor his parents. How can he when they come from different classes and ways of life? The only solution, which the son adopts after his sophistic education, is to *dishonor* them both. Here the fluidity, egalitarianism, and hybridity of democratic culture has a darker side: dispossession, confusion, and loss of ground.

By the fourth century, the growing specialization of culture meant a separation between popular and elite culture, seriousness and humor, education and entertainment. As popular theater developed into a form of entertainment the new genres of rhetoric and philosophy took over the paideutic function drama, including comedy, had once possessed.[21]

## II

Given all this, comparisons with television can only be absurdly tendentious. There was indeed a time before the triumph of industrial
capitalism, consumer culture, and the commodification of leisure when
one could find less tendentious parallels between ancient and modern
*theater.*[22] Before nineteenth-century state building and industrializa-
tion, churches, lodge halls, and community centers were sites for theatrical productions designed to make occasions such as weddings and
holidays more festive. The new commercial theaters that replaced
them, George Lipsitz points out, "needed no special occasion nor ritual activities" to justify their existence. Such performances "became
commodities sold to strangers for an agreed-upon price rather than
collective creations by communities enacting rituals essential to group
identity and solidarity." Unlike previous conditions and Athenian
drama, performers in these theaters lacked direct ties of kinship, pro-
pinquity, and history with their audiences.[23] The new audiences did
not share a history, reciprocal responsibilities, and obligations.

Lipsitz is careful not to tell a moralizing story of decline. Thus he
recognizes how the new commercial theater created a kind of social
space for working-class men to escape the surveillance of moral authorities and institutions, and for women to escape parental supervision and patriarchal domination. This theater also encouraged audiences to pursue personal desires and passions outside their socially
prescribed responsibilities, and because of the audience's unfamiliarity,
provided a cover for feelings and emotions that could be aired without
explanation or apology.[24] Nonetheless, he regards the new theatrical
forms as creating the "psychic conditions for the needy narcissism of
consumer desires,"[25] and goes on to argue that by "establishing commodity purchases as symbolic answers to real problems," the new
theater lay the basis for a commodity culture "where advertisers and
entrepreneurs offer products that promise to bring pleasures and fulfillment." Though nineteenth-century theater may have emerged in
part as a rebellion against sexual repression, "its greatest long-term
significance lay in shaping the psychic and material preconditions for
Americans to shift from a Victorian industrial economy to a hedonistic
consumer one." It is precisely the triumph of this culture and the material conditions that accompanied it that makes comparisons with ancient theater seem so far-fetched.

But what about the idea of television as a form of democratic political education? Like Greek drama, television is, in Neil Postman's
words, "our culture's mode of knowing itself. Therefore, how television

stages the world becomes the model for how the world is properly staged."[26] But this "stage "is a mass medium that constitutes a spatial and temporal organization of collective life no longer linked to the sharing of a common locale and face-to-face dialogue. To talk about contemporary public spaces we need to rethink both the idea of space and publicness in a way that reflects the complex interdependencies of the modern world with its highly mediated forms of communication.

Moreover, contemporary democracies are liberal or representative rather than participatory. There is no rotation in office, selection by lot, or absence of semi-permanent elites with their own corporate interests. Democracy now does not mean maximum self-rule (unless it is maximum "feasible" rule) and the mutual accountability of citizens, but a mechanism to ensure some degree of accountability of rulers to the ruled. Indeed, one could argue that even this minimal notion of democracy has been eroded in the past twenty years as American society has grown more and more inegalitarian, more divided by extremes of wealth and poverty, and more systematically dominated by corporate power. Insofar as this has meant increased power for elites bent on appropriating the conduct, knowledge, and procedures of public life, it is the inverse process of the democratization Jean-Pierre Vernant traces when he describes the evolution of democracy in classical Athens.[27] In any case, what seems clear is that since very few of our citizens actively share in the opportunities and responsibilities of power as Athenian citizens did, they can hardly bring the experience of direct participation in politics to the watching of television. Still less does television seem to provide the occasion and the place to reflect on public life with the depth and comprehensiveness present in Greek theater.

Television is frequently blamed for the attenuation of even this pallid form of democracy as well as for the corruption of public discourse generally. Some thirty-five years ago, Newton Minnow called television "a vast wasteland" (pinpointing situation comedies as the worst offenders). Television, he and his fellow critics claimed, was vulgar and one-dimensional rather than complex and edifying; sordid, prurient, and mean-spirited rather than uplifting and realistic. More recently, television has been named as a significant cause of the erosion of social capital, civility, and deliberative democracy, the trivialization of private and public life, and of political voyeurism replacing political judgment.[28] For such critics television is and must be a form of antipolitical education which corrodes democracy. There are ten elements to this general condemnation.

1. Television transforms citizens into consumers, political freedom and power into consumer sovereignty, and the public sphere into a realm of media manipulation and spectacle.

2. In its search for ratings, television homogenizes culture,[29] in effect imposing a form of censorship on what can be produced. Cable does not substantially change the situation since the parts imitate each other rather than offer real alternatives.

3. Television fosters and represents a closing in and down of public spaces. Given VCRs and Pay Per View, there is no need to go out to the movies. Given the Home Shopping Network, there is less reason (for mostly women) to go out in public and be in the company of, if not in conversation with, friends.[30] At the same time, television penetrates the home, helping to order domestic space, leisure time, and family identity, all of which are reconfigured around commodities and possessions rather than ethnicity or class. Finally, it colonizes intimate areas of gender and personality by exacerbating anxieties about sexuality and personality, all in the interests of selling products.[31]

4. In this world of private men and women the good life is the consuming life. Unable to think as citizens, public responsibilities are regarded as distractions from and intrusions on the world of banal utopian visions where all needs are instantly met, conflict is nonexistent, and poverty has evaporated into thin air.[32]

5. Television fosters political cosmeticians, image managers, spin doctors, and ad experts who sell candidates as they do other products. Almost all candidates are now bound to the commercial form and are presented as commodities.[33] No wonder people are cynical and anti-political.

6. Television worships power and devours those who have it. On the one hand, it displays obeisance to the sacred offices of the state.[34] But on the other, it subjects holders of power to a contemptuous scrutiny that is more voyeuristic than substantive.

7. Television makes the workings of power invisible. This is as true of its own form of power as of the larger structures of power in which it participates. Television presents itself as providing direct, unmediated, instantaneous reports of events as they are occurring, obscuring both the framing force of the medium, for instance, the way stopwatches organize the images that constitute "the news," and its own place within a capitalist economy; for

instance, the unprecedented corporate consolidation of the media during the Reagan and Bush administrations.[35]

8. Where television does not misinform or underinform us about its own power and complicity with the dominating economic and political powers of our time, it distracts us from power's effects by substituting what Pierre Bourdieu calls an "imaginary participation" which is "only an illusory compensation for the dispossession people suffer to the advantage of experts" and professionals.[36] This pseudo-power is symbolized by the "remote control" which allows (usually men) to change the world by changing channels.[37]

9. Television news precludes thoughtfulness, depth, and analysis.[38] It relies on sound bites in which images compete with each other for 90-second slots and leap from one issue to another in a way that flattens all distinctions and differences. By moving instantly from protests in Bosnia to football in Brazil, from floods in California to spelling bees in Pennsylvania, from research on the AIDS virus to an outing of the Royal Family, hierarchies of significance are eliminated and each fragment is related to another only by the medium itself.[39]

10. Television is ahistorical and moralistic. In his study of the medium's coverage of the Ethiopian famine, Michael Ignatieff shows how its "brief, intense and promiscuous gaze"[40] provided no opportunity for historical background and no reason to think one would be relevant. It was not only that television ignored the food shortage until it became a famine of epic proportions and so worthy of voyeuristic coverage, but also that, absent any analysis of imperialism and colonialism, the crisis appeared to be a natural phenomenon outside of history and politics. Thus real human suffering was seen as an elemental unmediated moment of connection between human beings outside of time, power, or ideology.

There is much to be said for this critique of television. Yet it is an exaggeration and itself antipolitical in its assumption of technological determinism, supposing that the medium *is* the message and that the aggregate of such messages does and must define the quality of public life. More than that, it is self-fulfilling and demonizes television rather than allowing it to be seen as a problematic whose contradictory forces and democratic possibilities need to be explored rather than preemptorily foreclosed.

This is not meant to deny that the medium contains a powerful cultural logic and that regarding it as a neutral instrument to be used for good or ill is superficial. But the challenge is to specify the medium without reifying it, to see it as a cultural form embedded in historical and material practices and shaped by decisions taken by particular groups in specific circumstances. This means studying television both as a vehicle of corporate capitalism and as generating forces that move outside or even subvert the hegemony such capitalism seeks to assure. It also means, following Marx on religion, looking at how television salves the wounds and disappointments of daily life, and at how its power may be symptom and sign of our powerlessness. "Even if we could safely dismiss every program on television as artistically worthless," George Lipsitz writes, "we would still need to understand the ways in which television presents the illusion of intimacy, how it intervenes in family relations, how it serves the consumer economy, and how its hold on the viewing audience is related to the disintegration of public resources, the aggravations of work, and the fragility of interpersonal relations that characterize our lives."[41]

Once we see television as part of a larger cultural dialectic, it becomes possible and necessary to ask whether television invented the superficiality and triviality of public discourse, political sloganeering, and distracting pageantry that defines our public life or has become dominant because of that development. If we could transform the vulgarity and shallowness of the medium or even eliminate it altogether, would that restore or let flourish a more acceptable form of discourse? Do charges of television being anti-democratic nostalgically ignore the parochialisms, hierarchies, and exclusiveness present in previous forms of public life and communication?

It also becomes necessary to look more closely at the assumption that what corporate sponsors and television executives or producers want to communicate is what is in fact communicated; that, in Todd Gitlin's phrase, media "operates hypodermically," injecting the proper ideas into the unsuspecting bloodstream of the masses. Like those critics who suppose that Aristophanes wrote for two audiences, the sophisticated few who recognized his real intentions and the gullible many who did not, critics from Plato to Adorno, Postman, and Habermas assume that the masses are manipulable fodder for elite control through the latter's domination of the media.[42] But there is evidence that the effects of programming are more various and dispersed and the audiences more savvy than this,[43] which means that we need to know how programs are read rather than just what is watched. "Pre-ferred readings," Stuart Hall writes, do not preclude "oppositional ones."[44]

## III

While these responses qualify and complicate the critique of television, they do not, nor are they intended to, undo it.[45] What they do is to pro-vide interpretive space for thinking about the ways in which television might become something other and "better" than it seems necessarily to be, or, more precisely, about the possibilities of television as a mode of democratic political education. And that opens the door, if only slightly, for reconsidering the apparent absurdity of comparing Old Comedy with television sitcoms.

For the door to stay open or open wider it is necessary to find op-portunities for contemporary citizens to experience the pleasures and opportunities of sharing power and responsibility and for them to bring such experiences to the watching of television.

The first set of opportunities is present in multiple sites of citizen-ship, both formally and informally defined. They exist in various envi-ronmental, human rights, and gay liberation movements, in women's health collectives, union organizing, mobilization of the poor, and the frequent complex negotiations in multi-ethnic neighborhoods that gen-erate vibrant effective local political associations. Of course, one must be careful not to romanticize civil society and social movements by as-suming that their politics will be wholly congenial. And one must avoid assimilating even such neighborhood politics to the Greek polis, though the idea of "the parallel polis" generated by Vaclav Havel and Vaclav Benda, and Hannah Arendt's suggestion that we think of the polis not in its physical location or historical configuration, but as "the organization of the people as it arises out of acting and speaking to-gether," does provide a language for seeing some analogues.[46]

But even if many of our fellow citizens bring some form of political experience to the watching of television, what about bringing the expe-rience of watching television to that political experience? For reasons already adumbrated, any conclusions on the subject must be very specu-lative, which will not of course stop me from doing precisely that in the concluding section.

**IV**

In many respects, stand-up comics such as Eddie Murphy, Phyllis Diller, George Carlin, Richard Pryor, Margaret Cho, and Chris Rock, each of whom appears on television regularly, would fit comfortably in the world of Aristophanic comedy. They, like he, violate the normative taboos against toilet talk and vulgarity, give ferociously self-deprecatory first-person accounts of sex and sexuality, and refer to orgasms and flatulence, genitalia and fantasies with casual abandon. Such violations of "decorum" seem especially shocking in the case of younger women comics, which suggests how much a double standard remains in effect. (To watch the very different reactions of most men and women to these comediennes is itself pretty funny.) Then there is the willingness to say what is unsayable in other contexts and polite company about corporate greed and military posturing, the personal peccadillos of politicians, and the romanticizing of marriage, parenthood, and family values (epitomized in Roseanne Barr's gum-chewing nasal proclamation that she is a "Domestic Goddess").

The lampooning of cultural icons and political rituals, the ridicule of what has unobtrusively become banal solemnities legitimating suspect power, and (as with the Gulf War) the mocking of national narcissism and government manipulation echoes Aristophanic comedy. These comics unite high and low entertainment with edification in a way that reminds us of Simon Goldhill's claim that Athenian democracy was the precondition of comedy and Nicole Loraux's argument that the reverse was also true.[47]

Nowhere is comedy's informally sanctioned privilege more obvious than in the "handling" of racial issues. With very few exceptions, comedy allows a frankness of expression found nowhere else. On the comic stage people are willing to see their carefully screened racial attitudes exposed and mocked. Whether it is Richard Pryor's parody of white walking and white talking, Margaret Cho mimicking her overly protective, fiercely achievement-driven Korean mother, or Archie Bunker explaining the nature of "the coloreds" or "the Hebes," comedy can present forbidden sentiments in public and perhaps unite (an admittedly self-selective) audience in laughter at its own prejudices.

But situation comedies as a genre seem to deal with comfortable emotions and easy issues in a highly stylized format. Anything that disturbs their formulaic bromides is erased within the half hour. All divisions between sexes, generations, races, and classes dissolve in what

David Marc calls "a whirlwind resolution" which provides a "tantalizing illusion of structural order in family, community, nation, and cosmos."[48] Nothing illustrates the erasure of dissonance better than *Hogan's Heroes,* a comedy about allied prisoners in a World War II prisoner of war camp which manages not to mention Nazism or Jews. From this show to *Ally McBeal,* sitcoms are populated by generic protagonists and static characters whose principal role is spouting one-liners.

Of course there are exceptions that seem to share some of the aims and sensibility of Aristophanic comedy. The cartoonish characters on *Third Rock from the Sun* often reveal something provocative about the "real world" their more realistic counterparts do not. When we laugh at the Solomons it is because the absurdities and shifting boundaries of their lives mimic ours which means we wind up laughing at ourselves.[49] Then there is *Roseanne* on same-sex relations, generational conflict, teen pregnancy, obesity, and working-class life generally, *Beavis and Butthead* on the infantilization of culture (including television), and *Absolutely Fabulous* on the vacuity of consumerism and parental authority.

But I want to focus on two sitcoms that are different in mood and content and appear at very different moments in the development of television, popular culture, and political life. The first is *The Honeymooners,* the second is *The Simpsons.* Pompously put, one is modern, the other post-modern.

Writing about Aristophanes, David Konstan argues that "Where society is riven by tensions and inequalities of class, gender and status, its ideology will be unstable, and literary texts will betray signs of strain involved in forging such refractory materials into a unified competition."[50] I will argue that *The Honeymooners* can be read in these terms; that it both enacts while trying to expunge television's role in papering over the bitter divisions that surface in consumer heaven, and stands in contradiction to the show of which it was, for a number of years, a segment.

Most viewers were introduced to *The Honeymooners* as part of a variety show whose overall tone and frame could not have been more at odds with the life of Ralph Kramden. The show began with an overproduced dance number that seemed equally inspired by Busby Berkeley and Las Vegas. At its conclusion, Jackie Gleason made a leering entrance dressed in ostentatious finery that paid unembarrassed obeisance to his nouveau richness. When it came to booze and broads, this man lived like a king with a banner proclaiming "how sweet it is."

Following his royal entrance, Gleason did five minutes or so of stand-up and then asked for "a little traveling music."

The journey was multi-layered: from Manhattan to Brooklyn,[51] from present success to a Depression-era past, when Gleason left school to become a pool hustler in a working-class neighborhood like the one in which *The Honeymooners* is set, from Farouk-like royalty to the wounded machismo of a fat guy who drives a bus, from ostentatious display and conspicuous consumption to "a barebones flat the likes of which this consumer medium has not seen since."[52] The flat is a place barren not only of material comforts but of social and psychological ones as well—all this despite the name of the show. The Kramdens' poverty was present in what was in their apartment and what was not; in the antiquated oven and icebox that barely worked and the non-existent telephone and television. Such technological backwardness suggests people whom time and progress has passed by, who are cut off from others and forced to turn in and on themselves. This claustrophobic atmosphere, compounded by the absence of children and a bedroom and the choice of static camera positions, recapitulated their endlessly repetitive lives.

All attempts to open up this world fail miserably. They try to adopt a child, spend all they have to decorate their apartment to impress the adoption agency, only to have the charade demeaningly exposed. After going to such lengths to pretend to have what they do not and be what they are not, the iceman cometh to demand payment on an overdue bill. Their hopes destroyed, they lapse back into a world without a future. No new beginnings or culture of self-help here.

Ralph's get-rich-quick schemes—glow in the dark wallpaper, developing uranium mines on the Jersey shore—are no more successful and no less desperate. He is stuck in a dead-end job that brings him neither the material rewards nor the social recognition he craves. Though full of bluster, he is intimidated by the powerful and wealthy. The few moments when he tells someone off are always based on a false premise that force him into an abject apology later. In all other situations he stands before them hat in hand, looking down at the floor, overly earnest and fawning as if enacting the stereotype of the slave. For this sycophant with a hair-trigger temper there is no American dream; Horatio Alger might as well be a beer label.

The show is built around two unspoken ironies: its title and his work. As I already suggested, there is nothing honeymoonish about the show despite the deus ex machina endings of "Alice, you're the greatest." The moon we hear most about is the one Ralph threatens to send Alice to when he is in one of his typical rages. Indeed, the threat of domestic violence is omnipresent. Ralph's attempts to be master of his house (in contrast to his obsequiousness in the presence of his "betters") is continually frustrated by Alice, who remains "terrifyingly calm" and thoroughly unintimidated in the midst of his fury. Her "Now, listen to me, Ralph" is both motherly and caustic, advice as well as insult. Then there is his job as a bus driver. The idea of a man as impatient as he is driving a bus in Manhattan traffic is both frightening and funny. It is hard to know what would be worse: riding with him or being a pedestrian anywhere near him.

Finally, Ralph is a prime candidate for an early death. Dangerously overweight, constantly frantic, volatile, frustrated, and disappointed, he is heading for a stroke or heart attack. If one were to count up the victims of modernity or capitalism, then Ralph Kramden would be high on the list.

But this is all frog dissection. The show is often hilariously funny, particularly when Ralph hatches some plot with his sewer-tending pal, Ed Norton. Norton is everything Ralph is not: self-satisfied with an oblivious calmness that enables him to slough off life's insults and focus on what really matters—food. Moreover, there is some opening up of and to the world: a (disastrous) trip to Europe, Raccoon Lodge meetings, an appearance on a quiz show, and a classic train ride.

Though I can imagine Aristophanes writing for *The Honeymooners,* I am convinced, on the flimsiest of evidence, that should he come down (or more likely up) to earth, he would be a writer for *The Simpsons,* and not only because the patriarch of the family is named Homer. (*The New Yorker* had a cartoon of Rembrandt's "Aristotle Contemplating the Bust of Homer." You can guess which Homer it was.) Like Aristophanic comedy, the show is anarchic yet pointed, sophisticated, and raucous, anti-intellectual in an intellectual way, subversive and caustic about the excesses of its own subversions. As with Aristophanes' comedies, the issues are serious—greed and the passion to consume, nuclear power safety and corporate responsibility in general, the erosion of community and local control, the dangers of the therapeutic state, self-help programs and moralistic religiosity, high culture and television itself—while their treatment is farcical.[53] Finally, *The Simpsons*'s distrust of power remote from ordinary people, its suspicion of intellectual pretense (as when Mensa tried to establish a Plato-like utopia in Springfield), and its mocking of institutions, practices, and cultural forms that pretend to be natural while never fully endorsing its own sophistic impulses all recall Old Comedy.

Homer Simpson is the Strepsiades of his generation. He is ineptly self-interested, manipulative, and greedy, has low and vulgar tastes, tries to cheat his creditors, and is infinitely gullible. Homer's vision of the good life is a day in the hammock or owning a used grease concession. He is forever wanting things he'll never have, scheming to get them only to fail miserably (which is why one critic thinks Homer's struggle owes as much to Ralph Kramden as to "the poetry of Aristophanes").[54] Yet, like Strepsiades, Homer loves his family and, in his own morally bumbling way, is superior to those who proclaim their superiority.

*The Simpsons* has a cartoon within a cartoon which brilliantly satirizes popular culture of which it is a part. *Itchy and Scratchy* is its name and it is every parent's nightmare. Full of gratuitous violence that politicians rail against, it has episodes entitled "The Last Traction Hero" and "Remembrance of Things Slashed." In "Itchy and Scratchy Land," the Simpsons visit a Disney-like theme park divided into Torture Land, Explosion Land, Searing Gas Pain Land, and Unnecessary Surgery Land, with a state of the art chemical dependency center for mom and dad to visit while the kids destroy everything. In one episode, *Itchy and Scratchy* writers are running out of themes so they have a theme about running out of themes. In another, a panic about ratings leads to the creation of focus groups and co-optation of new trends (such as rap music) in order to keep their clichéd show on for a bit longer. Others are devoted to the cartoon industry, suggesting a self-reflectiveness also present in Old Comedy.[55]

*The Simpsons* has certainly had an impact on the "outside" world. Elementary schools tried to ban Bart Simpson T-shirts and George Bush attacked *The Simpsons* in his 1992 State of the Union address, telling Americans they should be more like the Waltons than the Simpsons. (A week later *The Simpsons* responded that they were indeed like the Waltons since they were also living through an economic depression.) But of course Bart's contempt for authority is as American as Tom Sawyer's or Huck Finn's, and while *The Simpsons* does indeed mock the idealized portrait of the 1950s family and the self-righteousness of the Religious Right, it ultimately endorses the family, as rag-tag as it may be, and, almost uniquely on television, recognizes the importance of religion in American life.[56]

But in what ways, if any, can we say that *The Simpsons* contributes to the political education of democratic citizens?

The great Marxist critic C. R. L. James thought television would be an art of the people and for the people; that it would, precisely because of the kind of medium it was, be able to dramatize the infinite complexity of modern life in "the manner of the Greeks." Television (as well as film, comic strips, and radio) could, he believed, "shake the nation to its soul" as Aristophanes did to the soul of the Athenians.[57] This has clearly not happened and perhaps it never could or will. Yet programs like *The Simpsons* do play what I have called an interrogatory role in our public life. It does not, any more than Old Comedy, provide solutions to particular problems or offer simple lessons to ameliorate the injustices that continue to dog even our (selectively) affluent times. But it does, as Old Comedy did, make fun of contemporary institutions, culture, and social practices in ways that might lead a citizen to think differently, perhaps even prod him or her to act differently. More certainly, it will make its audience laugh at itself in ways that maintain some space between our identities and our public commitments and in that way might help keep America whole, not to mention the frog.

## Notes

1. I chose TV comedy because, as David Marc has put it, "Television is America's jester. It has assumed the guise of an idiot while actually accruing the advantages of power and authority behind the smoke screen of its self-degradation" (see his *Demographic Vistas: Television in American Culture,* rev. ed. (Philadelphia: University of Pennsylvania Press, 1996), 7.

2. As anyone who has heard Jerry Lewis expound on the subject can attest. The White argument is in the preface to the Modern Library edition of *A Subtreasury of American Humor* (New York: Random House, 1948), xvii.

3. Rush Rehm, *Greek Tragic Theater* (London: Routledge, 1992), vii, 3–5. See Oddone Longo, "The Theater of the Polis," and John J. Winkler, "The Ephebes Song: Tragoida and Polis," in John J. Winkler and Froma I. Zeitlin, *Nothing To Do with Dionysos? Athenian Drama in Its Social Context* (Princeton, N.J.: Princeton University Press, 1990), 12–19 and 20–61, respectively.

4. See the "Introduction" to *Three Plays by Aristophanes: Staging Women,* translated and edited by Jeffrey Henderson (New York: Routledge, 1996), 5–7.

5. See his "Drama and Community: Aristophanes and Some of His Rivals," in Winkler and Zeitlin, *Nothing to Do with Dionysos?*

6. Thucydides I 142, and Josiah Ober, *Political Dissent in Democratic Athens: Intellectual Critics of Popular Culture* (Princeton, N.J.: Princeton, University Press, 1998), 135–40.

7. David Konstan, *Greek Comedy and Ideology* (New York: Oxford University Press, 1995), 8, 165–67.

8. As Anthony Grafton has argued, humor is "the most delicate of subjects in scholarship and everyday life." The phrase "we are not amused" is one of the most fearful we can hear and the disapproving comment, "I don't think that's funny," makes most intellectuals neurotic. No social task is harder "than explaining a joke to someone who does not get it and no intellectual task is harder than trying to understand what makes jokes funny in another society or in the earlier history of one's own." See his "Beyond the Joke," in the *Times Literary Supplement,* April 10, 1998, 4–5.

9. Ober, *Political Dissent,* 123.

10. Malcolm Heath (in *Political Comedy in Aristophanes,* [Göttingen: Vandenhoeck and Reprecht, 1987]) argues that Plato is not blaming Aristophanes here but ridiculing Meletus for constructing a travesty of Socrates no different than the purposeful caricatures of comedy.

11. See Stephen Halliwell, "Comic Satire and Freedom of Speech in Classical Athens," *Journal of Hellenic Studies* cxi (1991):48–70.

12. Jeffrey Henderson, "The Demos and the Comic Competition," in Winkler and Zeitlin, eds., *Nothing To Do with Dionysos?* (Princeton, N.J.: Princeton University Press, 1990), 293–97.

13. See Daphne Elizabeth O'Regan, *Rhetoric, Comedy and the Violence of Language in Aristophanes' "Clouds"* (New York: Oxford University Press, 1992), 132.

14. I make the argument at length in *Corrupting Youth: Political Education, Democratic Culture and Political Theory* (Princeton, N.J.: Princeton University Press, 1997). My discussion of comedy draws on Chapter V.

15. I take the idea of a "democratic ethos" and *some* of its substance from William Connolly, "Democracy and Territoriality," in Thomas Dumm and Frederick Dolan, eds., *The Rhetorical Republic: Governing Representations in American Politics* (Amherst, Mass.: University of Massachusetts Press, 1993).

16. Henderson, "Introduction," 13. Christopher Carey argues that comedy required radical democracy. Given the "scale, rigor and tone of comic attacks on powerful figures," there must have been a "patron" more powerful than any of the targets. That patron "was the demos." ("Comic Ridicule and Democracy," in *Democratic Accounts* (Oxford: Clarendon Press, 1994), 69.

17. Ibid., 12.

18. Halliwell, 66. Simon Goldhill, "Comic Inversion and Inverted Commas: Aristophanes and Parody," in Simon Goldhill, ed., *The Poet's Voice: Essays on Poetics and Greek Literature* (New York: Cambridge University Press, 1991), 167–222.

19. Henderson, "The Demos and Dramatic Competition," 307.

20. Anthony T. Edwards, "Aristophanes' Comic Poetics: TRUX, Scatology, Skomma," *Transactions of the American Philological Association,* 121 (1991):179.

21. Robert Wallace, "Poet, Public, and Theatrocacy: Audience Performance in Classical Athens," in Lowell Edmunds and Robert W. Wallace, eds., *Poets, Public and Performance in Ancient Greece* (Baltimore: Johns Hopkins University Press, 1997). Cf. Josiah Ober, *Political Dissent in Democratic Athens* (Princeton: Princeton University Press, 1998).

22. See George Lipsitz, *Time Passages: Collective Memory and American Popular Culture* (Minneapolis: University of Minnesota Press, 1990).

23. Ibid., Chapter 1.

24. Ibid., 7–11.

25. Ibid., 19. But see the provocative argument by Robert Meister in "Beyond Satisfaction: Desire, Consumption and the Future of Socialism," *Topoi,* 15 (1996):189–210.

26. Neil Postman, *Amusing Ourselves to Death: Public Discourse in the Age of Show Business* (New York: Penguin Books, 1986), 92.

27. Jean-Pierre Vernant, *The Origins of Greek Thought* (Ithaca: Cornell University Press, 1982).

28. See Robert Putnam, "Bowling Alone: America's Declining Social Capital," *Current* (June 1995):3–14.

29. Quoted in Eric Barnouw, *Tube of Plenty: The Making of American Television,* rev. ed. (New York: Oxford University Press, 1982), p. 300. Caren Kaplan argues that television "contributed to the rise of a consumer culture by flattening or homogenizing U.S. national identity; increasingly by eliminating or subduing the vaudeville-inspired ethnic comics and through the representation of middle-class, white, WASP suburban families in situation comedies" ("The Good Neighbor Policy Meets the 'Feminine Mystique': The Geopolitics of the Domestic Sitcom," Lecture delivered at the University of Southern California, April 1993). Robert Bork criticizes the same phenomenon for very different reasons when he laments how American popular culture has become a threat to democracy because it "trashes our values." See his comments in the *New York Times,* June 14, 1992, Section 1, 24. On the "balkanization" of TV audiences, see Chapter 6 of David Marc's *Demographic Vistas.*

30. See the discussion in Anne Norton's *Republic of Signs: Liberal Theory and American Popular Culture* (Chicago: University of Chicago Press, 1993), Chapter 2.

31. See George Lipsitz, *Time Passages: Collective Memory and American Popular Culture* (Minneapolis: University of Minnesota Press, 1990), 4–5, 18.

32. Ibid.

33. Norton, *Republic of Signs,* 116.

34. On television's role in levitating John F. Kennedy and his presidency into "an historiographic mythosphere," see David Marc's *Demographic Vistas,* 133–34.

35. Jim Cullen, *The Art of Democracy: A Concise History of Popular Culture in the United States* (New York: New York Monthly Review Press, 1996), 278–79.

36. Pierre Bourdieu, "Sport and Social Class," in Chandra Mukerji and Michael Schudson, eds., *Rethinking Popular Culture: Contemporary Perspectives in Cultural Studies* (Berkeley and Los Angeles: University of California Press, 1991), 357–73.

37. Why look at anything for longer than the duration of its allure, when dozens more *imagi mundi*—all of them bouncing and shifting through endless permutations—seductively tickle the fingertips? David Marc, *Comic Visions: Television Comedy and American Culture* (New York: Routledge, 1992), 204.

38. In *Seducing America: How Television Charms the Modern Voter* (New York: Oxford University Press, 1994), Roderick P. Hart warns of the peril to democracy "when its people do not know what they think they know and when

they do not care about what they do not know. Television miseducates the citizenry, but worse, it makes that miseducation attractive," p. 13. Postman makes a similar argument about how television changes the structure of discourse by encouraging certain uses of the intellect, by favoring certain definitions of intelligence and wisdom, and by demanding a certain kind of content—in a phrase by creating new forms of truth telling," 27.

39. Michael Ignatieff, "Is Nothing Sacred? The Ethics of Television," *Daedalus*, 4 (1985): 70–71.

40. Ibid.

41. Lipsitz, 18.

42. See Todd Gitlin's discussion in the introduction to his edited book, *Watching Television* (New York: Pantheon, 1986), and Andrew Ross, *No Respect: Intellectuals and Popular Culture* (New York: Routledge, 1989).

43. See the discussion in John Corner, *Television Form and Public Address* (London: Edward Arnold, 1995).

44. See Stuart Hall, "Notes on Deconstructing 'the Popular,'" in Raphael Samuel, ed., *People's History and Socialist Theory* (London: Routledge, 1981), and "Encoding and Decoding," in Stuart Hall et al., eds., *Culture, Media, Language* (London: Hutchinson, 1980).

45. As Gitlin argues, while television may not have invented the superficiality or triviality of American political or public expression and there may be precedent for a "shriveled politics" of slogans, deceit and pageantry, "precedent is nothing to be complacent about when ignorance is the product." See his "Blips, Bites and Savvy Talk: Television's Impact on American Politics," *Dissent* (Winter 1990):26.

46. For an example of this local politics, see Roger Sanjek, *The Future of Us All: Race and Neighborhood Politics in New York City* (Ithaca: Cornell University Press, 1998), Dolores Hayden, *The Power of Place: Urban Landscapes as Public History* (Cambridge: MIT Press, 1995), and, for the importance of hip-hop culture and music in these negotiations, George Lipsitz, *Dangerous Crossroads: Popular Music, Postmodernism and the Poetics of Place* (New York: Verso, 1994). For Arendt's discussion of the polis, see *The Human Condition* (Chicago: University of Chicago Press, 1958), esp. 192–99.

47. Goldhill, "Comic Inversions and Inverted Commas," and Nicole Loraux, *The Invention of Athens: The Funeral Oration in the Classical City*, trans. Alan Sheridan (Cambridge: Harvard University Press, 1986), 302–11.

48. David Marc, *Demographic Vistas*, Chapter 6, "What Was Broadcasting," 65–66.

49. Karen Hudes, "It's the Sitcom Cartoons That Have Character," *The New York Times*, Sunday, March 8, 1998, Section IV, 36–37. The quote is on 37.

50. Konstan, *Greek Comedy*, 5.

51. See Blaine Harden, "Ralph Had Dreams. Archie Had Opinions. Jerry Had Neuroses. But They All Told a Story about Life and Times in the Big Apple," *Washington Post*, May 14, 1998, Section C, 1, 8.

52. Marc, *Demographic Vistas*, 112; Marc has an excellent discussion of *The Honeymooners*.

53. I take these points from Paul A. Cantor, "The Simpsons: Atomistic Politics and the Nuclear Family," *Political Theory*, 27, no. 6 (December 1999): 734–49.

54. See Jeff MacGregor, "More Than Sight Gags and Subversive Satire," *New York Times,* Sunday, June 20, 1999, Section 2, 97.

55. See Paul A. Cantor, "In Praise of Television: The Greatest TV Show Ever ('The Simpsons')," *American Enterprise,* Vol. 8, no. 5 (September–October 1997).

56. Cantor (in "Atomistic Politics and the Nuclear Family") makes much of the fact and of what he sees as the Simpsons' post-modern traditionalism.

57. C. L. R. James, *American Civilization,* edited and introduced by Anna Grimshaw and Keith Hart, with an Afterword by Robert A. Hill (Cambridge: Blackwell, 1993), 123.

# Part II

## The Contemporary World:

## Media, Public Space, and Democracy

# The Contemporary World:
# Media, Public Space, and Democracy

So as not to arrive too quickly at the conclusion, we note with Heidegger that "the frantic abolition of all distances brings no nearness; for nearness does not consist in the shortness of distance."[1] We live in the modern age with technologies that make available information that in earlier times one would have only learned well after the occurrence of the facts that gave rise to it; we live with knowledge of cultures that one might have before thought of as unknowable but that now have the same proximity as those of one's own state. Our statesmen, or at least politicians, get their information from the news media. (When asked what was happening in Iraq during the Gulf War, a spokesperson for the Pentagon suggested that one should watch CNN.) All of this corresponds to a transformation in the manner by which information is made part of the human life.

Yet there is little thought and less agreement about the significance of these developments for the existence and well-being of public space and its attendant democratic implications. Some lament it; others celebrate it; like Mark Twain's weather, little is done about it. The essays in this part of the volume are careful and incisive dissections of various aspects of these developments, neither praising nor condemning, neither accepting nor fatalistic.

They raise what seem to us central questions for our time. With the essays that follow, we must think of how the political process of representation, so central to democratic politics since the seventeenth century, is affected by the explosion of speed in the media. We must look at, and see if and how, new media encourage a tendency to theatricality and thus hypocrisy, a state of activity where one cannot tell and soon cannot care whether truth is involved. We must raise the question of the degree to which the information presented by these new media can be self-referential, that is, can be understood as calling itself into question, much in the manner that some of the essays in Part I show that it did. And finally, we must ask if these new media change not only the playing field but also the players on it: do they offer new spaces for interaction, with concomitant new interstices and thus new kinds of privacy. Here, developments in the digitalization of modern communication and the easy access to virtually public spaces both present new opportunities but also new enticements to reclaim public space for one's own power.

In "Stages of Democracy" (chapter 6), Sylviane Agacinski addresses the question of the effect of new media technologies on democratic politics. She makes two important moves. First, she reminds us not to confuse the preconditions for thought with the preconditions for democratic politics. Thinking does not require a priori that we seek agreement with others, nor even that we enter into conditions of reciprocity with them. Second, for Agacinski, the foundation of the public is in plurality, hence in disagreement, and not in consensus. Her targets are, on the one hand, theorists such as Habermas who posit a reciprocal public sphere as resting on the assumption of the possibility of agreement and, on the other, (ex?)left-wing thinkers such as Régis Debray, for whom the realm of reading and writing retains a political priority over that of images.

Associating the media with classical appreciations of the importance of rhetoric, Agacinski asks if there is any reason that "democratic debate cannot pass through mediatized spaces." She suggests that there is no reason in principle that this need be so. Some of the distress about contemporary media relies on a false romanticization of the past: if it is the case that a person who watches television cannot respond directly to the speaker on the screen, the same was true for the reader of a newspaper. What is important is that the spectator-experience can start a dialogue, that is, can lead us to ask or talk to someone else or ask ourselves about what we have seen and heard.

The work of Hannah Arendt serves as a quiet sounding board for Agacinski's recasting of contemporary theatricality. In his contribution, "Theatricality in the Public Realm of Hannah Arendt" (chapter 7), Dana Villa takes up these questions by focusing on the thought of Hannah Arendt. Villa argues that the two dimensions of Arendt's thought—the expressive and the communicative—are not, in fact, in tension. Arguing against most of the standard interpretations, Villa convincingly shows that Arendt is centrally concerned with worldliness—with what it means to be a human being-in-the-world as that world changes in different societies and epochs.

As with Agacinski, the opponent is Habermas, joined here by his disciple and collaborator, Seyla Benhabib. Habermas's story of the rise and decline of the public sphere is, while detailed and impressive, by and large a standard story. From him, the public has lost its critical-rational function; it has an increasingly only symbolic role; what passes for consensus in contemporary democracies is by and large an uncritical acceptance of passively consumed media clichés. Only the reintroduction of rationality into the public sphere will save us from being subject to the seductions of the media.

For Habermas, as Villa (and Agacinski in her way) points out, the enemy is rhetoric, as embodied by contemporary media. Habermas and Benhabib are in effect fighting their version of a supposed old battle[2] between Socrates and rhetoricians but without a supposedly saving polis. Drawing on the work of Richard Sennett, Villa seeks to show that what Arendt was doing can be understood as a rehabilitation of rhetoric and theatricality in the contemporary world. What is destructive of public space is the replacement of theatricality by an ideology of "intimacy and community, authenticity and what [Sennett] calls 'destructive Gemeinschaft.'" To the degree that contemporary media reinvigorate theatricality and rhetoric, they may restore a central dimension to the possibility of public space.

Similar themes shape the essay "Replacing the Body: The Question of Digital Democracy," by Samuel Weber in chapter 8. As with all authors in this book who look to the Greeks, antiquity provides neither nostalgia for what we have lost, nor a goal to which to return, but a critical edge upon our own contemporary blindnesses.

Weber starts by raising Plato's anxieties in the *Laws* about "theatrocracy." Plato associates theatrocracy with the introduction of heterogeneity and unpredictability and thus the disruption of knowledge and competence. It tends to break down boundaries. Weber argues that Plato's analysis was taken over and radicalized by Nietzsche in *The Birth of Tragedy*. What Nietzsche thought important was precisely the ecstatic division that occurred within the spectator as he saw himself on the stage while retaining his presence in the audience. Delocalization—being out of a place—is, however, as Weber goes on powerfully to show, associated with the experience of new media. What we experience with the new media is the possibility of gesturing, reaching out, touching an other, but not as an embodied self, rather only in and as a gesture. The question thus posed by the digitalization of democracy is thus what it would mean to point to the analogical body of the *demos*.

As we work this out, we will, avers Weber, have make a step along the path laid out by the history of theatrocracy.

In chapter 9, "Writing Property and Power," Anne Norton turns our attention to the ways in which the modern city (and, by extension, the modern state) seeks to control the realm of public visibility, in effect to shut down the "open" dimension of public space. She is interested in the way that sight is governed in the modern city, such that it seems perfectly permissible that advertisements intrude upon our vision but not graffiti, even and perhaps especially when those graffiti are aesthetically satisfying. The campaign against graffiti that she details in the city of Philadelphia, is, in effect, a desire to transform the public realm into private property. Significantly, during a period in which unemployment continued to rise and Philadelphia and the police were named in several scandals involving the framing of innocent African Americans and the beating of children, graffiti was pronounced the "most serious" problem in the city.

Norton sees in graffiti the efforts of a class that many would rather ignore to declare its visibility, its presence in the world. One graffitist told an interviewer that he wrote "to prove to people where I was." As such, in Norton's reading, graffiti at bottom reflects or may reflect the most ancient political drive: to be seen by others in public.

If the modern city tends to control what might be public space, what can be done about it? In the last essay in the volume, Benjamin R. Barber, in "Malled, Mauled, and Overhauled: Arresting Suburban Sprawl by Transforming Suburban Malls into Useable Civic Space," addresses the question of what might be done to transform the spaces into which contemporary Americans and Europeans (and not just them) gather into actual *public* spaces. His case is the shopping mall and, more generally, the trends in American architecture and planning associated with the development of the suburbs. Barber associates these developments broadly with the rise of consumerism and its concomitant retreat into privacy in a manner antithetical to democratic public space. The point, however, is not to lament the rise of Wal-Marts and pre-planned cities such as the Disney Corporation's Celebration in the state of Florida, but to ask how one might turn consumers into citizens. If people go to the Internet, argues Barber, and "become passive consumers of what is supposed to be an interactive technology, we need to reactivate the net." There is no reason in principle, even if there may be economic and interested resistances, that malls and other phenomena of suburbia cannot become actual public spaces. To effectuate this transformation will require both political will and the use of existing political institutions. What needs to be thought through—and such thinking is a public matter and will produce a public space as a result—are matters such as the sizes of stores, the kind of parking, the presence or absence of public transportation, the integration of residential housing, and so forth. Even small things—a large-scale chess set in the center of a mall—can produce important differences as to what kind of space the mall is. Barber concludes his essay with a description of a political program, the Agora Coalition, that has as its aim to reconstruct the possibilities of public space that Marcel Detienne identified in the first essay in this book.

So we come full circle (as it were). For the authors in this section, as for those in the first, the will to encounter another human being is not made impossible by the conditions of modernity. The reality of public space, as we argue in the Conclusion, has always been virtual. All we need is imagination.

## Notes

1. Martin Heidegger, "Being Dwelling Thinking," in *The Question Concerning Technology and Other Essays* (New York, 1969).

2. We say "supposed" because there is good reason to doubt this understanding. See Gary Shiffman, "The Practical Uses of Mortality: Citizenship and Solidarity in Classical Athens." Ph.D. thesis, Department of Political Science, University of Michigan, 1994.

# 6

## Stages of Democracy

**Sylviane Agacinski**

Questions concerning the new forms of public space and the effects of audiovisual media technologies have already been the object of considerable debate. Jürgen Habermas attributes the decline of public space to the media, arguing that they have replaced a genuine public sphere involving reciprocal communication with a manipulative mass culture.[1] In France, Régis Debray, suspicious of public opinion, maintains that "the moral and political State apparatus" is "humiliated by technology" and is transformed, willy nilly, into a *seductive state*.[2] I will later return to the question of reciprocal communication. I would like first, however, to point out that political power did not wait for the arrival of television in order to be seductive. The marriage of democracy and the necessity for persuasion has always allowed for this kind of "diversion." (Or perhaps we might call it "drifting"?) I also don't believe, and it is certainly not clear, that the screen is by nature more detrimental to political life than ancient public speech or the written word.

What is certain is that the arenas of democracy, their public and political spaces, have changed and thus transformed the relations between power and the people in both directions. These transformations obviously touch upon the nature and practice of democracy itself, if one takes democracy to be constituted by concrete procedures through which actual power is linked to a sovereign authority, namely the people, and indirectly, to public opinion.

These new public spaces have led not only to fear of a perversion of democracy but perhaps also to the fear of its expansion. What is seen as a disquieting "democracy of opinion" is indeed emerging and it is spreading beyond the circle of the "enlightened public," as it used to be called, or of the "elite," as we now call it. It is not wrong to think that public opinion, as it is constantly put into play and evaluated in the media, exerts permanent pressure on power and prevents it from falling back on the autonomy that representational democracy in principle allowed it. It is clear that the media expands public space—and in so doing expands democracy—but at the same time, this new public space tends to absorb the political space of institutions, parties, and, to a certain extent, the State itself; it partially destroys the old framework of political life, pushing it onto the stage of media communication.

Under the French Third Republic, the space of printed publications played its role of counterpower. It kept its distance from the political sphere, strictly speaking, and constituted both an "intellectual" sphere and an organ of opinion. This distance is blurred, however, when, as is now increasingly the case, journalists, politicians, rulers and their opponents, unions and experts, intellectuals and other members of "civil society" share the same screen, the same television and radio studios. This expanded public sphere and the political sphere thus become superimposed on one another, while the space of thought and reflection remains that of writing.

At this point several opposed positions become possible. For one, public opinion has often been denounced for being irrational or naïf, seduced or manipulated by the media. This position is rather undemocratic but is quite common with "republicanism," in the French sense of the term. Or second, the originating link between democracy and the people is recast such that the media counts as the new rhetorical technique of modern democracy. Democracy "in the age of mediatization," as Walter Benjamin might have said, still needs to be rethought.

I tend to the second position, albeit with several stipulations:

First, there must never be a confusion between the spaces where real thinking transpires, takes risks, is elaborated independently and even in solitude, and the political sphere in its widest sense, where a common ground and principles for coexistence must be established. Of course, all thought wishes for exposure and seeks to be shared. But intellectual, artistic, philosophical, or scientific life does not have the a priori requirement of agreement with others.

Second, the above implies, conversely, that political and democratic space must be given its own responsibility, through public debates oriented around the necessity of making collective societal choices. Democratic life and intellectual life share a common resistance to the claim of authority.

Third, democracy must expand the exercise of citizenship at all levels, increasing the opportunities to vote, in particular at the local level, so as to preserve the political responsibility of public opinion.

Last, inasmuch as it is possible, public space must be protected by laws and institutions from purely private economic interests, as well as from the influence of the State. By this I mean the influence of governments and not the desirable fact of legislation that provides democratic rules for public space—enforcing respect for pluralism, for example. If public opinion wishes to protect plurality and diversity, it must give itself, through the voice of its legislators, a right to observe the workings of its public spaces. (There are, of course, many public spaces, not only one.)

The real issue citizens should concern themselves with is the question of the financing and regulation of the media. Without this, there can be no contemporary democratic public space. The citizens should think about the responsibility of the media in terms of how it serves the *ends* of democracy.

### The Republic and Public Opinion

In France, mistrust of the media and public opinion is part of a tradition that stands for representational democracy, but that mistrust is, in fact, more republican than democratic. The republican way of thinking tends toward the belief that the State must form public opinion on the basis of its rationalist certainties. "Either the Republic teaches—or it does not *even* exist," as it has been said.[3] This is a nice epigram, but one must defend such a "secular" conception of teaching, dissociated from political opinions. In point of fact, the Third Republic was democratic enough not to want to go against public opinion—but only on the condition that it first be able to educate it. The philosophy of the Republic in fact follows closely the history of rationalism. Its sources are found first in the Enlightenment and then in positivism, such that political progress was understood to be based in scientific progress, hence the expression "political science."

I am not able here to undertake a full-blown critique of reason, but I am able to discuss the notion that politics is a science or whether there is even a rational foundation of politics. One may make a distinction between a rational *mode of conduct* that serves natural tendencies (in Spinoza's sense, for example) and a purely rational *foundation* of behavior that establishes a dualistic opposition between reason and nature or between reason and passion, as does Kant. (Such a dualism often leads to an opposition of the reason of the elite to the passion of the people.) Politics must undoubtedly be rational in its behavior, but it must, for this reason, understand the fears and the hopes of men. "He who has neither hope nor fear cannot see what is useful for him," claimed Spinoza. "He will be insensitive to any reason, and nothing will be able to make him obey." This is why, in politics, one cannot simply rely on oppositions: reason versus passion or truth versus opinion.

It must also be said that any power exercised in the name of a truth is necessarily dogmatic and potentially authoritarian. In any case, a notion of politics that is purely rational or scientific never fares well with the vicissitudes of heterogeneous points of views nor, therefore, with certain democratic freedoms.

We can see, for example, how the French Revolution, albeit in a very particular historical situation, recoiled from the freedom of the press. The revolutionaries of 1789, who had inherited a strong belief in the judgment of public opinion from the Enlightenment, initially gave full freedom to the press. But they were forced to recognize, especially after the fall of the monarchy, that opinion was divided, contradictory, and counterrevolutionary; freedom of the press was then curtailed, and already in 1792, a "Bureau de l'esprit public," a Bureau of Public Spirit (or Opinion), was created whose goal was to re-establish a unified public opinion, one that was favorable to the authorities. The whole problem that public opinion posed within the Republic is summarized in this abandonment of the agitated and conflictual space of public debate in favor of a uniformization of opinion under the perfectly chosen heading of *esprit*.[4] By calling it esprit, the public was reduced to a simple and unified entity, always in agreement with power. The use of the adjective *public,* as in the expressions *Salut public* or *esprit public,* thus itself became coercive, as Mona Ozouf explains, and was used as an alibi for despotism.[5]

Democracy can thus be bypassed in two manners. First, modern powers (who base their legitimacy in the sovereignty of the people) often try to attribute to the people the fictitious image of a simple unity, because if the people is one, in terms of spirit, will, opinion, or whatever, the people can then speak in one voice—that of a leader or of a party. Second, if power is based on philosophical or scientific knowledge, it then will be understood as belonging to an educated elite whose role it will be to govern and to educate the people in order to form a homogeneous public opinion. This is another sort of unification, again a bypassing of democracy.

Here, as is often the case, we must invoke Aristotle against Plato: the city is not one, it is a plurality *(plêthos).* Democracy is different from other regimes only when it also contains a pluralist and differentiating concept of the people, if it affirms, for example, its "mixed-ness." We can say that the two main obstacles to democracy are the fictitious unity of the people, and the idea of basing politics in a truth. Drawing from Aristotelian sources, Hannah Arendt has shown that politics doesn't have to be this "tyranny of truth" that has always attracted philosophers, but rather depends upon opinions and choices that must gain the consent of the people. We do not necessarily have to position ourselves within alternatives such as that between a necessarily reasonable and responsible representational power and a mediatized democracy that is necessarily direct, sentimentalist, and seductive. Democracy is never direct, and those who conceive of it ideally in this way, as did Jean-Jacques Rousseau, are quick to say that it is in fact not feasible. For my part, I would rather say that between the fiction of sovereignty and the reality of power, there are nothing other than "representations" or, if one prefers, nothing other than ways of configuring the designs of a political community that does not exist outside those figures it constructs of itself.

I therefore in no way endorse the idea that the distance between "the people" and power can be abolished; but I believe that any democracy is a way of *regulating this distance* in such a way that the people in its concrete reality remain, as much as possible, the organ within which a political "will" is formed. The way in which a people, by nature multiple and diverse, participates in public and political life therefore always requires a very complex art. Public spaces and political spaces must interconnect; that is why, in each of these spaces, one cannot do away with debate or with techniques of persuasion and dissuasion.[6] I will come back to this theme after a brief detour through the time when public opinion was born—the eighteenth century.

## Public Space and the Enlightenment

Before the Revolution, the public was never thought to be the same as the people and was indeed explicitly differentiated from it. The public was seen as literate and educated, as opposed to the multitude or the populace. The contemporary idea of a public (re)arises in the seventeenth century in relation to the arts. In fact, as in antiquity, it is at the theater, where spectators attend a spectacle together, that public space and indeed the very notion of the public was created. (Let us remember that in Greek, *theater* designated primarily the place from which one sees.) But the public is also that of letters, the public that reads—and often writes: art critics and literary critics in particular. The public is that group of men and women who judge works of art and who will extend its judgments to political life. As during the time when dramatic works were the object of public competitions, one can no longer separate the idea of the public from that of judgment, and as we have already mentioned with respect to democracy, the question is always that of determining how many people can judge together and whether one judges better alone or with others.

It is rightly said that the Enlightenment underscored the "tribunal" of the public sphere to the point of seeing in it the touchstone of the soundness and the rationality of opinions. Thus, in "What Is Enlightenment?" (1784), Kant calls for the "public usage of reason" whereby each person can freely put his or her thinking to the test of the judgment of the reading public.[7] Can the public usage of reason, which implies the fact of reasoning before others and testing our thoughts against the judgment of others, help us understand the nature of political judgment and democracy? I don't believe so at all; the "publicness" of thought must be given its proper place. The recourse to the judgment of others, as we know, is not relevant in philosophy for Kant: it is only necessary from the pragmatic point of view, which is of interest to anthropology.[8] Let us consider this from a political perspective.

In "What Is Enlightenment?," Kant declares that his goal is the freedom for each person to think on his own, that is to say, to use one's own understanding. Perhaps paradoxically, the public sphere constituted by the written word is not, as in an assembly, one that ensures contact with others but rather one that allows for a retreat from all institutional spaces in which speech is always kept under supervision. The written word can and must provide a space that is free from all institutional powers, namely that of the church and the State, such that the use of speech is qualified by Kant as being private. Kant's manifesto thus mainly wishes to guarantee, "for the learned," a space of free thinking protected from power. That was perfectly legitimate, and still is.

Now what is the connection between this space, this lettered public, and democracy? It was expected of these learned men, who were supposedly advancing together toward rationality and universality, that they enlighten the king and lead him slowly but surely on the path toward reforms. (The French Revolution, which was very near, soon showed that popular public opinion had a different relation to time. The learned public, which was also well fed, and was neither cold, nor hungry, nor angry, didn't mind taking its time. That is not the case for the people in general, and this difference still exists today.) The illusion of universality to which this enlightened public aspired has been sufficiently criticized, so that there is no need to go over it again here. This public, believing that it represents "a universal civil society," mainly identifies its own political interests as educated property owners with what it calls "universal man." Kant himself says that his "universal man" is in fact quite particular when he restricts the political use of reason and, consequently, citizenship to property owners alone. Those who are not "their own masters," that is to say salaried workers, cannot be citizens.

In a later text, Kant commits us to judge in some sense before human reason as a whole in order to free ourselves from the illusions that come from our empirical subjectivity.[9] It is the famous passage on "common sense," defined as thought enlarged, since one is obliged in it to think of "putting oneself in the place of others." Hannah Arendt found in this passage a political concern "to share the world with others."[10] This seems to me to be a very generous interpretation, at least from a political point of view. For on closer scrutiny, you can see that those others in whose place I must put myself in order to judge are not real others at all; and it is not their real judgments that my ideas must confront but only their possible judgments—with empirical contingencies set aside.

What, then, does it mean to put oneself in the place of others, if any one of these others is as devoid as I am of the particular conditions of his or her own judgment and is thus as abstract as I am? This substitution is truly dizzying: I put myself in the place of others in order to know how they would judge in the place of others, and so forth. One believes one is turning in a circle, but in fact one needn't leave one's place: in rising above the subjective conditions of judgment, we place ourselves in fact, as Kant himself says, in a universal point of view. We believe that we determine and even test this universal by placing ourselves, through our thinking, in the point of view of the other, but the place of the other is nothing but this improbable "universal point of view"— and such is the philosophical trap. This point of view of everyone and no one, as disinterested as mine, is a pure place, a placeless place.

What does it mean to put oneself in the place of someone who is, ex hypothesi, already without place? The "Other" here designates a subject correctly understood as utopic and not as a real individual, who would be one to whom I would actually have to listen in order to know, rather than myself constructing an abstract figuration.

What we have here is a philosophical way of thinking before the fiction of the other but not a political way of thinking with others. *Before* others doesn't mean *with* others. Before refers to an ideal alterity, not an empirical alterity. It seems to me, on the contrary, that we must deal more directly with the empiricity of what men do with one another and therefore with judgment in democracy. It is only if an actual public participates in it that we are dealing with political judgment. It is only if we try to persuade the actual body of citizens and if we "court their consent" that we can speak of democracy: if we seek empirically, with others, the conditions of our being together. (What we cannot get from the experience or rules of democracy is the leap into democracy, the decision to replace the use of weapons with that of words. Moreover, speech is not all: behind words there are social forces. Democracy cannot abolish all relations of power.)

### The Arenas of Democracy in Greece

The Greek model of democracy constitutes a political technique that encompasses several spaces that are today separate and that links politics with rhetoric. When power *(arché)*, instead of being incarnated in a single person, is placed at the center *(to es meson)*, between the citizens, the question then becomes how are they going to share this power, that is to say, make decisions about the public domain, the domain of common interests. The Greek answer is a technique of assembly.

The citizens, assembled in one place, will judge the common good by practicing contradictory public debate, in which possible choices are set forth and argued, and then followed by a vote.[11] Public debate between citizens is thus also a technique of democratic judgment. On one hand, then, a debate, and on the other, a vote, which allows for the victory of one position over the others. Both moments must be combined: a vote without a debate would be blind, but a debate without a vote would be in vain.

Aristotle would often repeat that deliberation is only useful when a decision is necessary. It is indeed only when it aims for a decision that a deliberation can be a responsible one. The big mistake of polls today is that they take as "opinions" subjective preferences that are divorced from any responsibility. It is only when faced with the responsibility of making a decision for all that each person can take the common good into account. And this responsibility is not assumed in the same way if one deliberates alone, as Jean-Jacques Rousseau wanted, or with others, as the technique of assembly would allow. I will dwell on this point for a moment, since the technique of assembly characterizes both the most desirable and the most troublesome aspects of democracy at its origins. For if, indeed, it illustrates the idea of a public judgment or of a shared opinion, it also shows how this sharing can work within an assembly in different ways.

There appear to be three ways in which this sharing can work. *First,* following Aristotle, the plurality remains a better judge of works of art and poems, for each person judges partially, according to his taste and competence, and the public judges the whole work. The plurality of points of view enriches the all-around quality of the judgment (a bit like at a potluck: the meal is richer and more varied if everyone brings something different.) Here collective judgment adds up particular judgments. In politics as well, the soundness of democratic judgment does not come, according to Aristotle, from the high competence of each (an oligarchical criterion) but from the addition of "fragments of practical wisdom." The sum of many different points of view finally produces a sound judgment.

The *second* manner is an interpretation of public judgment different from the one requiring that an assembly judge only at the end of a contradictory debate. In this case, the idea is that opinions mutually rectify each other, rather than add up.

And finally—this is the third way—the judgment of an assembled public has more obscure origins: the contagiousness of feelings and emotions, the tendency toward fusion when an assembly perceives itself as a whole and takes pleasure in its unity. The technique of assembly never goes without the fusional effects of gatherings in general, such as meetings, celebrations, or demonstrations. These diverse effects of the technique of assembly are unavoidable. They must be taken into consideration in order to distinguish between two very different kinds of public: the *assembled public,* which doesn't always debate, and the *dispersed public,*[12] which includes readers and, today, auditors, television viewers, or users of electronic media.

The role of public debate in Greece leads us to the question of discourse. Speech does not function here as an injunction or a ritual. It is addressed to a public that it must convince, and thus it can be rightly perceived as a technique of proof or of persuasion. These are different things, as Aristotle tells us in his *Rhetoric.* Proof has to do with a logic of truth: it is founded on sure premises and employs the sort of reasoning that takes place in the elaboration of theoretical knowledge.

Whereas persuasion has to do with a logic of the plausible: it is founded on premises that are only plausible *(endoxa)* and relevant to domains such as law and politics, where one tries to persuade a public
that makes judgments. In this sense, rhetoric follows a partisan logic
(that of the client or the party). However, if one admits that politics
can neither be founded on established truths nor do without the consent of the people, persuasion plays an essential part in it, and one
finds oneself in a world of shared convictions. That is again what
Hannah Arendt says: "The statement that 'all men are created equal' is
not self-evident but stands in need of agreement and consent."[13] This
means: *we have to persuade* one another of this equality.

Rhetoric, as the art of finding, for each subject, the most persuasive
arguments, is thus not only a cynical way of defending any particular
viewpoint, nor is it a clever way of conveying an acquired truth (though
it can sometimes be used for this purpose). It is, when faced with the
necessity of making choices that no certitude can found in an absolute
manner, the search for persuasive arguments that will carry the consent
of those who judge (in this case, the citizens). That is why their fears
and hopes must always be taken into account. The bad reputation of
rhetoric comes from the fact that it is seen as merely an instrument
serving a choice that is already made, in which case it is the weapon of
partiality. But, if we recognize that politics is not a science and that
judgments must be made in uncertainty, we must also admit that the
best argument to convince all of the citizens is also the one that best
convinces me. In other words, my search for persuasive arguments in
political matters can serve the victory of my party or even my own par-
ticularities, but it can also help me find, for myself, though in uncertainty, that which may be preferred by all.

Rhetoric can thus be understood as a means of democratic polemics
on the one hand and, on the other, as a technique of thinking that seeks
for itself and, to test them out on others, the motives of its possible
choices.

Let us now return to modern public space.


## Publics and Masses

As we have seen, a distinction used to be made between the public and
the people. But with the spread of the media, the public is no longer
opposed to the people but to the masses, that is to say, a restricted and
cultivated public is opposed to a very large one. In fact, as is always the

case, new techniques create realities that can no longer be named with old concepts: just as it was said that "iron architecture is not architecture" or "photography is not art," it was also said that the public of the media is not the real public.

Thus, for Jürgen Habermas, the real public is the one that assembles and discusses, for there is no public space without "reciprocal communication." For Régis Debray, the real public is the one that reads and writes, that reasons, as opposed to the one that allows itself to be influenced by images.[14]

Dualist ways of thinking tend to separate reason and emotion and thus localize the techniques of seduction. But this is impossible, for these techniques operate as much in the art of images as in written and oral discourse. Politics cannot get rid of emotions any more than it can eradicate rhetoric from images or discourse.

Not only do people want to transpose the opposition between reason and emotion to modes of communication (print and screen media) but also to the different publics affected by these techniques. The notion of "masses" or of a "public at large" is not only used to define the extraordinary extension of the public of the media but also to specify what could be called a class of public that is susceptible to the seduction of images. Modes of communication would thus form cultural classes, just as modes of production used to define social classes.

This mythical mass called the general public is always blamed for the same thing: for feeling too much and thinking too little, for seeking pleasure instead of understanding. This was particularly true for a theoretician of modernity like Adorno, for whom the truth of art had nothing to do with the pleasure of the senses: "He who takes concrete pleasure in works of art is ignorant."[15] The concept of pleasure therefore had to be eliminated from the definition of art, and its pure spirituality had to be affirmed. This exclusion of pleasure is bound to distance art from the larger public, which in turn is said to seek only pleasure. Much of the art that claimed to be "modernist" thought of itself as an intellectual art, foreign to the pleasures of the senses and thus inaccessible to the uneducated masses. The intellectualism of someone like Marcel Duchamp was inscribed within this logic, when he denounced "physical painting" as stupid. (This was metaphysical thinking.) "Publicity always takes something away," he said,[16] and laboratory work must be protected from "consumerism."

Of course, I am not claiming at all that artists should seek the immediate approval of a large public. But neither should they seek that of a learned and restricted one that is also conformist in its own way. The question is whether one should put public judgment in doubt at the outset, on the grounds that it allows itself to be governed by its emotions. It is not only for economic reasons that "consumerism" has been denounced: this word was used in a derogatory manner in order to condemn the place of desire and pleasure in the vulgar taste of the common public. We should come back to desire and pleasure, in the arts at least.

The differentiation of a cultivated elite that judges with intelligence from masses that are overly emotional is the transposition to the public of the old dichotomy between the intelligible and the sensible—precisely what *can't be* dissociated in art. An artist (or any thinker) must not free him or herself from this or that public but from any public at all, at least during the time of creation. When creative work is being done, all opinions must be ignored so that risks may be freely taken. When one is struggling with the unknown, one has a right to secrecy. Communication and exposure to others belong to a different time. This matter of the time for secrecy and the time for publicity not only exists in political life but should be taken account of.

In addition to a place of secrecy that is sometimes necessary in certain domains in parties and in governments (diplomacy, defense, etc.), there must be time to work things out (projects or programs) as well as a time for consultation, which do not yet belong to public debate. That is why the extension of public space to all spheres does not necessarily entail the *permanent obligation to publicize*. In a democracy, one must also think the time and the place of the secret.

## The Transformation of Public Space

If the public sphere has actually been supplanted by that of the media, nothing thereby proves that democratic debate cannot pass through mediatized spaces. I say here "pass through," and I pluralize "spaces," for such space is never singular, especially given that it is itself refracted into a multiplicity of spaces. Written communications, information networks, gatherings of all sorts continue to exist. They cannot, however, simply continue on in the same manner as before, for all of these spaces interfere with and intrude into each other. No space is autonomous. For example, televised news in France draws largely from the printed press, whereas, inversely, the press considers every day what is happening in the media. Many journalists go from the written word to the screen and vice-versa.

Mediated public space—what Habermas calls "external public space"—interferes also with the public space of organizations that bring their members together physically, that is, to a public internal space. The distinction between internal and external loses much of its meaning when the press and their cameras penetrate into organizations and transmit their internal debates "externally." "Closed door" has become almost an impossibility, such that inside political organizations, for example, the external is often used to further internal goals of communication or of strategy.

Mediatization is thus in a sense a hindrance for internal discussion that should remain semipublic, as it is for the very life of these organizations. The public in the extended sense risks being satisfied with a mediated relation to the leaders, one that paradoxically appears more direct, more intimate than the internal institutional relationship. Mediatized space thus risks emptying political parties and trade unions of their substance and function.

It would still seem necessary to democracy to maintain the internal spaces for collective pursuits, for open debate and the elaboration of political programs that cannot be accomplished except on the inside of an organization, especially of political parties or government commissions. The power of the media—and already of the radio in Nazi Germany—is fearsome when it is monopolized by a one-party regime; it is also dangerous when it is subject only to the logic of the market. However, as long as it respects certain rules, it is not by nature incapable of making public what is at stake in a given economic or political choice, of exposing the position and arguments of one side and the other, of giving, that is, to public life a visibility that contributes to forming citizens' judgments.

For Habermas, all mediatized communication is necessarily manipulative, whereas discussion is necessarily democratic. This simplifies the working of each. Taking over a conception of the public from C. Wright Mills, he recalls that in a public, as opposed to a mass, "There are at least as many individuals who express an opinion as there are those who receive it." He notes also that "the system of communication authorizes an immediate and effective response to any expressed opinion."[17]

But where might one find such a public? Even in the midst of an assembly, the immediacy of communication is a myth, just as is that of the equality of the number of those who express opinions and those who judge. Any "live" public debate has all sorts of delays, slippages, and hindrances between an intervention and a response. Indeed, it could not be otherwise, for all cannot respond at once to all. Any exchange comprises procedures that entail mediations and delays.

Conversely, the fact that the public is dispersed does not entail that all discussion or "reciprocal exchange" is impossible. Exchange at a distance, in writing, or through the airwaves, neither forbids nor weakens argument. Of course, a television viewer does not answer a mediatized speaker directly, but neither does the reader respond to the author he or she is reading: the important matter is the public and responsive character of the positions and arguments. What is important is that in each of these spaces, as well as in others, responses are possible such that a published text gives rise to private or public debate, or that an oral debate gives rise to a written response someplace. No one is absolutely alone before a screen or a newspaper; a question from the screen can be relaunched elsewhere, in another public space as well as in a private meeting, anywhere. Dialogue starts with oneself, when the words of another arouse, in each, a new question.

The media are thus not simply an instrument of manipulation or of the "vassalization" of atomized individuals but rather effectuate a deconstruction of public spaces, that is, of the ancient techniques of communication and of traditional types of the public (such as the assembled and dispersed publics). The local and the global, the internal and the external, the public and the private, the near and the far are no longer opposed to each other: they are permanently in interference one with the other.

There is no reason to give way to a nostalgia for the old spaces and certainly no way to go back: we can only attempt to live democracy in the epoch of mediatization, knowing that in a world that has technologically changed, our understandings of people and of opinions, as well as that of any exercise of power, cannot remain what they were.

## Notes

1. In Jürgen Habermas, *The Structural Transformation of the Public Sphere* (Cambridge: MIT Press, 1989).

2. Régis Debray, *L'état séducteur* (Paris: Gallimard, 1993).

3. Claude Nicolet, *La République en France* (Paris: Seuil, 1992).

4. The unity of the people is always a "spirit," a *Geist*.

5. Mona Ozouf, "L'esprit public guidant le peuple," in "Le Monde de la Révolution française," *Le Monde,* November 1, 1989.

6. Hannah Arendt, "Truth and Politics," in *Between Past and Future* (New York: Viking, 1968), 227–64.

7. Immanuel Kant, "What Is Enlightenment?," in *Kant's Political Writings,* ed. Hans Reiss (Cambridge: Cambridge University Press, 1977), 55.

8. Immanuel Kant, *Anthropology* (The Hague: Nijhoff, 1974), part one, chapter 2, "On Egotism."

9. Immanuel Kant, *Critique of Judgment* (New York: Hafner, 1968), chapter 40, esp. 136.

10. Arendt, "The Crisis in Culture," in *Between Past and Future,* 219ff.

11. Cf. Jean-Pierre Vernant, *Les origines de la pensée grecque,* volume 3 (Paris: P.U.F., 1983).

12. This distinction comes from Malesherbes, *Discours de réception à l'Acadèmie française* (1775).

13. Arendt, "Truth and Politics," in *Between Past and Future,* 246.

14. Debray, *L'état séducteur,* 87.

15. T. W. Adorno, *Théorie esthètique* (Paris: Klinsiek, 1982), 24.

16. Marcel Duchamp, *Duchamp du signe* (Paris: Flammarion, 1994), 170–72, originally published in *Bulletin of the Museum of Modern Art,* 13, nos. 4–5 (1946): 19–21.

17. Adorno, *Théorie esthètique,* 259.

# 7

# Theatricality in the Public Realm of Hannah Arendt

**Dana R. Villa**

What is the role of theatricality in the political theory of Hannah Arendt? Why does she persistently refer to the public space as a kind of "stage" upon which political *actors* disclose themselves "in word and deed"? Why does she rely so heavily on the metaphors of performance and virtuosity in articulating her concepts of political action and freedom? More to the point: Does Arendt's recourse to a theatrical metaphorics illuminate the nature of the public space and its problems in the modern age, or does it merely serve to obscure these by making the Greek polis the normative model of a robust public sphere?

Arendt's vision of the public realm as a "space of appearances" in which heroic individuals perform great deeds and speak memorable words is fully manifest in the Greek-inspired conception of political action set forth in *The Human Condition.*[1] However, there is another dimension to Arendt's conception of political action, one that emphasizes the deliberative speech of equals and the capacity to "act in concert." This dimension comes to the fore in *On Revolution* and the essays in *Crises of the Republic,* as well as the posthumously published *Lectures on Kant's Political Philosophy.*[2]

These two dimensions of Arendt's view of political action have led Maurizio Passerin d'Entreves and others to claim that there is "a fundamental tension in [Arendt's] theory between an *expressive* and a *communicative* model of action."[3] This tension introduces a basic ambiguity into how we interpret Arendt's broader conception of politics. As d'Entreves puts it:

> Insofar as Arendt's theory of action rests upon an unstable combination of both expressive and communicative models (or action types), it is clear that her account of politics will vary in accordance with the emphasis given to one or the other. When the emphasis falls on the expressive model of action, politics is viewed as the performance of noble deeds by

outstanding individuals; conversely, when her stress is on the communicative model of action, politics is seen as the collective process of deliberation and decision-making that rests on equality and solidarity.[4]

As Seyla Benhabib demonstrates in her essay "Models of Public Space" (and, more recently, in *The Reluctant Modernism of Hannah Arendt*), Arendt's internally divided view of political action generates two very distinct models of the public sphere: the agonistic and the associational.[5] The agonistic model of public space—an overtly *theatrical* model—"represents that space of appearances in which moral and political greatness, heroism, and preeminence are revealed, displayed, shared with others."[6] The associational, in contrast, represents "the kind of democratic or associative politics that can be engaged in by ordinary citizens who may or may not possess great moral prowess but who acquire the capacities of political judgment and initiative in the process of self-organization."[7]

Benhabib leaves little room for doubt as to which of Arendt's models is the more relevant. "The distinction between the agonistic and the associational models," she writes, "corresponds to the Greek versus the modern experience of politics." Arendt's theatrical, agonistic model places a premium on expressive action and the actor's achievement of a unique identity before his "audience." As such, it presumes, in Benhabib's view, a high degree of moral and political homogeneity; otherwise, the competition for excellence among peers could not take place in the *public* realm at all.[8]

Another drawback from Benhabib's perspective is that the agonistic model presumes a rigidly defined public realm, one that can serve its theatrical function of being a "stage where freedom can appear" only insofar as it is spatially delimited and its "substantive content" severely restricted. Only narrowly *political* matters, those concerning the founding and preservation of the polity's "constitution" (in the broad, Greek sense), are fit to appear in public. "Household matters"—which include a wide range of economic and social issues—introduce the taint of necessity and so must be rigorously excluded, in Arendt's view, from this "theater" in which freedom can appear and become a "tangible reality."

Because "the distinction between the social and the political makes no sense in the modern world," and because modern polities conspicuously lack the kind of moral/political homogeneity necessary for purely agonistic action, Benhabib concludes that Arendt's theatrical model of politics must be abandoned: "Arendt's agonistic model is at odds with the sociological reality of modernity, as well as with modern political struggles for justice" (95). The associational model of public space presents itself as the only viable alternative under the conditions of modernity.

Is this conclusion warranted, or is it perhaps premature? Does Arendt's theatrical conception of the public sphere have anything to teach citizens of modern democracies, or does it merely sum up those aspects of her political thought that are no longer tenable, the residue of a Grecophilic, Heidegger-influenced "philosophy of origins"?

It is my contention that Arendt's emphasis on the theatrical dimensions of public space and political action has, *pace* Benhabib, much to teach us about the nature of a healthy public sphere and the reasons for its contemporary decline. These reasons have little to do with what Benhabib calls Arendt's tendency toward phenomenological essentialism and the kind of "nostalgic *Verfallsgeschichte*" we find in Heidegger (76). By focusing on the theatricality of the public realm of the polis, Arendt is not positing a pure origin from which we moderns have fallen away. Rather, she is trying to teach us a lesson about the nature of *worldliness*—about a quality of human being-in-the-world that waxes and wanes in different societies and in different epochs. One reason Arendt so often appears to her critics as a nostalgic antimodern is that she felt the modern age unleashed forces (including capitalist expropriation, the "rise of the social," technological automatism, and a culture of authenticity) that have seriously, if not fatally, undermined our capacity for worldliness. Her emphasis on the theatricality of genuine political action and a robust public sphere is an attempt to get us to see how vastly different *our* "attitude toward the world" is from more political (read: worldly) cultures and times.

This chapter examines the close link between theatricality and worldliness in Arendt's writing. I hope thereby to demonstrate the continuing relevance of her "agonistic" model of public space.[9] In my view, following too closely Benhabib's advice on what is living and what is dead in Arendt's political theory would rob us of what is, perhaps, Arendt's most profound contribution to critical thinking about politics and the public sphere under contemporary conditions.

My argument proceeds as follows. First, I set out what Arendt means by "worldliness" and how she sees the theatricality of public life as its chief, and perhaps most important, expression. Next, I turn to the question of the distinguishing characteristics of "theatrical" political action as theorized by Arendt. Does this conception serve primarily expressive ends, as Benhabib and d'Entreves assert? In the fourth section, I contrast Habermas's description of the rise and decline of the "bourgeois public sphere" in his *Structural Transformation of the Public Sphere* with the quite different perspective provided by Richard Sennett's *The Fall of Public Man*.[10] My goal here is to broaden our understanding of the theatricality of public life. Sennett's work is helpful because it approaches the nexus of theatricality and publicness in a way that makes up for Arendt's much-criticized "sociological deficit."[11] In the Conclusion, I turn to the reasons why an associational model of the public space and a purely deliberative conception of democracy fail to provide an adequate critical model for the diagnosis of "the public and its problems" in contemporary society.

### Worldliness and Political Action

There is a strong temptation (as the quote from d'Entreves shows) to view Arendt's Burke-derived definition of political action—"acting together, acting in concert"[12]—as juxtaposing a solidarity-based model of politics to the heroic individualism of the agonistic model. Yet it is a temptation we should resist, and not only because Arendt herself was highly skeptical about solidaristic models of political action. More to the point, it obscures the crucial role the idea of worldliness plays in Arendt's view of political life, a role we lose sight of the moment we reduce her thought to civic republicanism or attempt to update this tradition for a social democratic politics.

This point is driven home if we turn to Arendt's essay "On Humanity in Dark Times: Thoughts about Lessing."[13] This remarkable essay, given as a lecture on the occasion of Arendt's receipt of the Lessing Prize in 1959, focuses on what happens to our feeling for the world in those "dark times" when the public realm either excludes us or becomes a source of shame and unease. Arendt plays the response of Lessing (who, as the subject of a monarch, was deprived of a public space for action) off the response of persecuted Jews and alienated Germans to the early (pretotalitarian) years of Nazi power.

What distinguishes Lessing from those closer to us in time is that he was never tempted to salvage meaning from his exclusion by means of a further self-withdrawal. Unlike victimized "pariah peoples," who could compensate for their exclusion from the public world by generating feelings of warmth and fraternity, or those who found this public world so stupid, base, and unendurable that they withdrew into the interior realm of thought and feeling, Lessing continued to uphold his "partisanship for the world" (8). Restricted to thought and writing, he attempted to humanize the darkened public world through discourse and argument and the peculiar "friendship" these engender. He eschewed the comforts of withdrawal, solidarity, and intimacy in order to remain "open to the world."

What is Arendt's purpose in drawing this contrast? It is, first and foremost, *not* a criticism of "pariah peoples" for being complicit in their exclusion (although Arendt's ambivalence about the "inner emigration" response—the response of her teacher and friend Karl Jaspers—is palpable). Rather, the example of these responses to "dark times" reveals an essential difference between the modern and late modern "attitude towards the world." For the early modern Lessing, a life lived in private or confined to a circle of intimates was not worth living. This attitude is similar to that of Arendt's beloved Greeks in that it values the human relation of friendship as mediated by the world (Aristotle's *philia*) over modern forms of intimacy and solidarity.

Like the Greeks, Lessing saw friendship as an essentially *worldly* phenomenon, born of discourse about the common world, rather than as a phenomenon of intimacy or a *fraternité* grounded in a shared humanity (24). Arendt focuses on his response to "dark times" because it reveals an attitude toward the world fundamentally at odds with the late modern retreat from a hostile public world. Lessing's response is colored throughout by an intuitive awareness of the cost to our very sense of reality that such a retreat from the world involves. Toward the end of her essay, Arendt writes:

> Lessing, too, was already living in "dark times," and after his own fashion he was destroyed by their darkness. We have seen what a powerful need men have, in such times, to move closer to one another, to seek in the warmth and intimacy the substitute for that light and illumination which only the public realm can cast. But this means that they avoid disputes and try as far as possible to deal with people with whom they cannot come into conflict. For a man of Lessing's disposition there was little room in such an age and in such a confined world; where people moved together in order to warm one another, they move away from him. And yet he, who was polemical to the point of contentiousness, could no more endure loneliness than the excessive closeness of a brotherliness that obliterated all distinctions. He was never eager really to fall out

with someone with whom he had entered into a dispute; he was concerned solely with humanizing the world by incessant and continual discourse about its affairs and the things in it. He wanted to be the friend
of many men, but no man's brother (30).

What does it mean when our alienation from the world makes a figure like Lessing (at least as rendered by Arendt) seem infinitely remote,
almost premodern? We can easily comprehend the desire for warmth
that draws "pariah peoples" together; we have no trouble understanding the phenomenon of "inner emigration." But how to understand a
passion for the world so intense that an individual would rather risk
self-destruction than face the prospect of an *unworldly* existence? How
to understand someone who, in the face of "dark times," eschews the
solidarity of the oppressed or the warmth of intimacy for the "friendship" of argument and discourse?

These questions lead us to *The Human Condition* and its evocative
passages about the nature of the public realm—"the common world."
For it is here that Arendt draws out her understanding of the peculiar
reality of the public realm, a reality that has become increasingly elusive
to us but whose traces Lessing doggedly clung to.

In section 7 of *The Human Condition,* Arendt states that "the term
'public' signifies two interrelated but not altogether identical phenomena." The first is that "everything that appears in public can be seen and
heard by everybody and has the widest possible publicity" (50). In the
public realm, "appearance . . . constitutes reality." The second phenomenon signified by the term "public" is "the world itself, in so far as
it is common to all of us and distinguished from our privately owned
place in it" (52). By "world" Arendt means neither the earth nor nature
but the "human artifact," the relatively permanent artifice created by
"the fabrication of human hands."

The reason these two senses of "public" are interrelated is that both
refer to something common, whether appearances that are seen and
heard by all, or to an "objective" context that is (in an extended sense)
inhabited by all. The difference between these two senses (and the phenomena they refer to) is that public appearances depend not only on
the availability of a public realm but also on the existence of a "human
artifice" that "relates and separates men at the same time" (52).

Arendt's thesis is that both phenomena designated by the term
"public" have, in the late modern age, ceased to perform their characteristic functions. As a "space of appearances," the public no longer

provides us with the same "feeling for reality" that it did for previous ages: "what appears to all" seems least real, while what is felt by the self or in intimate relations becomes the benchmark of reality (50–51).[14] Yet, as Arendt points out, when the subjective or the private is deprived of a strong contrasting term, it too loses much of its force. Hence the "weird irreality" that attends these experiences in the present, as they lose the sharp definition that juxtaposition with the "bright light of the public" used to provide.

Similarly, according to Arendt, the man-made world of things, the "human artifice," no longer fulfills its function as an "in-between." Under the conditions of mass society, the public world no longer serves to gather humans together, to "relate and separate" them (53). Indeed, as the human artifice is increasingly swamped by transient consumer goods and subjected to the rhythms of production and consumption, the "thing character" of the world becomes less and less tangible.[15]

These observations by Arendt lead to the obvious question as to why "the public" (in both senses) no longer seems able to play its characteristic roles in the modern age. I want to defer this question for now, focusing instead on Arendt's entry point into the discussion of the public realm. What is obvious in *The Human Condition*, but all too often overlooked by her critics, is that Arendt's discussion of the public realm centers on the experience of a particular sort of reality, a specific kind of "feeling for the world."

This feeling, born of a vivid "space of appearances" and the relative permanence of the human artifact, is what Arendt identifies with worldliness, which she sees as increasingly rare in the late modern age. The feeling for reality conveyed by the Arendtian notion of worldliness is obviously not reducible to public-spiritedness, a sense of community, or a participatory politics. Of course, all of these can be vehicles of worldliness, supports for a sensibility that is neither escapist/romantic or exploitative/capitalist. But what clearly matters for Arendt in these pages of *The Human Condition* is less politics than the "feeling for the world" itself. Indeed, one can say that Arendt's valuation of political action as the existentially supreme human activity flows from her desire to preserve worldliness at all costs. In this sense, even political action turns out to be of secondary importance, something of a means rather than an end in itself.[16]

How does political action promote and sustain worldliness? In answering this question, the first thing to be observed is that not all political action *does* contribute to worldliness. Arendt's highly selective approach to the question of what counts as genuine political action flows less from a misplaced purism than from an acute sense of the ways in which ostensibly political forms of action can contribute to our alienation from the world. Thus, in *The Human Condition* and "On Violence" she excludes violence, force, and domination as categories of *political* relations; in *On Revolution* she denies that struggles for liberation from domination, or the "instrumental" relationship between citizens and their representatives in representative democracy, constitute authentically political forms.

The common denominator linking all these "nonpolitical" forms of politics is that they undercut what Arendt, following Kant, calls our "common sense" of the world. Violence, force, and domination are mute: they are used to monopolize the public sphere (whether our examples are ancient régime monarchies or more up-to-date authoritarian regimes). By excluding the majority of subjects from any participation in the "space of appearances," they enforce and promote alienation from the world. Under the conditions of total domination—totalitarianism—terror destroys the very possibility of an "in-between," throwing individuals back upon themselves, depriving them of even the simulacrum of worldliness.[17] More surprising is Arendt contention that the politics of liberation struggles and representative democracy also do not contribute to worldliness. The former is "prepolitical," concerned solely with the overcoming of domination that is but the prelude to the founding of a new public sphere, while the latter encourages an interest-group politics that undermines a sense of the common or public.[18]

When we turn to Arendt's conception of "genuine" political action, that we begin to see how theatrical/agonistic action contributes to worldliness in ways that other, seemingly less exotic, forms do not. Yet Arendt's formulations have the effect of strengthening rather than easing the doubts raised by Benhabib and d'Entreves.

In her essay "What Is Freedom?" Arendt establishes a strong link between the freedom manifest in political action and the "virtuosity" of the political actor. She appeals to Machiavelli in order to illustrate the distinctive freedom of the political actor/performer:

> Freedom as inherent in action is perhaps best illustrated by Machiavelli's concept of *virtú,* the excellence with which man answers the opportunities the world opens up before him in the guise of *fortuna.* Its meaning is best rendered by "virtuosity," that is, an excellence we attribute to

the performing arts (as distinguished from the creative arts of making), where the accomplishment lies in the performance itself and not in an end product which outlasts the activity that brought it into existence and becomes independent of it. The virtuoso-ship of Machiavelli's *virtú* somehow reminds us of the fact, although Machiavelli hardly knew it, that the Greeks always used such metaphors as flute-playing, dancing, healing, and sea-faring to distinguish political from other activities, that is, that they drew their analogies from those arts in which virtuosity of performance is decisive.[19]

If we combine this passage with those from the chapter on action in *The Human Condition,* we seem to have ample confirmation of Benhabib's objections to the agonistic model. The more we focus on the theatrical or performative character of political action, the more the quality of virtuosity (or performative excellence) takes precedence in our evaluation of the political actor. As Benhabib points out, such a perspective—in which the consequences of any action of the motives behind it are rendered secondary—presupposes a high degree of "moral homogeneity." For it is only against the background of such a substantive agreement on positive virtues that the question of the excellence of the performance can come to the fore.

The emphasis on "virtuosity of performance" as the most important manifestation of the freedom of political action has another drawback. Insofar as it encourages us to see political action as a competitive agon between virtuosic actors striving for excellence before their peers, it also encourages us to view action as primarily expressive in character. This is the consequence noted by d'Entreves, and echoed by many of Arendt's critics.[20] Arendt seems committed (at least in *The Human Condition* and "What Is Freedom?") to a view that frames political action as the most important vehicle of the agent's self-disclosure or expression.[21]

But is the expression of excellence, or the disclosure of one's "unique identity," in fact the main reason for Arendt's choice of a theatrical metaphorics? Both Benhabib's and d'Entreves' analyses equate the agonistic Arendt with an overtly romantic Arendt, one perhaps overly influenced by Nietzsche. Yet if we turn to another of Arendt's texts, *On Revolution,* we see that the identification of agonism and expressivism is more than a little problematic. Arendt's appeal to theatrical metaphors in thinking about political action and the public realm is intended precisely to demolish the presuppositions of the expressivist model of action.

## Agonistic Action: Impersonal or Expressive?

In an important but somewhat obscure discussion in *On Revolution,*
Arendt addresses Robespierre's politics of virtue and the hatred of ancien régime hypocrisy that energized it (98–109). What, she asks, made
hypocrisy such a monster for Robespierre? Why did the unmasking of
*this* vice come to take absolute priority in the politics of the French
Revolution, and with what consequences? In answering these questions, Arendt juxtaposes two models of theatrical self-presentation to
the "corrupt" playacting of court society that Robespierre so reviled.
Her examples, surprisingly, are Socrates and Machiavelli.

For Arendt, Socratic moral integrity is not the opposite of playacting, a Greek version of Luther's "here I stand, I can do no other."
Rather, she views Socrates as taking his departure from "an unquestioned belief in the truth of appearances" (101). Operating within, not
against, this framework, Socrates taught, "Be as you would wish to appear to others." According to Arendt, by this he meant, "Appear to
yourself as you wish to appear to others" (101). Socratic conscien-
tiousness consists in the demand for self-agreement and exploits the
phenomenon of the "two-in-one" of consciousness in order to in-
ternalize the audience to one's actions. For Socrates, according to
Arendt, the agent and the onlooker "were contained in the selfsame
person" (101).

Machiavelli, in contrast, operated within the assumptions of Chris-
tianity; that is, he assumed a gap between appearances (how we appear
to our fellow human beings) and reality (how God perceives us).
Hence he taught, "Appear as you may wish to be"—by which he
meant (again in Arendt's "paraphrase"), "Never mind how you are,
this is of no relevance in the world and in politics, where only appearances, not 'true' being, count; if you can manage to appear to others as
you would wish to be, that is all that can possibly be required by the
judges of this world" (101).

The point Arendt stresses is that neither Socrates or Machiavelli,
however radically different they were in other respects, equated the theatrical presentation of self (to oneself or others) with hypocrisy. "Playacting," the idea of a distinct public self or the view of oneself as an
actor performing for an internalized audience, had yet to gain the connotation of deceit or corruption. Only when such acting becomes merely a vehicle of deceit—of oneself as well as others—does the hypocrisy
that Rousseau and Robespierre attacked so ferociously become the
defining characteristic of the public sphere. As Arendt presents it, the

court society of the ancien régime gave playacting—the conscious adoption of a role, the wearing of a public mask—a bad name. The response, manifest in Rousseau's theory and Robespierre's practice, was a cult of the "natural" man, the authentic (roleless) individual, coupled with a ruthless politics of unmasking.[22]

Arendt focuses on the way hypocrisy becomes a *political* topos for the French Revolution because she wants to reveal the relatively recent moment in our history when the idea of playacting, mask-wearing, or a distinct public self came to have a largely negative connotation. Once public role-playing or mask-wearing was no longer seen as the medium of a specific truthfulness—as the means by which the actor's voice could "sound through" while his private self remained protectively hidden—the notion of a public persona became permanently tainted. The very conventionality of the public realm now became the problem, with the result that an impersonal presentation of self became suspect and politically self-defeating. With the Revolution we enter an epoch in which public words and deeds are seen as either self-serving appearances (and therefore false) or the expression of the actor's "true," authentic self.

This way of viewing actions and speech, Arendt maintains, was simply impossible for Socrates or Machiavelli, both of whom thought of "acting" in a theatrical sense that did not *obscure* truth but rather enabled it to appear. Indeed, the example of Socrates' "theatrical" notion of conscience shows that there is no necessary connection between conscientious moral agency and the notion of an authentic self (however natural this connection seems to the heirs of the Reformation).[23] Even conscience can be theatricalized, divorced from the voice of God or the authentic (natural, virtuous) self.

Arendt's discussion of appearances, masks, and persona in chapter 2 of *On Revolution* is brief, but it highlights the assumption underlying Benhabib's and d'Entreves' characterization of her "heroic" agonistic model of the public sphere. The *last* thing Arendt wants to give us is a theory of political action that equates it with self-expression. Such a notion derives from the politics of authenticity invented by Rousseau. It is, in Arendt's understanding, fundamentally at odds with the kind of impersonality fostered by a theatrical conception of the self as a performer on the public stage. The fact that we, unlike Socrates or Machiavelli, equate impersonality with hypocrisy or "mere" playacting leads us to demand the performance of authenticity by our contemporary political actors. The result, as I shall argue below, is a shallow cynicism that further undermines of our sense of the reality of the public world.

That Arendt's appeal to the theatrical dimensions of the public realm is directed *against* an expressive model of political action is seen by returning to "What Is Freedom?" In a passage immediately preceding the one cited above on virtuosity and freedom, she explains what "acting from principle" means in terms of her theatrical conception. *Free* action, according to Arendt, "is neither under the guidance of the intellect nor under the dictate of will"; it is "free from motive on one side, from its intended goal as predictable effect on the other."[24] Arendt is not denying that intellect or will are necessary for the achievement of any action, nor is she claiming the motives and goals play no role in an agent's deliberations. Rather, she is claiming that the *freedom* of action does not reside in any of these categories, its "determining" factors. The freedom of action is manifest in the performance itself and in the *principle* that inspires it (152).

It is important to note here that Arendt's own "inspiration" on the question of principles is Montesquieu rather than Kant. Montesquieu analyzes forms of government and their respective inspiring principles (democracy and virtue, aristocracy and moderation, monarchy and honor). This analysis provides Arendt with a way of thinking about "acting from a principle" that is perfectly suited to the worldly, theatrical quality of political action. Principles in her sense are not defining self-conceptions, one's "core convictions"; rather, "they inspire, as it were, from without" (152). Too general to prescribe particular actions, they become fully manifest "only in the performing act itself": "The manifestation of principles comes about only through action, they are manifest in the world as long as the action lasts, but no longer" (152). Following Montesquieu, Arendt cites honor, glory, love of equality, distinction, or excellence as examples of "inspiring" (rather than determining) principles.

What is Arendt trying to get at with this idiosyncratic (and decidedly non-Kantian) rendering of "acting from a principle"? First, she is trying to reformulate "principled" action in a way that detracts nothing from the *performance* itself; that does not reduce the meaning of action to the motivations of the actor or his success in achieving his goal. "Principles" in her sense are immanent to actions. They inspire "from without" but are only fully real when embodied in action. But the main reason she links the freedom of action to the "inspiration" of principles is that she is trying to *depersonalize* political action, separate it from the inner determination of "the assertive will, the calculating intelligence, the impassioned heart, or the urges of the body or spirit."[25]

Arendt's dual emphasis on the depersonalized quality of acting from a principle and the impersonal quality of adopting a public persona or "mask" should make us question interpretations that see an expressive model lurking behind her agonism. Yes, "self-disclosure" is an undeniable part of what George Kateb calls the "existential achievement" of political action as theorized by Arendt. But such self-disclosure is not the externalization of an inner potential nor an expression of one's "true" self.[26] Arendt's focus on the impersonal qualities of political action do not promote the idea of selflessness; rather, it serves to highlight the distinction between the public and the private self. This distinction is undermined by the expressivist model of action we have inherited from Rousseau and Romanticism, which stresses the achievement of an integrated, "whole" human being.[27] Arendt's understanding of the performance of political action links it to the achievement of a "unique identity," but this identity is shaped by the discipline and depersonalization that come from adopting a specific public role or mask.

This is why the distinction Benhabib draws between agonal and narrative models of action is somewhat misleading (*Reluctant Modernist*, 126–27). Benhabib deploys this distinction in order to distinguish the expressivist or "essentialist" Arendt from the more intersubjectively oriented Arendt. Benhabib frames the contrast in the following terms:

> whereas action in the agonal model is described through terms such as "revelation of who one is" and "the making manifest of what is interior," action in the narrative model is characterized through the telling of a story" and the "weaving of a web of narratives." Whereas in the first model action appears to make manifest or to reveal an antecedent essence, the "one who is," action in the second model suggests that "the one who is" emerges in the process of doing the deed and telling the story. Whereas action in the first model is a process of discovery, action in the second model is a process of invention. In contemporary terms, we may say the first model of action is essentialist while the second is constructivist (125–26).

The force of this contrast is to drive a wedge between the deliberative, plurality-oriented Arendt (who views meaning and identity as functions of intersubjective narrative constitution) and the agonal

Arendt (who sees action on the public stage as the expression of one's unique identity). Benhabib draws attention to the fact that *all* action (including agonal action) is narratively constituted, which is to say it is articulated and defined in terms of a "web of interpretations" (127). Her point is that Arendt's agonal model deliberately and mistakenly *obscures* this dimension by focusing so intently on the "rare deeds" of the virtuosic performer.

However, if we attend to the impersonal dimensions of Arendt's theatrical conception, we see that Arendt's agonistic model of the public space does not really reduce to yet another expression of what Habermas has dubbed the "philosophy of the subject." Arendt's emphasis on the importance of roles, masks, and principles demonstrates the presence of "intersubjectivity," but in the specific form of a theatrical conventionality. Arendt is drawing our attention to a "narrative web of interpretations" of a very particular kind, one focused on a distinct set of phenomena: public words and deeds. She is *not* trying to make a general point about social epistemology, about what Benhabib calls the "the deep structure of human action as interaction" (111). Benhabib reads her as doing precisely this, the better to assimilate her insight into the "narrative structuration of action" to the social epistemology of Hegel, Marx, Mead, and Habermas (127).[28]

Once *this* move is made, the specific characteristics of agonistic action—its manifest theatrical dimensions—are dissolved to make way for a larger point about the intersubjective constitution of the "lifeworld." According to Benhabib, "One of Arendt's fundamental contributions to the history of twentieth century philosophy is the thesis that the human space of appearances is constituted by 'the web of relationships and the enacted stories'" (112–13). The stage-like "space of appearances" is thus read back into the discursively constituted "horizon of human affairs." From here it is but a short step to questioning the need for Arendt's unpopular distinction between the political and the social. Not only does this distinction appear untenable under modern conditions; it ceases to do any theoretically important work once action is identified with interaction *tout court*. According to Benhabib, nothing about *political* action distinguishes it, generically, from other "narrative" modes of action, modes that exist and flourish without the presence of a theatrical "space of appearances."

In Benhabib's presentation, then, Arendt's agonistic model—the public realm as theater or stage—emerges as superfluous and needlessly constricting. If the important point about human action is that it is narratively constituted through a communicative web of interpretations, then the need for a bounded, ocular space of appearances dissolves. We are then free to use Arendt's insight into the narrative structure of action to discover public/political spaces throughout the social body. This is precisely what Benhabib does when, for example, she asks us to view Rahel Varnhagen's nineteenth-century Berlin salon as a proto-public sphere, one that brings different social types (women, Jews, intellectuals, and aristocrats) together and establishes a quasi-egalitarian space of discourse between them (14–22).

Turning to the present, Benhabib demonstrates how the emphasis on action as interaction rather than agonistic performance enables us to see various contemporary social movements for gender, wage, and racial justice as forms of *political* action. The thrust of her argument is that the shift from an agonistic to a communicative/deliberative or "narrative" model of action fundamentally alters our sense of what a robust public sphere looks like. There is no longer any need to see a strong sense of the public as dependent on the availability of a "holistic" or theatrical public space. Rather, we can view these social movements as initiating a process of moral-political *Bildung,* one that forces their participants to transcend the narrow (individual or group) interests that drove them into the public arena in the first place. As Benhabib puts it:

> Whichever class or social group enters the public realm, and no matter how class or group specific its demands may be in their genesis, the process of public-political struggle transforms the attitude of narrow self-interest into a more broadly shared public or common interest (145).

The theatrical public space, then, no longer fulfills any important political function—or, rather, it fulfills a function appropriate only to "face to face" societies, namely, it provides a venue in which a community "becomes present to itself and recognizes itself through a shared interpretive repertoire" (201). Benhabib proposes to drop Arendt's apparently antiquated desire for such communal self-representation, extending her remarks about deliberation, judgment, and the Kantian "enlarged mentality" in order to "desubstantialize" the public sphere. Viewing the public sphere as "not just, or even principally, an arena for action but an impersonal medium of communication, information, and opinion formation" enables us to reconnect Arendt's theory of action and the public realm not only to the conditions of contemporary society, but to the question of democratic legitimacy as well (200). According to Benhabib, such a critical appropriation has already been performed, by Jürgen Habermas's *Structural Transformation of the Public Sphere.*

## Genealogies of the Present: Habermas vs. Sennett

Habermas's study of the rise and decline of the bourgeois public sphere is at once Arendtian and at odds with the spirit of her work. It is Arendtian in that the story Habermas tells about the decline of the public realm in the nineteenth and twentieth centuries emphasizes the role played by the rise of the social welfare state and plebiscitary democracy (*Structural Transformation*, 177–78). In telling this story, he gives historical and sociological flesh to Arendt's somewhat vague thesis about "the rise of the social" in the modern age.[29] Yet the public sphere whose rise and decline Habermas charts is decidedly different in character from the agonistic, theatrical public realm depicted by Arendt.

What is the heart of this difference? There is the obvious point that Habermas's analysis focuses on the rise and decline of the public sphere in Europe between 1640 and 1960, with nary a glance to the public sphere of the polis. But this difference in period is also a difference in the origins, character, and role of the public sphere. Unlike the public realm of the Greeks, the bourgeois public realm was, from its inception, a decentered public realm, occupying sites separate from both state and the economy. It emerged when property-owning private subjects (the bourgeoisie) began to question the regulations laid down by autocratic rulers for the realm of civil society (28). This nonpolitical challenge, which took the form of subjecting such regulations to rational-critical public debate, gradually expanded to become a full-scale ideology of critical publicity and democratic legitimacy, in which the force of the better argument and public opinion informed by arguments rationalized the exercise of political power. Politically speaking, then, the bourgeois public sphere introduced a historically unprecedented medium for the confrontation with power: "people's public use of their own reason [*offentliches Räsonnement*]" (27).

The first part of *Structural Transformation* is devoted to describing the process by which an independent, critically reasoning public begins to emerge in the coffee houses, salons, and *Tischgesellschaften* of the eighteenth century. Excluded from participation in public decision making, private individuals began to develop their capacity for critical judgment and public argument in these sites through the discussion of cultural and literary matters (29). From its beginnings in a secularized world of letters and literary-cultural debate, the principle of critical publicity widened to include the rules governing civil society, giving rise to the idea of law as a body of abstract and universally valid rules (54–56).

With the emergence of a critically reasoning public in the eighteenth century came the idea of public opinion as a critical filter, the carrier of a deliberative rationality that could distinguish between the parochial interests of elites and the common good (90–101). "Publicity" became the test for all legislation and enactments; only those that could survive free and open discussion could claim legitimacy.[30] The great theorist of "publicity" as the moral test of policy was, of course, Kant, whose formulation in "What Is Enlightenment?" serves Habermas (despite its obvious limitations) as the normative ideal of the bourgeois public sphere. It was Kant who first showed how the "public use of one's reason" contributed to the constitution of a critically reasoning public, one whose consensus would be built on the force of the better argument—now the "pragmatic test of truth" in moral-political affairs (106–7).[31]

The Kantian idea of a critical publicity deployed by a community of independent, rational citizens has, of course, never been fully realized in any political society. In terms of the story Habermas tells, however, the striking thing is how quickly the idea of public opinion as a force opposed to power became the object of theoretical anxiety as well as empirical skepticism. In Tocqueville and J. S. Mill, the idea of public opinion already begins to take on the negative connotation that it has today, the connotation of an irrational and conformist force, one that is easily manipulated and impossible to escape (132–40). Stripped of its critical, rational form, public opinion quickly came to be seen as "one power among other powers" (135).

The fears expressed by nineteenth-century liberals do not render the ideal of a critically reasoning public obsolete for Habermas; rather, they anticipate what he calls the "structural transformation" of the public sphere that occurs in the context of mass society. Here, the instrumentalities of a bureaucratized, plebiscitary democracy combine with the media of mass culture to produce a "pseudo public sphere," one stripped of its critical (rationalizing, universalizing) function.

Habermas describes this transformation in the second half of *Structural Transformation*, providing a peculiar synthesis of Arendt's arguments from *The Human Condition* with those of the essay "Culture Industry," from Horkheimer and Adorno's *Dialectic of Enlightenment*. In a section entitled "From a Culture Debating to a Culture-Consuming Public," Habermas traces how the rise of mass culture destroys the sites of cultural discussion and debate in which the bourgeoisie had learned "the art of critical-rational public debate" (159–74). "Since the middle of the nineteenth century," Habermas writes, "the institutions that until then had ensured the coherence of the public as a critically debating entity have been weakened" (162).

Hence, the private arenas of reading and debate that developed an "audience-directed subjectivity" are either destroyed (as in the case of the salon) or colonized by the passive consumption of mass culture (as is the case with the family, which becomes the primary site of such consumption) (163). Moreover, the proliferation of panel discussions and media-staged debates turn public argument itself into an object of consumption. As Habermas notes, "Today the conversation itself is administered" (164). Critical debate, "arranged in this manner," may serve important "social-psychological functions," but it is increasingly bereft of its publicist (authentically critical) function.

As the public shifts from being an arena for critical debate and argument to the passive consumption of prepackaged news (on the one hand) and entertainment (on the other), we can no longer speak of a *critical* publicity. In politics, publicity now means the advertising efforts necessary to generate plebiscitary support for particular leaders or policies, the manufacture of a (non-rationalized) consensus from on high (177). As Habermas puts it:

> Publicity is generated from above, so to speak, in order to create an aura of good will for certain positions. Originally publicity guaranteed the connection between rational-critical public debate and the legislative foundation of domination, including the critical supervision of its exercise. Now it makes possible the peculiar ambivalence of a domination exercised through the domination of nonpublic opinion: it serves the manipulation *of* the public as much as legitimation *before* it. Critical publicity is supplanted by manipulative publicity (178).

Citizens are transformed into consumers in the political realm as well as in private life. The public sphere is "refeudalized" in the sense that publicity loses its critical-rational function and increasingly takes on a purely symbolic role (195, 5–8). Worst of all, the public sphere becomes a kind of "show" set up for "purposes of manipulation and staged directly for the sake of that large minority of the "undecided" who normally determine the outcome of a election" (221). Stripped of its active, argument-oriented character, public opinion ceases to play a rationalizing role in the political arena, with the result that what passes for consensus in contemporary democratic societies has no real relation to the idea of justice implicit in "the standard of a universal interest" (234).

The story of decline Habermas tells is by now a quite familiar one, to the point of taking its place among the very media clichés we passively consume. The point I wish to emphasize here, however, is how Habermas's focus on the Kantian idea of the "public use of one's reason" reduces Arendt's notion of the public sphere to its formally deliberative dimensions. These are valued, while the agonistic or theatrical aspects are denigrated as either anachronistic or mere "show." Publicity deprived of its rational, argumentative form is, and can only be, manipulation. With this observation, Habermas tacitly evokes the original Socratic-Platonic critique of democratic politics as "mere" persuasion, performed by unscrupulous demagogues before an audience gathered in the assembly.[32] Habermas, in effect, provides an updated, democratic version of this critique, one in which the prospects for a more robust and democratic public realm hinge on our ability to "re-rationalize" the public sphere, making it the scene of a critical, deliberative formation of popular will once again.

If Habermas strives, in this early work, to separate the deliberative kernel of Arendt's conception of the public realm from its theatrical shell, Richard Sennett draws our attention to the way theatricality is itself constitutive of public life. Moreover, he does so in a way that demonstrates that such theatricality does not rely on a "holistic" public sphere of the sort Benhabib describes. His historical analysis enables us to question the quasi-rationalist opposition of argument versus theater erected by Habermas and Benhabib, for not all theatricality is spectacle, and not all performance is manipulation. Indeed, Sennett's thesis is that the manipulative forms of theatricality that Habermas points to are relatively late inventions, functions of a pervasive personalization of the political realm.

Sennett's study, like Habermas's, traces the decline of public life in the period between 1750 and the present. Unlike Habermas, he is concerned with the health of public culture in a broad sense and therefore is far less restricted in the range of phenomena he investigates. The presentation of self in everyday life; the rise of a culture of intimacy;

the role that the "psychological imagination of life" plays in our constitution of public and private reality: all of these figure centrally in Sennett's work, while they appear peripherally, if at all, in Habermas's.[33]

The transformation Sennett depicts, then, is not the functional one of the role of public opinion in political life. It is, rather, the much larger change from an Enlightenment-era society built on theatrical codes of self-presentation to a contemporary Western society in which place a premium is placed on intimacy, directness of emotional expression (in public and private), and community. As Sennett notes toward the end of his book, "Warmth is our god" (259). An ideology of intimacy, which assumes that "social relationships of all kinds are real, believable, and authentic the closer they approach the inner psychological concerns of each person," rules our public as well as our private lives (259). Indeed, it has contributed mightily to the dissolution of any strong sense of the distinctiveness of the public realm or self, to the point that political action is routinely read back to the "character" of the actor (his "real" self) and its evaluation made a function of the actor's personal characteristics and believability. The rise of a culture of intimacy systematically transmutes "political categories into psychological ones" (259).

It was not always so. In the first half of his book, Sennett describes the emergence of a secular "society of strangers" in the great urban centers of eighteenth-century London and Paris. The unprecedented concentration of strangers in one place created a "problem of audience": how to know and to judge the appearances—the words and deeds—of individuals encountered in this new, anonymous public. According to Sennett, the eighteenth century dealt with this problem by drawing on the venerable tradition of *theatrum mundi,* the image of society as itself a theater or stage. Expanding on this analogy, urban life in the eighteenth century built a "bridge" between the stage and the street, transferring a set of theatrical conventions and criteria of judgment (of dress, utterance, and believability) to the "theater" of the city.

To move in the public space of the eighteenth-century city was, almost by definition, to be an actor, a performer (107). A shared set of conventions governed the presentation of self and emotion to strangers, enabling the growth of an "impersonal sociability" distinctive to the time. These conventions (of gesture, dress, and speech) opened a communicative space that worked by creating a distance between the actor and his acts or appearances. Within this conventionally defined space, judgment and understanding focused on the act, the gesture, the word, rather than the agent behind them. If the "world is a stage," then "character of acts and the character of actors are separate, so that a man of the world 'can censure an imperfection, or even a vice, without rage against the guilty party.'"[34] When the common sense of public life was theatrical in this sense, one could disagree with the position held by another (often to the point of comical, polemical excess[35]) without feeling the need to demonize the *person* of the opponent.[36] One's opponent was simply an individual who had taken an evil or blameworthy role. In sum, it was the role that was condemned, not the person's *nature*.

This eighteenth-century notion of "man as actor" thus placed a premium on masks, role-playing, and appearances as the medium of an impersonal sociability. Such theatrical devices created a distance between the "natural" and social self, a distance that conduced to an impersonal but, paradoxically, easier and more expressive sociability. As Sennett remarks, "Wearing a mask is the essence of civility. Masks permit pure sociability, detached from the circumstances of power, malaise, and private feeling of those who wear them. Civility has as its aim the shielding of others from being burdened with oneself" (264). With the aid of such conventions, the urban space of the eighteenth century created a distinctive public geography, one defined, in large part, by its highly artificial nature, its distance from the "natural" world of the home and family (40–41, 90–92).

The public space of the Enlightenment, then, was conventional through and through. Even the coffeehouses—one of Habermas's favorite examples of a proto-public space of rational discourse— "worked" as the result of establishing a strict set of conventions governing the form of discourse and sociality allowed within their doors: "The art of conversation [among social unequals in the coffeehouses] was a convention in the same sense as dressing to rank of the 1750's, even though its mechanism was the opposite, the suspension of rank" (82). The kind of impersonal sociability enabled by these theatrical devices is no longer available to us, for we have lost the art of playacting. Conventionality and theatricality are condemned, from Rousseau to the present, as inhumane and antiegalitarian. The transition from the world of the eighteenth century to our own time charts a dialectic of public theatricality and intimacy. In Sennett's words:

> In the theater, there is a correlation between belief in the persona of the actor and belief in conventions. Play, playacting, and acting, all require

belief in conventions to be expressive. Convention is itself the single most expressive tool of public life. But in an age wherein intimate relations determine what shall be believable, conventions, artifices, and rules appear only to get in the way of revealing oneself to another; they are obstructions to intimate expression. As the imbalance between public and intimate life has grown greater, people have become less expressive. With an emphasis on psychological authenticity, people become inartistic in daily life because they are unable to tap the fundamental creative strength of the actor, the ability to play with and invest feeling in external images of self. Thus we arrive at the hypothesis that theatricality has a special, hostile relation to intimacy; theatricality has an equally special, friendly relation to a strong public life. (37)

The rise of a culture of intimacy means the decline of (social) theatricality; the decline of theatricality means the decline of public life. Focusing on the nineteenth century and the disruptions created by the rise of capitalism and an increasingly secularized culture, Sennett traces how the family ceased to be "a particular, nonpublic region" and became, instead, "an idealized refuge, a world all its own, with a higher moral value than the public realm" (20). As public life in the urban centers of the nineteenth century came to be seen as morally inferior to intimate life, public/political credibility became a matter superimposing private upon public imagery (25). Political actors still performed in public, but what they performed was their character, their feelings, the force of their personal convictions.

Sennett argues that this shift first comes to light in the revolutions of 1848, when virtuosos of romantic subjectivity like Lamartine challenged and pacified hostile street audiences through the sheer force of their personality and charisma. Distrustful of convention, such audiences became passive spectators, convinced that what the truth of what any public speaker had to say reduced, finally, to the kind of person he was (25). The more adept at performing "genuine" emotion, at displaying the private self in public, the politician is, the more believable he becomes. As Sennett remarks with regard to Lamartine: "The hidden power of a speaker like Lamartine is that he harnesses mystification. He has no text, and so escapes being measured by any standard of truth or reality. He can make the quality of his intentions and sentiments a self-sufficient basis of his legitimacy to rule" (237).

While the age of both proletarian revolution and the romantic performer may be over, this distinctive cognitive structure survives. For us, as for the revolutionaries of 1848, "A believable public event is created by a believable public person rather than a believable action" (237). With the death of the dispersed, participatory theatricality of the eighteenth century, the performative dimensions of politics are confined to the calculated presentation of individual character to a silenced audience: "The genuine aesthetic qualities of the meeting of politics and the arts having disappeared, what remains is only the obscurantist, paralyzing effect of a 'politics of personality'" (237). In contemporary politics, impersonality is death; the wearing of masks, deceit. In a culture of (faux) intimacy, politics reduces to what, for the eighteenth century, would have been a contradiction in terms—"personality in public" (261). While Americans may be a bit more savvy than they were when Nixon gave his "Checkers speech," we remain firmly within the grid described by Sennett, one he equates with "the end of public life."

## Conclusion

Sennett's descriptions of the decline of social theatricality and the rise of an ideology of intimacy and community (or authenticity and what he calls "destructive *gemeinschaft*") resonate powerfully with Arendt's observations on modern alienation from the world. Set against the backdrop provided by Sennett, her distinction between Lessing's "attitude towards the world" and the warmth sought by "pariah peoples" or the *fraternité* trumpeted by the French Revolution becomes even sharper. Neither intimacy nor solidarity, she is claiming, can provide a tenable substitute for lost worldliness. The public sphere is not merely the sphere of politics, of action or deliberation; it also has an irreducibly cultural dimension.[37] Hence the apparent paradox presented by both Arendt and Sennett's work: the spread of democracy in the modern age can also coincide with the decline of the public realm.

Of course, neither Arendt nor Sennett blame democracy for this state of affairs, despite their common and profound debt to Tocqueville. Their shared point is that the decline of public culture, of worldliness in various forms, undercuts the promise of democracy. Benhabib and Habermas are also concerned with the public sphere's decline but view this sphere in so narrowly formal terms that the "recovery of the public realm" is identified with the achievement of a more "deliberative" democracy. This would, to be sure, be a great advance. However, the expansion of opportunities for public deliberation and debate in itself cannot guarantee a more robust sense of the public. Here, it seems to me, Benhabib and Habermas fall prey to a familiar delusion, namely the idea that the more opportunities people have for debate and deliberation, the more their moral horizons expand, the more likely (in the end) they will come to a reasonable consensus.

This faith in the power of public discourse to raise individuals from the merely personal and idiosyncratic to the common or universal runs deep in the Western tradition. One finds traces of it in the account of public judgment Aristotle gives in Book III of the *Politics*; it receives classic formulation in Rousseau and Kant (the former's phobia of factional argument notwithstanding); and inspires even liberal theorists such as J. S. Mill (his worries about the tyranny of the majority aside). Yet, we must ask, is it really the case that (to cite Benhabib's formulation once again) "the process of public-political struggle transforms the attitude of narrow self-interest into a more broadly shared public or common interest"? Isn't it just as likely that, as Charles Larmore puts it, "the more we converse, the more we disagree"?[38] Recent appeals to a revived civic virtue or procedural forms of rationality are all attempts to offset both the pluralism and the privatism of contemporary society. Yet the possibility of generating consensus, whether through neo-Aristotelian or neo-Kantian means, cannot make up for our lost "feeling for the world." This, I take it, is a lesson that flows from both Arendt and Sennett, and we would be wise not to discount it.

Reading Arendt through the lens provided by Sennett does not merely make us skeptical of Habermas's and Benhabib's claim that the sine qua non of the public sphere is "the public use of one's reason." It also reveals just how off-target many of the objections to Arendt's "agonism" are. If Arendt's appeal to virtuosity and "rare speech and deeds" were merely a function of a misplaced hero worship, Benhabib's either/or of agonistic versus associational democracy would make sense. The heroic dimension is certainly there, but Arendt's focus on the impersonality of political action (a dimension Sennett's serves to highlight) helps us see that an agonistic public need not be confined to the rare deeds of those who possess "great moral prowess," like Pericles.

Nor, for that matter, must such a public space be "holistic" or "ocular." As Sennett demonstrates, theatricality can be every bit as dispersed as rational argumentation or information gathering, perhaps even more so. Reading Arendt's emphasis of the impersonal, theatrical quality of political action through Sennett, we are able to envisage multiple and fluid public sites of contest and debate. Indeed, Sennett's analysis warns us that our public sphere is becoming more "ocular," more bogusly "holistic," all the time.

This is not to say that either Arendt or Sennett encourage us to find thriving public spaces where we least expect them (an activity currently popular among political and cultural theorists). By tying worldliness and theatricality so closely to culture and convention, both Arendt and Sennett deliver disillusioning news. They force us to acknowledge that the health of the political public sphere is inseparable from the health of public culture generally, and that no appeal to contemporary social movements or grass-roots politics can redress this fundamental shift in Western culture. The (currently depleted) energies of social democracy may be occasionally stimulated by such movements as feminism or environmentalism, but the "return of the political" that so many expect to be generated by the associational life of civil society will be far less transformative than presumed.

Indeed, it may be doubted whether single-issue movements or identity politics do anything to transform the interests they politicize into "a more broadly shared public or common interest," at least in the quasi-Rousseauian sense both Benhabib and Habermas give this term.[39] It seems more likely that they contribute to the dialectic described by Sennett, largely by fostering an affinity group culture, one that is inclined to view moral-political virtues as a function of "who one is" in the most rudimentary sense. The inner connection between narcissism and the rhetoric of community has become increasingly apparent in identity politics, as community is ever more tightly defined in terms of those like oneself. The psychic demands filled by the rhetoric of community also make it less likely that one's political opponents will escape demonization on the basis of who *they* are, whether male or female, straight or gay, white or black, etc.

This returns us to the quandary raised by Arendt's characterization of Lessing in the quote cited above. Our inability to comprehend a figure like the one presented by Arendt flows from our inability to make the crucial distinction between actor and role a distinction that both Sennett and Arendt identify as one basis of a *worldly* culture. We simply cannot understand how it is possible to "humanize the world by incessant and continual discourse about its affairs and the things in it." In a culture of intimacy/community, polemics and argument only divide people; they cannot provide the medium of an impersonal sociability, let alone "friendship."

So long as we personalize the political in the sense described by Sennett, the ability to distinguish words, acts, and policies from a person's nature, character, or "identity" will elude us. Slaves of the simplifying moral epistemology of the culture of intimacy/community, we have virtually eliminated the dimension of worldliness from our lives.

When Hannah Arendt focuses our attention on the agonistic "sharing of words and deeds" in the public realm of the polis, then, she is not promoting hero worship or yearning for the days of communal self-representation. Rather, she is trying to present this vanished dimension of worldliness in its most intense theatrical and political form. That she is so often misread as succumbing to the lure of romantic subjectivity ("the performance of noble deeds by outstanding individuals") testifies to the accuracy of her diagnosis of modern alienation from the world. It may well be that *amor mundi* presupposes the "common sense" of *theatrum mundi*. It is this possibility, rather than any "nostalgic *Verfallsgeschicte,*" that makes Arendt (and Sennett) speak of the loss, destruction, or end of public life. The lesson they teach us is that politicization as such has no particular connection to the recovery of the public sphere. This is a hard and not particularly welcome lesson, but one we would do well to learn if we really care about the fate of the public realm.

## Notes

1. Hannah Arendt, *The Human Condition* (Chicago: University of Chicago Press, 1958).

2. Hannah Arendt, *On Revolution* (New York: Penguin Books, 1963); Hannah Arendt, *Crises of the Republic* (New York: Harcourt Brace Jovanovich, 1972).

3. Maurizio Passerin d'Entreves, *The Political Philosophy of Hannah Arendt* (New York: Routledge, 1994), 84. I note a similar tension in my own work: see Dana Villa, *Arendt and Heidegger: The Fate of the Political* (Princeton: Princeton University Press, 1996), 54–55.

4. D'Entreves, *Political Philosophy of Hannah Arendt,* 85.

5. Seyla Benhabib, "Models of Public Space: Hannah Arendt, the Liberal Tradition, and Jurgen Habermas," in *Habermas and the Public Sphere,* ed. Craig Calhoun (Cambridge: MIT Press, 1992), 77–78; Seyla Benhabib, *The Reluctant Modernism of Hannah Arendt* (Thousand Oaks, Calif.: Sage Publications, 1996), 125. Benhabib also cites the passage from d'Entreves.

6. Benhabib, "Models of Public Space," 78.

7. Benhabib, *Reluctant Modernism,* 125.

8. Benhabib, "Models of Public Space," 78, 79.

9. I have attempted a similar project, albeit from a very different direction, in my essay "Postmodernism and the Public Sphere," *American Political Science Review,* 86 (1992): 712–21.

10. Jürgen Habermas, *The Structural Transformation of the Public Realm,* trans. Thomas Berger (Cambridge: MIT Press, 1989); Richard Sennett, *The Fall of Public Man* (New York: W. W. Norton, 1976).

11. See Jean Cohen and Andrew Arato, *Civil Society and Political Theory* (Cambridge: MIT Press, 1992), chapter 4.

12. Hannah Arendt, "On Violence," in *Crises of the Republic,* 143.

13. Hannah Arendt, "On Humanity in Dark Times: Thoughts about Lessing," in Arendt, *Men in Dark Times* (New York: Harcourt Brace Jovanovich, 1968), 3–31.

14. The phenomenon Arendt is tracing in these pages, and in *Human Condition* generally, has much in common with the "subjectification of the real" addressed by Heidegger in such texts as "The Age of the World Picture." For a discussion of this relation, see Villa, *Arendt and Heidegger,* especially chapter 6.

15. See Arendt's discussion in her essay "The Crisis in Culture" in *Between Past and Future.*

16. This is an aspect of Arendt I did not see clearly enough when writing my study of the relation of her political theory to Heidegger's philosophy. It also makes me dubious of the definition of worldliness George Kateb gives in his fine study, *Hannah Arendt: Politics, Conscience, Evil* (Totowa, N.J.: Rowman and Allanheld, 1984), where he calls worldliness "a common commitment to the reality, beauty, and sufficiency of the culture or way of life that sustains political action, as well as a commitment to political action itself" (2). By so framing worldliness as that which contributes to the sustenance of political action, Kateb overly restricts the resonance of Arendt's term.

17. Hannah Arendt, "Ideology and Terror," in Arendt, *The Origins of Totalitarianism* (New York: Harcourt Brace Jovanovich, 1966). As Benhabib notes, even under totalitarian regimes, it is a bit misleading to say that the public realm is destroyed, or that worldliness becomes impossible. More often than not, there is a kind of migration of the public sphere, the creation of a kind of "underground" public (see Benhabib, *The Reluctant Modernism of Hannah Arendt,* 69–75).

18. Arendt, *On Revolution,* 74–75, 269.

19. Arendt, *Between Past and Future,* 153.

20. See, for example, Hanna Pitkin, "Justice: On Relating the Public and the Private," in *Hannah Arendt: Critical Essays,* ed. Louis Hinchman and Sandra Hinchman (Albany: State University of New York Press, 1994), 272.

21. See Arendt, *Human Condition,* 176–79.

22. For Arendt, this politics has no built-in stopping point: everyone, including the original unmaskers, can be revealed as hypocrites. Hence the origin of revolutionary terror and the phenomenon of the revolution devouring its own children.

23. In her essay "Civil Disobedience" in *Crises of the Republic,* Arendt gives a reading of Socrates at odds with the one outlined here. The later essay presents Socratic moral integrity as a kind of self-interest, to be contrasted with the worldliness of Machiavelli's civic republicanism. Machiavelli's cri de coeur—"I love my city more than my soul"—obviously stands in stark opposition to the lesson Socrates was trying to teach his fellow Athenians. All the more reason, then, to be surprised by the use she makes of this pair in attacking the emergent politics of authenticity in the French Revolution.

24. Arendt, *BPF,* 152, 151.

25. Kateb, *Hannah Arendt,* 12.

26. See Villa, *Arendt and Heidegger,* 90–92, for a discussion of this point.

27. It's fairly clear that Arendt is writing against the Rousseau-Schiller-Hegel-Marx sequence, which attempts to overcome the dichotomy of *homme* and *citoyen.*

28. As Benhabib puts it, "Narrative action is ubiquitous, for it is the stuff out of which all human social life . . . is constituted." Benhabib draws this point out more fully in chapter 4 of *Reluctant Modernism* (107–113). Cf. her earlier discussion of the Arendtian idea of plurality in Benhabib, *Critique, Norm, and Utopia* (New York: Columbia University Press, 1986), 241ff.

29. See Arendt, *Human Condition*, 38–49.

30. Habermas cites Guizot's classic formulation in this regard; see Habermas, *Structural Transformation*, 101.

31. Habermas of course criticizes Kant for his limitation of the public sphere to those who are property owners, and turns to Hegel and Marx in order to draw out the "contradictions" of the bourgeois public sphere (see *Structural Transformation*, 110, 117–29). Nevertheless, his enthusiasm for the Kantian formulation of legitimation through a public test of universalization is unmistakable, and forms the basis for much of his subsequent work on "deliberative democracy."

32. See, especially, the critique of rhetoric in Plato's *Gorgias*.

33. See Sennett, *Fall of Public Man*, 31–32, for how he distinguishes his approach from Habermas's.

34. Henry Fielding quoted in Sennett, *Fall of Public Man*, 109–110.

35. Sennett cites, amusingly, a French pamphlet from 1758 against a floating loan, in which the author's opponents are described as "Scaly monkeys, slaves of the dung hill on which they gibber" (*Fall of Public Man*, 100).

36. Sennett contrasts this attitude with the "trial by character" evident in both sides of the Dreyfus Affair, with particular attention to the rhetoric of Zola's *J'accuse* (*Fall of Public Man*, 240–51).

37. See, in this regard, Arendt, "The Crisis in Culture" in *Between Past and Future*.

38. Charles Larmore, *The Morals of Modernity* (New York: Cambridge University Press, 1996), 12.

39. See Habermas, *Structural Transformation*, 234–35. For a sympathetic critique of this strand of Habermas's thinking, see Thomas McCarthy's essay, "Practical Discourse: On the Relation of Morality to Politics" in *Habermas and the Public Sphere*, ed. Calhoun.

# 8

## Replacing the Body: An Approach
## to the Question of Digital Democracy

### Samuel Weber

Aristotle, it is well known, stated that philosophical thinking originated in wonder or surprise, *thaumazein*. Although the remarks I offer here are far too preliminary and tentative to make any claim at being philosophical, they do originate in a sense of wonderment. In an age increasingly dominated by electronic media, a certain *theatricality* seems not only to survive but even to reemerge with renewed force and transformed significance. From military or strategic thinking to the more rarefied realms of post-Hegelian philosophy, theatrical perspectives assume an importance that could be qualified as paradigmatic, if the notion of paradigmaticity were not itself called into question by the theatrical. For it seems as if the notion of theatricality emerges precisely in response to an uncertainty about the conditions under which anything can be exemplified or indicated, *alongside* something else (*para-deiknúnai*: to show side by side).

How, why, in what ways, and with what consequences has such a theatricality re-emerged *alongside* theory, strategy, politics, and the media? And what of a space that is determined by this *juxtaposition* and *contiguity*? These are the questions to which I want to begin to respond. And the emphasis, for me at least, has to be on the word *begin*.

I began by commenting not just on theatricality per se but on a "certain" theatricality. This qualification recalls the banal but all too forgettable fact that the same words do not always mean the same things. The history of "theatricality" is there, among other things, to remind us of this important truism.

To begin to understand what is at stake in the history of theatricality, it is helpful to turn to a text of Plato's—one that, significantly enough, does not concern theater as such but rather music, dance, and song—specifically, a passage from Book III of the *Nomoi*, generally translated as the *Laws*. The Athenian has just recalled that his countrymen were able to resist the onslaught of the Persians only because of two interrelated factors, both involving *fear*: first of all, their fear of the enemy and of the consequences of defeat; and second, "that other fear instilled by subjection to preexisting law," which allowed them to turn fear into disciplined resistance.[1] "The Athenian then, however, concludes his historical review with a rather enigmatic remark: Despite the obvious differences in their respective political histories, consisting above all in the fact that "they reduced the commonality to utter subjection, whereas we encouraged the multitude toward unqualified liberty," the Athenian nevertheless appears to deny that difference by asserting that "our fate has, in a way, been the same as that of the Persians" (699e). Megillus, one of his interlocutors, is understandably puzzled and asks for clarification. In response to this request, the Athenian, somewhat surprisingly, cites the history of music as exemplary for the degeneration of liberty into license and for the collapse of a state of law. Formerly, he remembers,

> our music was divided into several kinds and patterns . . . these and other types were definitely fixed, and it was not permissible to misuse one kind of melody for another. The competence to take cognizance of these rules, to pass verdicts in accord with them, and, in case of need, to penalize their infraction was not left, as it is today, to the catcalls and discordant outcries of the crowd, nor yet to the clapping of applauders; the educated made it their rule to hear the performances through in silence and for the boys, their attendants, and the rabble at large; there was the discipline of the official's rod to enforce order. Thus the bulk of the populace was content to submit to this strict control in such matters without venturing to pronounce judgment by its clamors.
>
> Afterward, in the course of time, an unmusical license set in with the appearance of poets who were men of native genius, but ignorant of what is right and legitimate in the realm of the Muses. Possessed by a frantic and unhallowed lust for pleasure, they contaminated laments with hymns and paeans with dithyrambs, actually imitated the strains of the flute on the harp, and created a universal confusion of forms. . . . By compositions of such a kind and discourse to the same effect, they naturally inspired the multitude with contempt of musical law, and a conceit of their own competence as judges. Thus our once silent audiences have found a voice, in the persuasion that they understand what is good and bad in art; the old sovereignty of the best, aristocracy, has given way to an evil "sovereignty of the audience," a theatrocracy *(theatrokratia)*. (700a–d)

"Theatrocracy," as the rule of the audience, is, for the Athenian, far worse than a democracy:

> If the consequences had been even a democracy, no great harm would have been done, so long as the democracy was confined to art, and composed of free men. But, as things are with us, music has given occasion to a general conceit of universal knowledge and contempt for law, and liberty has followed in their train. . . .

> So the next stage of the journey toward liberty will be refusal to submit to the magistrates, and on this will follow emancipation from the authority and correction of parents and elders; then . . . comes the effort to escape obedience to the law, and when that goal is all but reached, contempt for oaths, for the plighted word, and all religion. The spectacle of the Titanic nature of which our old legends speak is reenacted; man returns to the old condition of a hell of unending misery. (701a–c)

A democracy, although obviously not the political form of choice for the Athenian, would at least have respected certain "confines": it would have been "confined to art" and it would have confined its *demos* to "free men," thus excluding (but also presupposing, for its freedom) slaves. What is so frightening and fearful about the *theatrocracy*, by contrast, is that it appears to respect no such confines. And how, after all, can there be a *polis*, or anything *political*, without confinement? The previous divisions and organization of music into fixed genres and types is progressively dissolved by a practice that mixes genres and finally leaves no delimitation untouched or unquestioned. And if the driving force of such a development seems to be hedonistic, the fact that the "lust for pleasure" is qualified as being "frantic and unhallowed" suggests that here, no less than in its military struggles, the Athenians are driven as much by fear as by desire or, rather, that fear and desire are difficult to separate.[2] The theatrocratic usurpation of the rule of law is driven by desire and fear as much as by the search for pleasure. At the same time, this drive appears to be associated not by accident with an acoustical rather than a simply visual medium: it is song, dance, and music that break down most effectively the sense of propriety and the barriers that are its condition, giving the "silent" majority a voice and producing a hybrid music bordering upon noise. The emergence of the theatrocracy thus necessarily and essentially involves what today we would call *multimedia*. It is against this background that the reference to *theater* acquires a special significance. For the theater that is here referred to is not at all that of tragedy or comedy, and yet, it is still designated as theater. The *theatron*, as one knows, designated the place from which one sees, but if the notion of theatrocracy retains this reference to a specific place or site, it is perhaps above all to underscore how the stability of that site is being increasingly undermined. In other words, the theatrical dimension of theatrocracy would define itself in relation to the unsettling of all institutional stability, beginning with the organization of the space of the theater itself and of the *sights, visions (thea, theasthai, theorein)* that it seeks to situate. Indeed, the force and fascination of the theatrocracy suggests that the disruption of the theatrical site is marked by a resurgence of a *thauma*, a wonder that draws one's gaze irresistibly, without in turn fully submitting to its control.

This impression is strengthened by a second passage from the *Laws*, from Book VII. In it, the Athenian sketches another nightmare scenario, illustrative of the political hell into which Athens, in his eyes, has descended:

> A magistrate has just offered sacrifice in the name of the public when a choir, or rather a number of choirs, turn up, plant themselves not at a remote distance from the altar, but, often enough, in actual contact with it, and drown the solemn ceremony with sheer blasphemy, harrowing the feelings of their audience with their language, rhythms, and lugubrious strains, and the choir which is most successful in plunging the city which has just offered sacrifice into sudden tears is adjudged the victor. Surely our vote will be cast against such a practice. (800c–d)

Public rites are thus disturbed by mobile choirs who lack all respect for constituted authority and who show this lack of respect through their very movement, refusing to stay "at a remote distance from the altar but often enough" entering "in actual contact with it."[3] Through such proximity, the voices of these mobile masses can "drown" out the "solemn ceremony," just as the noise of the audience overwhelms the voices of reason and competence in the theatrocracy.

If we reflect on what elicits condemnation in these two passages, we come to the following two conclusions. *First*, theatrocracy, which replaces aristocracy and is not even democratic, is associated with the dissolution of universally valid laws and, with them, of the social space that those laws both presuppose and help maintain. The advent of theatrocracy subverts and perverts the unity of the theatron as a social and political site by introducing an irreducible and unpredictable heterogeneity, a multiplicity of perspectives and a cacophony of voices. This disruption of the theatron goes together, it seems, with a concomitant disruption of *theory,* which is to say here, of the ability of *knowledge* and *competence* to place and keep things in their proper place and thus to contribute to social stability. Furthermore, it should also not be overlooked that theatrocratic subversion originates not so much in the audience itself, which only follows the example set by the poets and composers, whose experimentation with established rules in their own artistic practice set the fateful precedent of undermining the stability of all rules and laws. Thus, the exclusion of poets and artists from the Republic finds a powerful vindication in this account of their responsibility for the rise of theatrocracy.

But it is only in the *second* passage, or scene—since, as the Athenian himself notes ironically, his own arguments are themselves often quite theatrical, despite (or because?) of his aversion to theatrical spectacle—that the subversive force of the theatrocracy actually reveals itself: it resides in its power to *move* and disrupt the consecrated and institutionalized boundaries of place, for instance, those that separate the "altar" from the public. Theatricality demonstrates its subversive power when it leaves the theatron and begins to wander. At that point, it is no longer confined by the prevailing rules of representation, aesthetic, social, or political; its vehicle is irreducibly plural and, even more, heterogeneous: not just "a choir" but rather "a number of choirs" that turn up in the most unexpected places, disorganizing official sacrifices, not so much through brute force as through the seductive fascination of their chants, "harrowing the feelings of their audience with their language, rhythms, and lugubrious strains" and thereby subverting the success of the sacrificial ceremony. They do not storm the altar from without, as it were, but simply sidle up *next* to it, in "actual contact with it," brushing up against it without overrunning it; *touching* it and touching all those who cannot resist the insidious force of their "lugubrious strains." The power of such choruses is seductive, contagious, hypnotic. It breaks down the borders of propriety and restraint in others and, at the same time, is difficult to control or to classify. For these "choirs" are composed neither of amateurs nor of professionals. And yet, since the need to which they respond seems undeniable, the Athenian is led to make the following, exasperated suggestion:

> If there is really any need for our citizens to listen to such doleful strains on some day which stands accursed in the calendar, surely it would be

more proper that a hired set of performers should be imported from abroad for the occasion to render them, like the hired minstrels who escort funerals with Carian music. The arrangement, I take it, would be equally in place in performances of the sort we are discussing. (800d–e)

This "arrangement would be equally in place in performances of the sort we are discussing" for the simple reason that the relation of employer to employed, the "hiring" of professional musicians, would impose a recognizable social role on the parties involved. Hired, professional musicians can be expected to know their place. And it is precisely this that is at issue in the theatrocracy: knowing one's place. Or rather, having a place that is stable enough that it can be known.

It is such stability of place and of placing that theatrocracy profoundly disturbs. In this respect, its perverse effects are only the culmination of Plato's worst fears concerning mimesis in general:[4]

The mimetic poet sets up in each individual soul a vicious constitution by fashioning phantoms far removed from reality, and by currying favor with the senseless element that cannot distinguish the greater from the less, but *calls the same thing now one, now the other.*

Imitation destroys the self-identity of the "same" and the fixity of values by implanting "in each individual soul" a propensity that confuses phantoms with reality and "calls the same thing now one, now the other." The exemplary space in which such a "vicious constitution" can unfold to the extreme is none other than the theater, in which mimesis is, as it were, (dis-)embodied in the audience:

And does not the fretful part of us present many and varied occasions for imitation, while the intelligent and temperate disposition, always remaining approximately the same, is neither easy to imitate nor to be understood when imitated, *especially by a nondescript mob assembled in the theater.* (604e, my italics)

Assembly in a theater is, for Plato, the sinister parody of the assemblage of citizens in the forum. For in the theater, everyone tends to forget their proper place. And, as already suggested, the fascinating power of theatrical mimesis cannot be explained simply by an appeal to "pleasure," not at least in any univocal sense of the word. For, as the words of Socrates just cited make clear, it is the "fretful part of us" rather than the "intelligent and temperate disposition" that presents the most "varied occasions for mimesis." The power of those errant choirs, we recall, was displayed in the irresistible appeal of their "lugubrious strains," which defied and defiled the official ceremonies of sacrifice. It is as much through the appeal to fear, care, and mourning as to simple "pleasure" that theatrocracy seduces and establishes its rule.

In the example of the choirs, the result was an audience moved to tears. But there is another aspect of mimesis gone wild that marks the power of that theatricality that Plato, himself the consummate dramaturge, knew only too well: the power of laughter.

> There are jests which you would be ashamed to make yourself, and yet on the comic stage, or indeed in private, when you hear them, you are greatly amused by them and are not all disgusted at their unseemliness . . . there is a principle in human nature which is disposed to raise a laugh, and this which you once restrained by reason, because you were afraid of being thought a buffoon, is now let out again; and having stimulated the risible faculty at the theatre, you are betrayed unconsciously to yourself into playing the comic poet at home. (*Republic*, X, 606)

Laughter "breaks out" and breaks down the barriers of propriety, transporting the stage from the theater to the home, undermining the division of public and private space, disturbing domestic tranquility. In the outbreak of laughter, articulate, reasonable discourse is progressively drowned out by the reiterative amplification of gesticulations that can, on occasion, suggest a body out of control.

It is precisely this link between theatricality and laughter that marks what I have referred to as the re-emergence of the theatrical paradigm. Were I to pursue this matter further here, I would try to sketch out the broad lines of this re-emergence, passing by way of texts such as Kierkegaard's *Repetition*, Nietzsche's *Birth of Tragedy*, Benjamin's *Origin of the German Mourning Play* and his essays on Brecht, and culminating, perhaps, in the writings of Artaud, or more recently, in Derrida's *Specters of Marx*. The list could obviously be extended at will. Instead, however, I will limit myself to extrapolating just one or two motifs from these texts in order to suggest how this re-emergence of theatricality might bear upon the cultural, political, physical, and metaphysical effects of what, for want of a more precise name, we call the "new media."

First, from Nietzsche's *Birth of Tragedy*:

At bottom the esthetic phenomenon is simple; one need only have the ability to see continually a living play and to live perpetually surrounded by hosts of spirits, and one is a poet; one need only feel the drive to alter oneself [sich selbst zu verwandeln] and to speak out of alien bodies and souls, and one is a dramatist.

Dionysian excitation is capable of communicating to a whole multitude this artistic power to feel oneself surrounded by such a host of spirits, with whom one knows oneself to be inwardly one. This process [Prozeß] of the tragic chorus is the originary dramatic phenomenon: seeing oneself altered before one's very eyes [sich selbst vor sich verwandelt zu sehen] and now acting, as though one had really entered into another body, another character. This process stands at the beginning of the development of drama. . . . Here already the individual gives itself up by entering into an alien nature. And what is more, this phenomenon arises epidemically: a whole crowd feels itself enchanted in this way.[5]

Nietzsche's account of the tragic chorus as dramatical *Urphänomen* both radicalizes and transforms the Platonic nightmare vision of the theatrical: contrary both to certain other statements of Nietzsche himself, in the *Birth of Tragedy,* and even more, to a certain reception of this text, the "dramatical phenomenon" described by Nietzsche never loses its theatrical dimension, which is to say, it never simply results in a mystical, ecstatic union with "the Lord and Master, Dionysos." The chorus, Nietzsche insists, does not cease to "look at" this God, even if the sole way he can be seen is not as a figure but rather as a split or doubled phenomenon, as a *process* of *Verwandlung*: metamorphosis, transformation, or as a movement. The German word used here by Nietzsche *(Verwandlung)* suggests, moreover, that this movement is not simply locomotive in character, does not simply involve a change of place. The root of Verwandlung is *wandeln,* which comes from the verb for *turning, wenden,* in turn related to *winden,* to wind, also in the sense of to twist, coil, or twine. In short, the movement Nietzsche is alluding to is more like a twisting and turning, a spasm or a tick, than a goal-directed linear and continuous process. At the same time, throughout the *Birth of Tragedy,* Nietzsche never ceases to insist on the inseparability of the Dionysian from the Apollonian, which is why this text is concerned ultimately more with theater than with religion. The "visionary" dimension of the theatron is conserved but also altered, and it is altered precisely insofar as the nature of its *site* (in the sense of *situs,* but also its *sight*) is changed. Instead of functioning as a closed container of equally self-contained bodies,[6] the theatrical site splits, stretches, twists, and turns into a space of alteration and oscillation, of Verwandlung. It is the space of a body that no longer takes its orders from the soul.

One consequence of this state of affairs is that the relation of life and death is no longer construed according to the logic of simple opposition. When Nietzsche writes that the "individual" gives itself up to this movement of alteration both by entering into alien bodies and souls and at the same time by *seeing* itself thus splitting apart, he describes a reflexive movement that does not come full circle. In the gap opened by such noncircular reflexivity, the *scope* of life and death is altered. For what ensues is not just a plurality of individuals but the fracturing of each individual. And in the space of this irreducible divisibility of the "individual," no simple "collection" or "collective" can take place. This transforms the relation of the living to the dead by disrupting the place of each. The "lively play" to which Nietzsche refers (in the passage just cited) therefore requires an observer who lives "surrounded by a host of spirits." The perspective from which this spectacle must be seen is thus that of not just an irreducible plurality, of a "host," but of an irreducible spectrality. As a "host of spirits," the individual does not merely cease to exist: it exists, but dividually, divided between spectator and actor, alien and identical, entering into an alien body and soul, on the one hand, and remaining sufficiently detached to see itself in the process. The individual thus altered is both here and there, and yet neither simply here nor there, simply itself or simply other. It is the movement of a certain errancy and oscillation, and it is *this* that makes it something like the *ghost of itself,* lacking an authentic place or a proper body.

Such traits begin to indicate just how and why a certain theatricality could be compatible with the spread of contemporary, electronic media. As Marshall McLuhan has observed, "Nothing can be further from the spirit of the new technology than 'a place for everything and everything in its place.'" This phrase served as a motto for a book published in 1985 that bore the telling title *No Sense of Place.* In it, Joshua Meyrowitz sought to investigate "the impact of electronic media on social behavior" by interpreting that "impact" in terms of the changing sense of place. Since then, it has become more or less accepted to speak of the "delocalizing" effects of electronic media. But the notion of "delocalization" tells only part of the story, and taken by itself it can be highly misleading. For what is at stake in the changes being brought about by the spread of the new media, and in particular by their electronic varieties, involves not just a "delocalization" of "*physical* settings: places, rooms, buildings and so forth," as Meyrowitz wrote in the preface to his book[7] but rather a change in the very structure and function of such settings. The passages we have been reading, from Plato and Nietzsche, remind us of what is not any less decisive for being evident: namely, that there can be no movement of *delocalization* without an accompanying *relocalization*. And moreover, that the two need not be construed as being simply symmetrical: what results from the self-abandonment of the individual as described by Nietzsche is not simply another individual, in the sense of an alter ego. What ensues is a dynamic spectacle that both offers itself to sight while at the same time eluding any simply perceptual grasp. This is why Nietzsche, in the text we have quoted, stresses the traversing of limits and frontiers rather than the emergence of a new figure, be it an alien one: the individual sees itself "*as though* it had *entered* into a foreign body and character." In short, the spectacle is one not just of a movement from one place or body to another but of a splitting, a fracture whose only proper place seems to be that of the interval or . . . of the *interruption*.

A similar insight informs the approach of Walter Benjamin to theater. Although it is in his book-length study, *Origins of the German Mourning Play*, that Benjamin elaborates most extensively the relation between theatricality and modernity, here I want instead to discuss very briefly a later and shorter text that seeks to respond to the question, "What is epic theater?" Brecht's epic theater offers Benjamin a point of departure for reflections on the general situation of theatricality in the twentieth century:

> What is at stake today in the theater can be more precisely determined with respect to the stage than with respect to the drama. It involves the filling-in *[Verschüttung]* of the orchestra pit. The chasm which separates the players from the audience *[Publikum]* like the dead from the living, this chasm, whose silence in the play heightens the sublimity . . . this chasm, which among all the elements of the stage most indelibly bears the traces of its sacred origin [this chasm] has lost its function. . . . The stage is still elevated, but it no longer rises out of fathomless depths; it has become a podium. This is the podium upon which one must settle *[sich einzurichten]*.[8]

What begins as apparently a fairly familiar gesture of defining theater in terms of what today would be called a level playing field—one in which the aesthetic sublimity of fiction is brought down to earth—reveals itself to be in the Nietzschean tradition, not that of Dionysian ecstasy but that which confounds the living with the dead. The level playing field that is established by the "filling in" of the orchestra pit paradoxically puts the living on almost the same level as the dead. To reduce the bottomless pit separating players from audience, stage from orchestra, was, for Benjamin (if not for Brecht) not so much to create a "Living Theater" as what Tadeusz Kantor years later was to call a "Theater of the Dead."

The primary virtue of Benjamin's text, in our context at least, is that it begins to "flesh out" just how theatrical spectrality can be concretely construed. At the center of Benjamin's response to the question "What is Epic Theater?" is the notion of *gesture*. Epic Theater, Benjamin asserts, is above all *gestural* theater. Or rather, it is a theater in which gestures have been made *citable*. *Citable*, and not just "quotable," as we read in the published English translation. Even in English, to "cite" is not simply the same as to "quote." And this is all the more the case in German, where even today the verb *zitieren* still carries its etymological resonance of *citare*, to set in movement. In English, this resonance is buried in verbs such as "incite" and "excite." And yet movement is only half the story. For in both German and English, "to cite" has yet another meaning that is crucial for Benjamin. *To cite* means not simply to set something in movement but also—as American drivers know only too well—*to arrest* movement. As in the sense, of course, of *receiving a summons* to appear before a tribunal in order to account for an excess of speed.

In short, for Benjamin, the "stage" in respect to which epic theater and theater in general, must be situated today, is determined as the site *(situs)* and as sight but also and above as a space of citable gestures. Why, however, this emphasis on *citation* and why, precisely, *gesture*?

Concerning the first part of this question, Benjamin's response brings together the two dimensions of *citation*, that of inciting and arresting, by retracing their common origin to the fact that "the basis of citation" in general is "interruption." Citation, then, involves not simply a setting-into-motion or a setting-to-rest, but a disruption, a detachment, a dislocation and a relocation from which the violence of a certain legality is never entirely absent. And "interruption," Benjamin reminds his readers, "is one of the fundamental procedures through which form is given" (536). In other words, if we have reason to regard "form" as the constitutive category of modern aesthetics, then Benjamin here is indicating that the origin of the work of art, its very "formation," is based not so much on a model of creativity or construction, much less on one of expressivity, but rather on a process of *separation,* by which an intentional, teleological movement—call it a "plot"—is arrested, dislocated, and reconfigured. Reconfigured as what? Precisely as *gesture.*

Gesture is the category that replaces the aesthetic concept of *form* in Benjamin's rethinking of theatricality. Like the notion of form, that of gesture for Benjamin has as one of its essential attributes that of being "fixed" and "delimited":

> In contrast to the actions and undertakings of people [gestures have] a definable *[fixierbaren]* beginning and a definable end. This strict, frame-like closure of every element in an attitude *[Haltung],* which however as a whole is caught up in the living flux, is even one of the basic dialectical phenomena of the gesture. From this results an important conclusion: we obtain gestures all the more, the more frequently we interrupt someone in the process of acting *[einen Handelnden].* (521)

A gesture, then, is a bodily movement that interrupts and suspends the intentional (teleological) narrative progression toward a meaningful goal, thus opening up a different kind of space in which an incommensurable singularity can emerge. As the site of a citation, this place is never closed or self-contained, since it must inevitably refer to another place, an elsewhere or alibi, the place from which it has come and which remains to be discovered in a future altered state. This is why the gestural movement of Epic Theater in re-citing the past simultaneously points forward toward a future that might be otherwise. Brecht's theater, Benjamin notes, places its accent not on great decisions, situated along the expected lines of perspective *(Fluchtlinien der Erwartung),* but rather on the incommensurable, the singular. "It can happen that way, but it can also happen entirely differently *[ganz anders].* . . . This is the basic attitude of anyone who writes for the epic theater. He relates to the story the way the ballet teacher does to his pupils. His primary concern is to loosen her joints to the limit of the possible" (525).

The essence of gesture, then, is not its goal but the joints that make all bodily movement possible while at the same time also making possible their interruption, for instance through loss of coordination. To experience the body, not simply as a continuous medium or entity, but as the possibility of an imperfect machine, as the potential disjunction of its constitutive members, is what Benjamin seems to be pointing to in and through Brecht's notion of "citable gesture": or, as it might also be translated, of "gesture on the move."

For the function of the theatrical in an age of electronic media is above all to raise precisely the question of the site (and the sight) of the body—or rather, of bodies, for there are more than one, more than one kind, and above all, more than one way of construing those bodies. To speak of *the* body, in the singular, gendered or not, almost inevitably entails the more or less surreptitious privileging of the human body over all other kinds. To emphasize the citability of gesture as determining mechanism of theatricality, by contrast, is to call attention to the body as something other than an organic whole, as something other than a container of the soul, as something other than what today is so often and so confidently referred to as "embodiment" (the correlative of "empowerment"). It is precisely the self-evidence of this "in" or "em-" that the notion of theatricality as citable gesture calls into question. And in so doing, such theatricality calls into question one of the chief axioms of Western modernity: that of the immanence of subject, object, and the world they are held to constitute. This can be illustrated, in conclusion, by going back to one of the earliest discussions of "digitality," long before the age of binary computation. In his discussion of place and its relation to the body, in Book IV of the *Physics,* Aristotle distinguishes the way place can be said to "contain" bodies from the way these in turn "contain" their organs:

> The next step we must take is to see in how many ways one thing is said to be *in* another. In one way, as a finger is in a hand, and generally a part in a whole. In another way, as a whole is in its parts; for there is no whole over and above the parts. . . . Again, as the affairs of Greece are in the King, and generally events are in their primary motive agent. . . . And most properly of all, as something is in a vessel, and generally in a place.[9]

What happens, however, when the function of the finger is no longer determined primarily through the fact that it is located "in a hand" as "generally a part" is located "in a whole"? What happens then to the "in," the hand, and the body? It is precisely the possibility of such dismemberment that fascinated Benjamin in the new media and their technologies, just as its "uncanny" and "automatic" aspects fascinated Freud. If Aristotle regarded the relation of hand and finger as that of whole to part, then what Freud discovered to be profoundly "uncanny" was the separation or disjunction of that relationship. What could be more familiar than the fingers of a hand? Unless those fingers, or that hand, no longer form a whole, over and above its individual members. It is in this context that the notion of "digitalization" reveals its curiously ambivalent character. For the "digit" is, on the one hand, a model of discreteness: the clearly defined unit of the finger, serving as model for the no less clearly defined and discrete numerical unit. And yet, the numerical unit does not necessarily relate to the combinations it constitutes as does a part to a whole. A "digit" does not relate to a numerical operation as does a part to a whole. It is a relational element in a combinatorial process. In the case of computers, that relation is one of binary opposition: 0s and 1s, shorted and opened circuits, positive and negative, each only "meaningful" as the other of the other. It is this combination of otherness that constitutes the binary relation that exemplifies "digitalization" in computers. There is no intrinsic limit to the combinatorial sequences that constitute such digitalization. Just as there is no intrinsic limit to the combination of letters and words and their sequencing, their syntax, in language. This lack of intrinsic quality is what excludes the relation of part to whole that Aristotle saw as defining the bodily organ, the "finger" and the "hand." And a fortiori, the body itself as the exemplary occupant of that "vessel" known as "place."

Nevertheless, all of those bodily organs have always had divergent functions, which anticipate and reflect the tension between organic whole and combinatorial series. The hand is the organ of grasping, of appropriation, of perception and conception, of seizing and of controlling. In this, it relies upon the fingers doing its bidding. The fingers must be subordinate to the intention embodied in the hand. And yet, the finger is also discrete, separate from the hand, not merely its integral part. If it is required for all grasping, it can also engage in a very different kind of contact: that of touching, for instance, or that of pointing. Pointing can be a means of anticipating the seizure and appropriation of what is being pointed at or out, but it can also entail a movement away from the familiarity and control of the hand, and the body. In pointing, the finger can move the body elsewhere. And a finger can be recognized as a finger, even and perhaps especially when it is severed from the hand, from the body. It still remains discrete. Something quite similar is happening to the sense of body, and the notion of identity that it supports, with the spread of "digitalization."

What is "digitalized" points away from itself, is "allegorical" in the sense given the term by Benjamin: it signifies something radically other than what it represents. Visual, verbal, acoustic "qualities," the objects of "sense impressions," are produced by sequences of relations that have no intrinsic relation to anything other than simplest form of relationality itself: that of binary opposition. The most familiar manifestation of human identity, the individual human body, comes therefore to be regarded with increasing suspicion and even fear. Popular films, from *Invasion of the Body Snatchers* to *Alien* to the series of *Terminators*, bear witness to this becoming-uncanny of the most familiar, the body. And this in turn is not without the most profound political ramifications. Ever since the 18th century, at least, the "body politic" has been more or less explicitly the informing metaphor for the political subject, whether construed as "nation," as "people" or as "class." A "democracy" is only conceivable insofar as the demos—the people—is presupposed, which means presupposed as the founding basis of the unity of the political community. How can a people "rule," be democratic, it if is not in principle unified and whole? And yet, precisely these notions of unity and wholeness have been progressively undermined by the spread of what I have been describing here as "digitalization," in turn tied to the spread of a certain type of "mediality."

The issue, then, of whether or not, or to what extent, such "digitalization" is compatible with the notion of "democracy" must, I would argue, be treated at the very least as an open question. The search for principles of unity and foundations results today in the spread of religious and ethnic "fundamentalisms," which in French is designated by the significant term "intégrismes." The spread of media that subvert the immanence and integrity of place and of body, together with the rise of transnational centers of power and wealth, produce as reaction-formations the resurgence of claims to transcendent principles of identity: religious, ethnic, racial. These in turn draw much of their power from their ostensible ability to reinstate as arbiter a certain level of sense-experience: the perception of facial or bodily characteristics (real or imagined) and the possession of shared beliefs. The relativization of place, domestic, public, and political, through the electronic media, brings forth the reactive response of an affirmation of place, especially when "transcendentalized" through appeals to more or less distant historical or religious histories and traditions.

Against this reactive reaffirmation of transcendental schemes of identity and of identification, which both mirror the subversion of immanence involved in the electronic media and at the same time seek to extract from it the fantasy of reappropriation, the resurgence of theatrical motifs, it not of theatrocracy, underscores the irreducible and yet problematic status of a place whose entire determination depends upon its relation to other places and times, and to alterity tout court. Such a place is nothing other than what has long been known as a scene. And it is this that distinguishes theatricality from theatrocracy. There can be no "rule of the theatron" where every place is seen as a scene that exceeds all possible containment. A scene, unlike a place, and unlike the bodies that occupy it, is not simply a vessel, if by vessel we mean a self-contained container. The scene situates but without containing. In this, it is eminently mediatic. But is also involves the most profound and far-reaching challenge to all forms of "rule": to every -cracy, be it theatrocracy or be it democracy.

To challenge rule, however, is in no way to eliminate it as a possibility. On the contrary: to the extent that the economic, political, and cultural dimensions of contemporary social life are organized and informed by the value of appropriation, and hence of identity, the theatrical-mediatic challenge to all forms of rule can easily provoke the most desperate efforts to reinstate such forms. This is the danger that ever more palpably threatens political life today, in an age when the loudest appeals to a New Order bring intolerable disorder in their wake, and when transnational geopolitical Unions appear increasingly designed as instruments of the most self-destructive forms of social disintegration.

## Notes

1. Book III, lines 700a–d, from Plato, *Laws,* trans. A. E. Taylor (Princeton: Princeton University Press, 1973).

2. See Socrates' discussion of "pure and impure pleasures" in the *Philebus,* 52c and passim.

3. One is reminded of Walter Benjamin's account of the tendency of the modern "masses" to break down distance in "bringing closer" all things (*Das Kunstwerk,* GS I.2, p. 479).

4. Plato, *Republic,* Book X, lines 605b–c (my italics), in *op. cit.,* trans. Paul Shorey.

5. Friedrich Nietzsche, *Das Geburt der Tragödie,* chapter 8, in M. Montinari and G. Colli, eds., *Werke: Kritische Gesammt Ausgabe* (Berlin: Gruyter) 196ff, vol. III$_1$, pp. 56–57.

6. "The place of a thing is the innermost motionless boundary of what contains it. . . . If then a body has another body outside it and containing it, it is in place" (Book IV, line 212a, from Aristotle, *Physics,* trans. R. P. Hardie and R. K. Gaye, in

Jonathan Barnes, ed., *Aristotle: Complete Works* (Princeton: Princeton University Press, 1984).

7. Joshua Meyrowitz, *No Sense of Place* (New York: Oxford University Press, 1985), ix.

8. Walter Benjamin, *Gesammelte Schriften*, volume 2, part 2, sections 519–39, unter Mitwirkung von Theodor W. Adorno und Gershom Scholem hrsg. von Rolf Tiedemann und Hermann Schweppen (Frankfurt am Main: Suhrkamp, 1972); also in *Illuminations*, ed. Hannah Arendt, trans. Harry Zohn (New York: Harcourt, Brace and World, 1968), 154, translation modified.

9. Lines 210a, 14–25, from Aristotle, *Physics,* in *Complete Works,* ed. Barnes.

## 9

# Writing Property and Power

**Anne Norton**

Graffiti is the inscription of property and power on the walls of the city of the senses. One experiences the city through the senses. It is on the dimensions of sight and sound and touch that the boundaries of the city are marked. As Heidegger reminds us, it is through the marking of boundaries that something is called into being.

There is a politics of sensation in the city of the senses. Touch is one dimension on which the boundaries of the city are marked. Through touch we feel the limits of contact in the city. The city is a place of great physical intimacy. Contact is inevitable. We are reminded of the boundaries of our bodies in the press of people on the streets and on subways. We are obliged to think of whom we must touch and whom we cannot touch. We are obliged to think of how we must touch, and when. We must shake hands, we must not step on other people's feet. We may pat a friend on the back, we may not pat a stranger on the ass. We move our bodies carefully, so that we touch those we press against only in a certain, acceptable way.

The city is shaped on the plane of sound as well. Sound is given boundaries. There will be sound. That sound is another dimension of the shape of the city. Sound must be kept within bounds. It cannot become too loud, or too pervasive. The boundaries of that sound mark the zones of the city: center and periphery, areas of industry and areas of commerce. Sound marks day and night, times of work and times of leisure. We hear the city we are in. In Cairo or Tunis we hear the call to prayer flow through the city. We can hear the city in the style of the muezzin. We hear the sounds of popular preachers on the street and on cassette and pop songs with the refrain "Muhammed is our prophet." We also hear the syncretic, multilingual pop of the transvestite Israeli Dana International and the secular mockery of the call to prayer, "allahu snackbar."

In Europe (and America), there is the sound of church bells and silence: the absence of the call to prayer.

The city is shaped and reshaped in the explosion of sound and then the silencing of boom boxes on city buses.

The city is shaped on the plane of sound by the sounds we can't hear and the sounds we must: the ubiquitous muzak of mall and grocery and medical offices, the advertising message while we are put on hold.

Whether they are spoken or silent, there are always the questions: Who can be heard? Who is heard? How do these sounds mark the city? To whom does the city we hear belong? These sounds declare "this city is Muslim," "this city is Christian." Sounds are commanded: "You must hear the muzak the store chooses." Sounds are forbidden: you cannot hear the rap your fellow traveler chooses. Sounds declare who holds power in the city, and exclusions echo in the silence.

The sense most recognized as a dimension of power and authority is the sense of sight. We are accustomed, we scholars we citizens, to the government of the visible. We are accustomed to reading the inscriptions of authority on the city. There are flags and seals, the familiar grandeur of city hall, the courthouse, and the museums. In these we see the grandeur of the state and know ourselves to be within its power. We see, too, whose streets are cleared and whose are left obstructed. We can read in those cleared streets the avenues of power and access to power. We see who is permitted to be visible in the city and who must be concealed.

We know—from Foucault and Certeau, Lefebvre and Virilio—if we did not know it from our own experience of the ordinary, that sight is power. The government of sight entails the power of concealment, to determine what is invisible to us, and the power of commanding the gaze. The government of sight determines what we must see and what we cannot see. The reach of power does not end here. Sight is governed not only through the eye but through the mouth. There are things we see but are instructed not to notice or, if we notice them, not to acknowledge. There are sights we cannot speak of and sights we are commanded to see only in a certain way. In this way, zones of the plane of sight are fenced off from critique, challenge, and debate.

Look at graffiti with these in mind. Who governs the visible? Who is permitted to command our gaze?

Look first at what we must see. Perhaps we should look first at what we can. For those on the ground, the city may be a set of narrow canyons, fenced in by buildings to which they are denied entrance.

There is always the question, as Patricia Williams has observed, of who can see the inside of the shops they pass. This holds for office buildings as well. Those who enter, if they merit an office, or merely a windowed cubicle, may see the city stretched before them. Here, as elsewhere in the city of the senses, sensory access suggests political access. Zoning regulations limit what one can see. Private enterprise is more powerful. Architectural works like la Sagrada Familia, the Centre Pompidou, and Bilbao impose themselves equally on the awed and the indifferent, the reverent and the irritated. So, too, do works of public art. The controversy over Richard Serra's work and the Vietnam War Memorial speak to the question of what must be seen. Yet we are imposed upon more pervasively and less intrusively by the ordinary buildings, sidewalks and roads, of urban architecture. Corporate advertising is more obtrusive. We must see billboards, ads on buses, buses wholly painted with ads, advertising in store windows, on kiosks. We cannot escape these sights. We must see the visual assertions of capitalism, whether we wish to or not. We should not see the inscriptions of graffiti artists and taggers. One might, standing outside city hall, wonder which effects the greatest imposition. There on a building across the way is a mural seven stories tall of a woman shooting a basket and wearing Nike's insignia. As a headline in the *Philadelphia Inquirer* reported, "City never signed off on mural."[1] The mural had gone up without permits from the department of licenses and inspection and the nominally requisite approval from the arts commission. There was, the *Inquirer* noted, "No evidence of any application for a permit." Three years later, the mural remains.

Sight is governed in the city of the senses, but it is not governed by the government. It is not, in fact, seen as a political matter at all. Politics does, of course, intervene through zoning requirements and obscenity laws, but much of the governance of sight remains concealed, insulated from politics and from critique. It rests in the hands of architects and technocrats. These hidden governors of sight determine the forms of the buildings we walk past, the buildings we work in, and the buildings we inhabit. Technology determines not only the shape of the computer screen and the form of the telephone but also the placement of lines and cables . . . and the color the city has at night. We are obliged to live (without much reflection or objection) within the limits these invisible governors draw around us. We must see what they build. We must see their walls. And we ought not to write on them. Not as graffitti artists, nor as academics.

The architects and technocrats who fashion the city are not the only people who impose themselves on our eyes. Corporate advertising is ubiquitous, insistent, and naturalized. It is identified not as political speech but as "economic speech," and this identification shields it from political critique. In the economic zone of the visual there is no free speech at all. There is, however, all the speech money can buy. Normally, that speech echoes in the silence of opposing speech. All we hear is the speech of the billboard and the display window. In all this din, rarely is there objection or dissent.

There are practical differences between corporate speech and the speech of the graffiti artist. One is expensive, one is free. One is legal, one is a crime. One may be seen as an advertisement, an act of advertising creativity, or an informative convenience. The other must be seen in a certain way. We must not see graffiti responses as part of a political debate. We must see these as defacement of property rather than as public responses to public speeches.

Conceptions of property govern—and are further empowered by—the government of sight in the city of the senses. The privileging of property makes the *Show Girls* poster a movie advertisement on a billboard rather than a piece of pornography or a public declaration on the bodies of women. The Hooters billboard is an advertisement. The Hooters restaurant sign identifies a business. These are property properly paid for, not political texts or statements on women. Stores, signs, and billboards command our gaze in the city of the senses. We must see them, and we must see them as saying only what they purport to say. We must not see them as subject to debate.

This is an instance of the power of money, certainly, but it is also an instance of power *as* money. The advertising image has become currency. Like money, it must be taken for what it purports to be. As with money, defacing it is illegal. As with money, the status of the image as the sign of property and value evacuates/silences all the other things it says and stands for. In such signs the signifier cannot be spoken of, only the signified can be acknowledged.

Look then, to what we should not see and may not speak of. One may look at graffiti in many ways. In most, three dimensions are present: aesthetics, property, and speech.

The aesthetic opposition to graffiti argues that graffitti is ugly, and we should erase it. The sleek modernism of the subway car is marred by the colorful inscriptions on its corrugated exterior. The city wall is "defaced" by spray-painted tags. Here, graffiti is an aesthetic offense, marring the beauty of the city. Cleaning it up is tantamount to picking up litter. The eye speaks against this.

More telling testimony to the absence of aesthetic criteria are the murals of the antigraffiti network. Rarely does one see a piece of graffiti so lacking in aesthetic merit as these. In my town, Philadelphia, the antigraffiti network has contributed several murals. These tend to follow two aesthetic schools. In the tradition of socialist realism, one set of murals is relentlessly hortatory and didactic. Another school comprises murals painted by schoolchildren. Apparently, all things done by children are beautiful by definition. To the eye, however, these are grim indeed, the people ill-proportioned, the colors badly chosen, the subjects hackneyed and saccharine. Despite this license, one tends to sympathize with the children. They are, after all, under some duress. They are not generally permitted to decide what they will paint. They are more commonly obliged to "paint by numbers" some icon of childish sentiment: baby animals or blooming flowers. The antigraffiti network has been vigorous in opposing certain subjects: guns, for example. It has also opposed certain styles identified with dissident subcultures. The children, and other participants in mural painting, are directed away from styles that might themselves be mistaken for graffiti or that might lead the confused to take graffiti for art.

Aesthetics is, however, no longer commonly given as the reason for opposing graffiti. Opponents of graffiti frequently acknowledge the beauty of certain compositions. They object to graffiti not on aesthetic grounds but on semiotic ones, showing us once again that in the city the image serves as currency. They oppose not the graffiti but what the presence of graffiti signifies.

There are also those who claim to object only to the location of the work, not its content. In this view, some graffiti is beautiful, but all graffiti defaces.

The categorization of graffiti as defacement reveals a larger aesthetic that finds graffiti objectionable. This is an aesthetic position linked to a political one. In it we see why graffiti offends not only tradition but modernity. Graffiti not only spoils the patina of federal-era brickwork, it also mars the pristine surfaces and (at least nominally) functional forms of the subway car and the overpass. Contrary to one's first expectations, graffiti is not readily assimilated within an industrial aesthetic.

One might imagine that liberal modernism would delight in graffiti. It is, after all, the work of an individual. The defiant individuality of the composition—in conception, execution, and content—confirms the modernist myth of the singular artist. This figure, whose creativity knows no bounds, who is unfettered by convention, transgressive in the pursuit of artistic expression, not only manifests the modernist myth of the artist, he (it is always he) might also be taken for an icon of liberal individualism.

The graffiti artist and the tagger would seem exemplars of this myth. Each is an avatar of the singular individual acting autonomously. His agency is manifest; he is willful. His indifference to law and convention prove his freedom, like Picasso or Gauguin. He inscribes that will and that authority on nature and culture alike.

That was, after all, how Kilroy was received. Chaka, whose inscriptive interventions—on the courthouse wall as well as the freeway overpass—testified to ingenuity, daring, and perhaps a similar collective constitution, was not.

Why is Kilroy accepted, even idolized? Why isn't Chaka? Why does the myth fail to accommodate Wahid or Superman or Eros? There is a simple answer to this question. If it is not the final answer, it is nevertheless one worth attending to: race matters. Kilroy was white. An omnipresent white Everyman can reassure. An omnipresent Chicano or black man is too often read as a sign of omnipresent danger.

There is also the question of authority on the plane of nationalism. Writing on walls in Europe may seem to advance state and nation. Kilroy's inscriptions evoked an American omnipresence. The identification of that presence with an unknown common soldier or civilian accords with the American desire to present American dominion as democratic, peaceable, and unthreatening. The presence within American boundaries of a similarly faceless, unknown, and ubiquitous presence is less acceptable.

Graffiti calls forth all the anxieties of liberal modernity. The tension between property rights and the right to free speech is clear enough when the striker writes on the factory wall. The condemnation of such graffiti points out the radical disparity of power between capitalists and workers, and reveals how the seemingly neutral categories of art and speech and property reinforce the hierarchical relation of those who own and those who labor. Graffiti also makes it apparent that those with more property may also have more speech. It raises difficult questions about freedom of speech as well.

There are graffiti I have loved. The alterations made by a passing satiric hand on billboards and advertisements are, to me, reassurances of popular suspicion and resistance. I loved the inscription "Dream

Fast," written many feet high in thin red lines on a grey wall in Chicago. I do not find all graffiti so appealing. White supremacist graffiti, misogynist graffiti offend me. The efflorescence of fundamentalist graffiti on southwestern campuses, should I see it, would make me feel distant and alienated. Because it evokes an indeterminate, perhaps a very large, presence, graffiti is particularly able to inspire a sense of alienation and unease, even where its content is inoffensive.

Whatever it is, graffiti is not neutral. It cannot present itself as universal. It is never for everyone. It has none of the neutrality that buildings claim in the name of form or function.

Liberals and modernists don't like graffiti for much the same reasons they don't like postmodernism. Graffiti argues that form and function are not adequate in themselves. These random ornamental inscriptions actively contend that the elegant white wall and the architectural form can be improved by ornament: ornament that is hybrid and syncretic, that borrows from pop culture. In this respect, graffiti belongs to the postmodernist aesthetic of Michael Graves and Ettore Sottsass. One might regard it as the visual equivalent of rap: hybrid, syncretic, and aggressive. Like rap, it uses icons of pop culture and mass-marketed commodities. As in rap, with its use of sampling, the assertive self-presentation of the author is surrounded by techniques and quotations that call that authority into question.

Graffiti challenges the conception of the liberal subject and the text. It blurs the distinction between the individual and the collective. It extends, indeterminately, the distance between the name and what it names. It obliges us to notice layers of reference. My favorite Philadelphia tagger is Eros, whose tag marked the rail line all the way from my house to the airport. Eros seemed to me to be an admirable name for a tagger, for as Plato wrote, Eros was born of the union of poverty and resource.

Graffiti is excessive. There is always something added, something extra. Often, the extra is race. That extra, that excess works as a supplement in the Derridean sense. Eros becomes not Eros, a single tagger, but the ungovernable black underclass. And as with the supplement that adds only to replace, the addition of Eros's tag doesn't add beauty or value to the wall on which it is written; rather, it replaces its value with a lower denomination.

The opponents of graffitti argue that it may be beautiful, it may be art, it may be speech, but that whatever it is, graffitti lowers property values. And, they would ask, "Would I want it on my house?"

The canonical answer to this question is given by Vachel Lindsay in the poem "Factory Windows": "Factory windows are always broken/ Other windows are left alone/ No one throws through the chapel window/ The bitter, sharp, derisive stone."

It is in this question of value that the relation of graffiti to property and power becomes suspect. Graffiti lowers property values. Where? On abandoned buildings? In railyards and subway tunnels? On tenements? On the abandoned worksites and factories that litter the inner city? I think not. It is not the graffiti but the abandonment that lowers property values. Within its familiar urban context, graffiti inscribes a trenchant and straightforward text on the underlying issue of economic power. The firms that leave the city (after tax abatements and other forms of corporate subsidies) are unquestionably "lowering property values." The McDonald's or the Burger King or the other strip-mall denizens that open in formerly upscale residential areas may lower property values as well. We assume that graffiti does the same. Notice, however, that the activity that does the most harm, that most lowers property values, is the least condemned and the least policed. In this suspect evaluation, class and race may be seen moving what is nominally an issue of market economics and property rights.

The construction of graffiti as an urban issue of the first importance is commonplace now. A *Philadelphia Inquirer* headline from March 6, 1997, in the discourse of war characteristically employed by the antigraffiti forces, declared, "Graffiti Gateway Targeted."[2] The subhead read, "The scrawl along the Amtrak lines is visible to nearly all who enter the city. Not for long." The expanse of wall along the Schuykill Expressway was, the reporter claimed, "Philadelphia's most visible 'rep wall'—the place where graffitti writers go to make their names—and it could soon lose its reputation." City officials hoped to replace the graffiti with "the city's biggest mural." "But the search for roughly $50,000 for the mural has so far come up short." The report, like Philadelphia's "war against graffiti," is full of ironies. Perhaps the most profound irony is the curious status of graffiti in a city whose economy is heavily dependent on tourism and whose reputation is heavily dependent on the arts. Graffiti is not only popular with the American underclass, with art critics and academics, it is also popular with European tourists. As the *New York Times* reported, viewing graffiti is a necessary component of the "American tour" for Europeans, and the creation of graffiti is an American activity on a par with cattle drives and Disneyland. "Visiting the city specifically to 'bomb' it has become a popular pastime for a few Spanish, French, Belgian and German tourists."[3] Graffiti belongs, however, not to New York but to Philadelphia. The distinctive lettering of postwar graffiti entered New York through an artist who readily acknowledged a Philadelphia graffiti writer as his source and teacher. Philadelphia is thus not only the site of an internationally lauded American art form, it is also the site of its continuing practice and evolution. The popularity of graffiti in quarters given to tourism should prompt a city dependent on tourism to reconsider its war against a potential source of profit and renown. Instead, we find the city prepared to spend a very great deal of money to cover it up.[4]

In Philadelphia, city hall and journalism are active allies in what both call "the war against graffiti." Both insist upon the importance of graffiti in the array of problems facing the city. The *Philadelphia Inquirer* linked "crime, education, and graffiti" in an article on the campaign against it. Mayor Rendell declared that "nothing is more destructive to the City."[5] Rendell made that statement in Philadelphia's eleventh year of job loss. This was the year in which the governor and the mayor lost the Meyer-Werftt shipbuilder's bid to replace the abandoned naval shipyard. In the same year, Philadelphia faced another of its recurrent police scandals, one involving the framing and beating of innocent African American citizens and the sexual assault of children. This year, we were told that Philadelphia's most serious problem is not jobs, not an undisciplined police, but graffiti.

The preoccupation with surfaces is not, it appears, a defect peculiar to postmodernists. In these ill-advised mayoral and journalistic statements, the signifier is taken for the signified, the symptom is taken for the cause. The war against graffiti (the symptom of poverty and declining property values) is deployed to distract attention from the cause of that decline: the political and economic failure of an increasingly conservative regime.

How then, should we should read graffiti? Should we write it?

Graffiti is an instance of building, dwelling, thinking. I recommend that we read it with Heidegger. Heidegger is particularly useful in revealing the meaning of taggers. Taggers are the most broadly condemned of graffiti writers. They write or scrawl a name or a tag on any available surface. Their inscriptions make no claims to beauty or artistic worth, and cannot be easily defended on those grounds. They affirm a presence but offer no other speech, and so cannot claim protection or merit on that account. All that we know of taggers is that they are an instance of the link between writing and dwelling, between presence and the marking of spaces. In tagging, one can see how the marking of spaces begins presencing.

I have said elsewhere that I think we (we Americans, we moderns, we of the West) see ourselves in our names, our writings, our letters and diaries, our photographs and school records. Taggers acknowledge writing as presence. The tag should prompt us to ask ourselves, What takes place here? Who dwells here? What is brought into being within these boundaries? For Heidegger, "Dwelling is the manner in which mortals are on the earth."[6] Mortality is the condition of those who find themselves limited in time and space. One who builds and dwells, who takes place, takes place in another sense as well. One who takes place, who marks out a site, creates a space, also takes place, becoming present in time, for a time. Making a place for oneself involves both the acquisition of a place of shelter that is one's own, a marked-out place, and making a place in thought, a presence in mind, to persist when one is absent. Taggers accomplish these things.

We are mortals. We take place. We have our partial presence (our definition and initiation) in time and space. We are bounded in time and space. That bounding is our vocation, that which calls us into being: "the boundary is that from which something begins its presencing" (154). We inhabit space and time. We live in a place. We mark that place, repeatedly. Our repetitions mark out intervals. In these intervals, thought enters (155). The interval is the absence that becomes the site of our presence, our coming into being. Taking place in time is being mortal, being toward death. Taking place in space is inhabiting: marking the boundaries within which one can dwell, marking the intervals within which one can think.

I read Heidegger in Philadelphia. Cool Earl told an interviewer that he wrote "to prove to people where I was." He recognized that writing was to be the medium of his presence; writing would call him up in his absence. Cool Earl was (or perhaps, is) a liberal individual and a modernist, and his will was thus both more and less effective than he thought. It is not the author alone who decides the meaning of what is written, but the readers. For many of those readers, Cool Earl was (and is) no one in particular. Cool Earl is a sign, an icon: a black man, a member of the underclass, rarely visible, but leaving signs of an ungoverned, ungovernable presence: a presence that insists on its own authority, a presence that should be erased.

"The basic character of dwelling," Heidegger writes, "is to preserve, to spare, to save" (150), to let something be. Heidegger's example of such a building is not, as one might expect, a house, but a bridge (152). Letting things be in one sense—permitting them presence—requires that one let them be in another sense: that one leave them to themselves. This version of tolerance, like Rorty's "taking things lightly," acknowledges that we do not exhaust what should be in the world.

Leaving the center of Philadelphia for the university, one crosses the South Street bridge. The bridge was marked, when I first came to the city, by a poem, with stanzas written on successive sections of the bridge, which told of casual gay sexual encounters under the overpass. The poem spoke of the hidden and the invisible, and gave them presence. The poem made visible, legible, the meaning of that space to others. Yet it let them be. In this respect, it was a peculiarly effective means for conveying the limits of experience and the multiplicity of space.

Graffiti is a sign, an evocation, of presence. My aim has been not to argue for the good of graffiti (though I am often tempted to do so), for its beauty, or for the manner in which it gives speech to the silent and makes visible that which is too often concealed. Rather, I want to conclude with the obvious (and with that which the obvious conceals so well). Heidegger tells us that language "tells us about the nature of a thing," but he also warns us that "language, in a way, retracts the real meaning." This is the case with the language of (and the language on) graffiti.

Graffiti is a matter of surfaces. The discourses of panic and distraction that invite us to debate the merits of graffiti should not distract us from what lies beneath it. These strategies of panic and distraction depend for their success on the isolation of graffiti from a broader visual economy. We should refuse this isolation and look instead to architecture, technology, commercialism, and advertising, to the vast complex of ways in which sight is governed in the city of the senses. We should ask: what are we commanded to see? What sights are concealed from us? Who rules sight in the city of the senses? And should we cede the governance of sight to them?

## Notes

1. Thomas Ferrick, Jr., *Philadelphia Inquirer,* July 21, 1996.
2. Marc Kaufman, "Graffiti Gateway Targeted," ibid., B1.
3. Lieut. Steve Mona, head of the NYPD Transit Bureau Vandal Squad, quoted in "Invasion of the Euro-taggers" *New York Times Sunday Magazine,* January 19, 1997, 12.

4. The mural was necessary, the *Times* article continued, because "in the city's graffitti subculture, say the city's graffitti-fighters, a mural is usually respected; a blank wall is not" (B6).

5. Marc Kaufman, "National Guard to Join Graffiti War" *Philadelphia Inquirer,* August 20, 1996, A1.

6. Martin Heidegger, "Building Dwelling Thinking," in *The Question Concerning Technology and Other Essays* (New York: Harper and Row, 1982), 146; subsequent citations are indicated by page numbers in the text.

# 10

## Malled, Mauled, and Overhauled: Arresting Suburban Sprawl by Transforming Suburban Malls into Usable Civic Space

**Benjamin R. Barber**

It may be that the relationship between time and space have been radically altered by what Manuel Castells calls the global network society.[1] We certainly can no longer think about space in conventional historical terms without thinking about the compression of time and the virtualization of our real places by the electronic networks that are creating a new cyber-planet shell around the age-old and still familiar world of real neighbors and historical nations. Our conventional notions of space-time are, in the fanciful term Jimmy Stewart used in the film about an imaginary rabbit named Harvey, quite literally pixelated. That "place for us" I employed as a title to my book on civil society is ever more difficult to locate in the suburban sprawl dominated by cars, malls, multiplexes, and held together, if at all, only by the net.[2]

Yet as close to new frontiers in space and time as we may be drawing in the abstract, we are a long way off from the kinds of virtual lives denizens of the electronic frontier fantasize about, and how we organize the old-fashioned physical spaces in which we exist and conduct our quotidian affairs in public and private remains the concern not just of architects and planners but of politicians and citizens as well. It is no accident that the Prince of Wales ended up enduring both aesthetic and political ridicule as a consequence of his traditionalist critique of British architecture; or that Vice President Gore has found it prudent to make suburban sprawl one of the issues by which he is defining his campaign for the presidency in the year 2000 (the operative phrase describing sprawl containment today is "smart growth"); or that the Disney Company's ongoing commercial assault on our sense of historical place has roiled a lot of people in Virginia, Florida, and New York. In Virginia, the company tried in vain to build a Civil War theme park next to the real Civil War battlefields; in Florida, it succeeded in building Celebration, its first residential new town; and in New York, it "saved" old-town Times Square but at a new-town price paid in the depreciated currencies of suburbanization, gentrification, and domestication.

Each of these examples suggests that how we organize, design, and then live in the spaces that define our physical lives matters profoundly—even in the networked society. It suggests that whether we segregate or integrate the public and the private, the residential and the industrial, and the recreational and the civic, makes a concrete difference in the character and quality of our culture and our democracy. So pressing has the challenge of suburban sprawl become that state governments have started to move more aggressively than ever before to contain it. With vehicle miles traveled outdistancing population growth four to one, suburban congestion has given new impetus to suburban planning. In Georgia, the Regional Transportation Act, passed in 1999, gave the governor extraordinary planning (and veto) powers few other governors can match.[3] Cities like Portland, Oregon, are actively encouraging dense, high-rise building to preserve open space and reduce sprawl but at the price of higher housing costs than free-market, "anything goes" towns like Phoenix and Las Vegas.

It should not, then, come as a surprise that the malling of America has sometimes entailed the mauling of American civil society and its public, multiuse spaces; or that a first priority of those who care about the impact of design, architecture, and planning on the quality of civic life is the overhauling of suburban malls in the name of civic goals.

### Malled or Mauled?

The mall has come to embody many of the dilemmas of a privatized and commercialized society that compels every institution to pay its own way as measured by monies earned and quarterly profits distributed. Although in practice the mall has achieved some of the variety and pluralism typical of all American institutions as they spread into distinctive regions and subcultures, I will focus on an ideal (if hardly ideal!) paradigm. Certainly, there are malls that offer relatively diverse fare, are not dominated by "big boxes," try to integrate restaurants and other more leisurely venues into their commercial space, and are accessible to public transportation. (Many of these exist in the vicinity of university campuses.) But the dominant model is a big-box-anchored enclosed space dominated by boutiques and specialty stores catering almost exclusively to shoppers and without significant public transportation access. Malls of this kind define the genre: they are not only the centerless centerpieces of suburbs (in which more than half of America now lives) but are becoming models for urban revival as well. Ironically, at the very moment when the city is reappearing in the suburbs under the sanitized guise of the new urbanism (the cosmetics of the city without the inner core of lively disorder that is the real key to its urbanity),[4] the suburbs are invading cities through the malling of commercial neighborhoods and the displacement of seedy authenticity by anodyne artifice.

The mall stands as a powerful embodiment of the privatization and commercialization of space associated with the forces of what I have called McWorld, turning our complex, multiuse public space into a one-dimensional venue for consumption. The sameness of the architecture and interior design, and of the goods and entertainment offered, no longer has the excuse Howard Johnson and the Hilton once offered the weary traveler: comforting conformity in an otherwise alien world. Sameness now is a matter of efficiency, volume, and cultural homogeneity. Even the tie-in with multiplex movie houses is about consumer conformity and the selling of films that are more and more closely tied to music, fast food, and other commodities in which the mall specializes. The multiplex is the mall's consumer academy. A film like *Titanic* that is an industry unto itself (at more than a billion dollars in revenues), puts a half-dozen books on the best-seller list, sells not only its prize-winning song but Celine Dion, music generally, and the hardware needed to play it, is typical of the vertical integration of modern commodities in what I have called the "infotainment telesector."

In the 1960s Herbert Marcuse prophesized the coming of a conformitarian world brought to heel not by terror but by technology, a world in which civilized humanity risked being reduced to one-dimensionality.[5] At the time, this struck many as hyperbole, and Marcuse's own preoccupation with the radical and subversive moment of negativity in Hegel's dialectic (see his *Reason and Revolution*) was equally well represented in the epoch's more subversive, countercultural manifestations. Nowadays, Marcuse looks prescient. The potential of the new global markets for assimilation of all distinctions and the blurring of all ideological oppositions, abetted by the fuzziness of borders between news and entertainment as well as information and amusement, give his perhaps overwrought sixties' fears renewed currency. The pervasiveness of consumer identity today is evident in market research profiles, which classify people not by race or gender or even traditional class, but by segmented market inclinations. Clarita, a Virginia marketing firm, charts potential customers and their behavior by reference to such nouveau niche categories as "pools and patios," "shotguns and pickups," "Bohemia mix," and "urban gold coast." Identity itself is increasingly associated with branding and commercial logos. If to be branded was once the melancholy fate of cattle and slaves, today business adviser Tom Peters (in his *Brand You*) tells his customers with satisfaction, "You're every bit as much a brand as Nike, Coke, Pepsi, or the Body Shop." The first step for someone who wants to brand himself is to "write your own mission statement, to guide you as CEO of Me, Inc."[6]

This consumerist one-dimensionality achieves a palpable geography in the controlled and controlling architecture of the shopping mall. Malls are the privatized public squares of the new fringe city "privatopia," which uses secession from the larger common society— deemed vulgar, multiethnic, and dangerous—to secure a gated world of placid safety. Cut off wherever possible from public transportation (and the suspect publics it serves),[7] denuded of political and civic activities (often with the help of State Supreme Court decisions declaring the enclosed space of malls to be private and thus not subject to the rights of assembly and free expression that would apply in public space), the mall becomes the cathedral of our new secular civilization.[8] It would be too much to call the mall's consumerist culture totalitarian, freighted as that term is with the twentieth century's most egregious horrors. But inasmuch as the mall replicates a one-dimensional life in which every activity other than shopping vanishes, there is certainly something totalizing about its defining activities. The mall refuses to play host to churches or synagogues, to community theaters or art galleries, to political speech or civic leafleting, to clinics, childcare centers, schools, granges, town halls, or social services of any kind.

On entering an enclosed mall, we are asked to shed every identity other than that of the consumer. Eating is about buying fast food and moving back into the stream of shoppers; entertainment means buying Hollywood's latest and all the commodities that go with them; hanging out and people-watching are discouraged by security guards and, more important, the architecture is designed to impede sitting or standing around and keep the traffic flow moving into the shops. On weekend evenings, teens may try to behave as they once did on Main Street strips, and in the course of rainy afternoons seniors may look to stroll and loiter as they once might have done at a town post office or corner barber shop or general store. But malls are neither designed for nor encouraged to serve such purposes.[9] Food is available in "fuel-up pit stops" but not in restaurants where shoppers might while away valuable shopping time over a social dinner. Clocks are nowhere to be seen— time stands still for the shopper who must, under no circumstances, be reminded that it may be time to be somewhere else.

Indeed, nowadays, malls do not even pretend to sell necessities. No dry cleaner's, no hardware store, no vegetable market, no laundry, no place to pick up eggs or milk or a bottle of sherry or a newspaper. Mall developers and their vendors prefer theme and specialty stores and ubiquitous boutiques like The Museum Store, Warner Bros., The Sharper Image, Brookstone's, The Nature Store, and The Disney Store that sell you nothing you want until you get inside and realize you need everything they sell.

The mall as concept is no longer limited to suburban shopping centers. Consumerism demands the commercial colonization of every location, the malling of every public space. Decaying downtowns (like New York's Times Square) are "saved" by yielding to the safe mall aesthetic and its cookie-cutter vendors. Airports and train stations have ceased to be merely gateways to other places and are now shopping destinations in their own right so that every journey becomes a shopping expedition from which, however, you don't come home but end up somewhere else. Public buildings (train terminals, post offices) are privatized and turned into shopping arcades, while the Internet is becoming an electronic mall where dot-com overtakes and outstrips dot-edu and dot-org. Gas stations become convenience stores and convenience stores morph into minimalls. Schools and universities, starved for funding by the dominant ideology of privatization, find themselves under pressure to sign contracts with fast food, cola, and sports apparel vendors. These contracts are quietly coercive and their terms are rarely disclosed. They not only subordinate the academic commitment to critical thinking and autonomy to corporate marketing goals but increasingly give to student unions and other public buildings the actual appearance of malls—but malls that lack even that elemental right to choose between different brands of the same generic athletic shoes or cola beverages or pizza. Pedagogy in the malled university is reduced to an exercise in subliminally learning how to be a consumer. Learning itself becomes an exercise in "shopping" for the right credential-bearing courses on the way to a career in production and consumption.

Clocks are already largely banished from the mall, and now time itself is increasingly under assault as blue laws fall and twenty-four-hour-a-day, seven-day-a-week shopping becomes the norm throughout the Western world. No second can elapse without some marketing director asking how it might be turned to the purposes of shopping. You are never far from the mall. Not when you await an answer to the call you place (in Sweden and Spain, free service is available to those who will listen to advertisements while the phone rings!); not when you watch your computer screen download web information (free Internet access—even free computers—to those who accept ribbon or banner ads as wallpaper for their screens); not even when you ponder the stars (satellite advertising is technically feasible and under discussion).

## The Example of Disney

The malling of America, and what it stands for in American life, is nowhere more evident than in the marketing logic of the Disney Corporation. Disney does not operate malls, it embodies and extends the consumerist philosophy undergirding the mall. The formula creates safe, sanitized spaces where people can experience the thrill of the different without taking any risks; where entertainment can pass as learning; where community can be synthesized in a manner that offers some of its benefits and none of its costs; where the boundaries between the vicarious and the real are blurred; and where, every step of the way, people are treated exclusively as spectators and shoppers who consume entertainment, information, and goods without knowing where one ends and the next begins.

Disneyfication has become a term of art for a host of sins, but it is not my object here to condemn the company in general or to fault its vision of becoming entertainer to the world.[10] The downside is not in what Disney does (which it often does very well), but in the totalizing nature of its ambitions. Nowhere is Disney's encompassing and let's-theme-park-the-world vision more evident than in Celebration, Florida, Disney's commercial experiment in the Disneyfication of a newly built all-American town. Celebration is a carefully planned, full-service town of about twenty thousand people founded in 1996. Although Disney's checkered experience in Celebration has prompted it to exit from the town-planning side of its business, the character of its mixed-success experiment in Florida is revealing.[11] Celebration is one third a typical American "new town" on the model of say Reston, Virginia, one third a typical exercise in American escapism via a gated community that walls off its residents from both the thrills and the risks of real urban life, and one third a typical Disney fantasyland simulation, in this case a simulation that reproduces life itself in its most cherished small-town incarnation. The convergence of these three aims allows Disney to boast, quite accurately, that in Celebration it is doing what "no one had ever done before."[12]

Some critics have accepted Disney's boast and have even welcomed Celebration as "a town that not only promises to be real but to be a model for others to follow."[13] To be sure, Disney's problem is not with its wish to market entertainment to the public but, as with the mall logic it mimics, its need to treat the public exclusively as an audience for shopping and entertainment—to make marketing the whole of its privatizing public philosophy. Hence, when Disney tries to co-opt history, as it did with its failed plan to build a simulated Civil War theme park on the sacred Virginia ground where the actual war was fought, it invariably profanes it. That it can enlist historians like Eric Foner to legitimize its animatronic robot presidents by providing the imprimatur of verisimilitude to their "speeches" reinforces rather than diminishes their confounding of the vicarious and the real.

What is new and riveting about Celebration is that the Disney company has taken the principles of comic book spectatorship and sanitized vacations and safety-conscious adventure and vicarious history and simulated multiculturalism from their entertainment venue and applied them to an environment for living. Such principles may seem apt to a theme park or even a mall—indeed, they define theme parks and malls—but in Celebration they are made the foundation for a place where people work and live and raise children and grow old and die. Just a few miles from Orlando, an urban home to poverty, racial bias, and crime, Celebration can boast "a signature golf course, tennis courts, acres of parks, ponds and open spaces," as well as "homes with front porches and a vibrant downtown where you'll see friends and neighbors."

Yet it is as if this friendly neighborhood were purchased in the Nature Store, since community in Celebration is not conjured from years of earned solicitude and hard communal work but is ready made and pret-a-porter, courtesy of its famous architects and town planners like A. M. Stern, Philip Johnson, and Robert Venturi. Community is, in effect, available for the price of your mortgage, protected by its gate-like economics (not too expensive, but no public housing, no potential slums). The community is there when you arrive, along with instant "Celebration traditions." The word *tradition* (like the word *community*) is clearly deployed for its emotive power to evoke nostalgia. There is nothing in Celebration to suggest that it earns its meaning. The root-ed sense of history to which the publicity materials refer turns out to de-note such "traditions" as a "fun-filled interactive orientation session" and an eighteen-hole golf course designed by Robert Trent Jones, Sr. and Jr.

In keeping with the dominance of marketing and the substitution of manufactured wants for real needs characteristic of malls, Disney of-fers a prefabricated "old-fashioned community life," forged not from hard times and the blood, sweat, and tears of common struggles lost and won, but "imagineered" by the same entertainment specialists who make the films and create the rides and design the pavilions. Disney dares to speak of community, with all its American overtones of self-government, without providing anything like real self-government. Daniel Kemmis, the former mayor of Missoula, Montana, and a thoughtful advocate of community democracy, is only echoing older democratic lore when he says: "I don't believe you can create genuine community in the absence of self government."[14]

Celebration celebrates the hard sell rather than local control. It of-fers life without risk, diversity without tension, community without pain, and tradition without history. Night comes in Celebration, but unlike Epcot or Disney World, the curtain never falls on the show here, because life is the show. The "cast" (the name Disney gives its theme-park employees) comprises Celebration's residents; like the denizens of *The Truman Show,* they are players and spectators alike, the enter-tained "front porch" watchers of the entertaining lives they lead. Cele-bration is reality TV in reverse: not real people living television-scripted lives, but television-scripted lives being lived by real people in the real world. Elsewhere, mall developers look to incorporate housing into their shopping centers to recreate the feel of a town by making shop-pers into residents.[15] In Celebration, the Disney Company turns the Disneyland fantasy Main Street that Walt Disney imagineered from his boyhood experience of smalltown, USA, back into a real residential street. Is it real? Yes. And no.

Will Celebration be truly diverse? Multicultural? In its look, yes. Its "archetainment" style is a Disneycletic hodgepodge on the surface with a comforting homogeneity underneath. Like the Hollywood whose defining spirit and alter ego it has always been, Disney is neces-sarily parasitic. Like mall storefronts that pretend in their windows and styles to a diversity belied by the homogeneity of the goods they sell, Disney creates nothing original in Celebration, living off other people's cultural capital. Like parasites everywhere, it consumes what it mimics and destroys what it imitates. It simulates the Mediterranean and the classical in its architectural cosmetics but assures neutral and common suburban interiors.

Disney makes no effort to avoid sounding faintly absurd (perhaps it actually is pulling our leg): the office park is "inspired by the artistry and beauty of Pisa, Italy," it brags. Its imagineered homes are designed in "classical, coastal, colonial, revival, French, Mediterranean and Victorian" styles, safe in the knowledge that the climates and cultures that inspired these stylistic choices will remain invisible, allowing the styles to "harmoniously blend with one another." The eclectic veneers barely conceal the reassuringly banal commonality, and this core commonality insulates home owners from anything that risks real distinctiveness (e.g., poor plumbing, period stoves, narrow staircases, bats in the belfry, a windowed pantry instead of a fridge) or foreignness (e.g., strange languages, alien habits, Sabbath no-shopping rules).

Disney's genius, sought after by prudent mall developers, is to domesticate the foreign, to sanitize blood and sweat, to homogenize diversity. We are inoculated against infection by the truly different with an immunizing shot of the superficially distinctive. Taco Bell style that gives us Mexico without diarrhea or Chiapas rebellion, French Mediterranean ambiance without snotty waiters or people who think their language is better than ours, German castle cosmetics without Turkish workers or Dachau. And so, Celebration can guarantee its residents community without either the vices of hierarchy or the virtues of hard work, tradition without either prejudice or roots, and friends without either vendettas or loyalty.

In Celebration, Disney also ventured for the first time into government. In order to create schools and a security system, it needed the cooperation of its host, Osceola County, and a degree of autonomy from the county's oversight.[16] As with malls, whose interior spaces have been treated by many state supreme courts as private space from which political and civic activity can be banned and whose rules and regulations can be privately enacted, Celebration considered its open town space to be private. Many quasi-governmental functions have been subordinated to town "guidelines and controls" enacted not by a town meeting but by Urban Design Associates, in conjunction with Robert A. M. Stern Architects and Cooper, Robertson and Partners. Ironically, this privatization of the public sphere publicizes private behavior, bringing under regulation such "private" issues as house paint colors and the placement of porches. Except that the trustee of these public decisions is a private corporation rather than a democratically elected government. This not the metaphoric displacement of the public domain by the private about which I have previously complained, this is the actual substitution of private for public authority—a virtual privatization of sovereignty that is in its essence not only destructive but oxymoronic. Even Celebration's public schools operated by the county are in many ways also private, helped by supplementary funding from Disney and a subsidized "teaching academy."[17] Such special funding has been found unconstitutional in some states, but it is the key to the secession strategy being pursued by Disney in Celebration.

My criticism here does not issue from some exogenous German dialectical critique. I am only echoing the words of a prescient *Boston Globe* editorial. "The Disney Dream machine is starting to sell reality," the editors warned back in 1996; "The scary part is that Americans have become so afraid of themselves that some people are turning to a theme park operator to build a country they can live in."[18] Indeed, this form of privatization and homogenization of public diversity has been the key to the withdrawal of middle-class America from its responsibility in the face of America's common social challenges, as well as to the fear of diversity that has accompanied it. As a symbol of the vision behind at least one aspect of the malling of America, Disney's Celebration makes clear why malls are at once so seductive and so corrupting, serving the wish for safety and familiarity but at the expense of the idea of a common community open to all that serves diversified interests and heterogeneous values. Unless we can have both, our American experiment in unity through diversity and liberty without inequality will fail.

## Overhauling the Mall

This is the challenge for those who are critics of the dominant trends in modern American architecture and planning and dissatisfied with the responses to date. Suburbanization has meant secession, sprawl, and the destruction of community. The new urbanism has addressed the loss of vitality in the suburbs in a primarily cosmetic way, opting for the appearance of cities but avoiding those essential urban traits such as class and race mixing, the delight real urban dwellers take in the unfamiliar, tolerance and even affinity for disorder, and the ubiquity of risk. Yet these are precisely the rough and vital substance of real cities.

Architects who romanticize suburban tawdriness and attack its critics as elitist snobs (Robert Venturi, for example) seem insensible to the social and civic costs of the anarchic styles they embrace for what appear to be mainly aesthetic reasons. They slum in suburban sprawl with little concern for the civic and social costs. Their eclecticism may reflect an admirable roadside-diner romanticism and an appealing American pragmatism. When Robert Venturi writes, "I like elements which are hybrid rather than pure, compromising rather than clean, distorted rather than straightforward . . . perverse as well as impersonal. . . . I am for messy vitality over obvious unity," he sounds intriguing.[19] But when, in Martin Filler's description, Venturi and Scott Brown decide since "young Americans today are most familiar with eating in fast-food restaurants, why not design a college dining hall resembling the neon-lit food courts of shopping malls?" and proceed accordingly with their design for Swarthmore College's Tarble Social Center, he sounds downright insidious.[20]

If Venturi celebrates the meretricious anarchy of the suburbs, confirmed haters of suburbanization tend to indulge a secessionist strategy of their own, withdrawing into boutiqued cities that have practiced "urban removal" where they can feel at home and leaving suburbanites to their tawdry little destinies. Or they dream of getting people out of the suburbs and back into small towns. They wage quixotic campaigns against big-box stores like Wal-Mart and the Home Depot, and yearn to close the malls so that downtowns will spring back to life—but at the expense of less economically privileged suburbanites who benefit from the low costs and multiple consumer options of the big-box megastores.[21] Nostalgia for small-town America dies hard in a nation where so many people spend the first twenty years of their lives trying to escape the parochialism of the small towns where they grew up, and the remainder of their lives wishing they could somehow go home again.

I would offer a less radical and more realistic approach. If a privatizing ideology and a consumerist culture have turned citizens into consumers, we need to go to where the consumers are and try to turn them back into citizens. If they go to the net and then become passive spectators to what is supposed to be an interactive technology, we need to "reinteractivate" the net.[22] If they go to the mall in search of public space and are seduced into privatized shopping behavior, we need to confront and transform the mall. The aim is not to get people off the Internet but to get civic, cultural, and educational activity on it, not to close the malls or lure people out of them but to make them more like the multiuse public spaces they have displaced.

Given the ubiquity of malls, it makes more sense to rethink the laws, politics, zoning policies, development incentives, and architectural predilections that have forged our particular version of suburban life. Which changes might encourage the reconfiguring of commercial space in the suburbs? There is considerable latitude even within the confines of purely commercial development for variety: big box or small store outlets? Open-space parking, parking deck, or traditional strip-mall doorfront parking? Public-transportation access or parking lots only? Integration of residential housing or purely commercial? Just shopping or subsidies for public art and traditional grocery store and dry cleaner vendors? The answer to these questions obviously impinges on the character of the public space a retail mall creates.

Cities have used tax incentives and building permit requirements to induce developers to offer public sculptures, park space, and a livable, environmentally accommodating architecture along with new retail and corporate space. Highway programs can have a powerful impact on outcomes. In the 1950s, ring roads were built around cities in the hope of diverting traffic from inner cities and creating pedestrian residential and shopping districts. Instead, they siphoned off potential residents and customers, devitalizing cities and helping to create the first ring suburbs of that era. Accommodating rising vehicular traffic with expanded highways in subsequent decades merely encouraged more traffic and accelerated the pace of sprawl. Planning has then to be done with an eye to unintended consequences.

There is plenty of room for experimentation. Malls have been overbuilt in the suburbs, some estimate by 30 percent or more. This means failed malls and empty stores even in the successful ones. Meanwhile, people have tired of the monotonous unidimensionality of the mall experience, and the average visit has declined from well over to well under two hours. In short, while flourishing in many ways, malls are troubled enough to incite anxiety in developers and vendors, who are looking for new forms of collaboration with the civic and residential communities they serve. In many cases this amounts to little more than a search for a new promotion concept, a gimmick that gets people back into the stores. But what looks like a gimmick to a developer may turn out to entail a relatively serious deprivatization of retail space. A renewed civic life instigated by, say, a second-hand bookstore or a community performance stage or a life-size chess set at the heart of a mall may give new hope to retailers even as it allows customers to think of themselves as neighbors and citizens. This has been the experience of Ron and Merritt Sher, whose "Crossroads" center in Seattle has become a gathering place not just for shoppers but for friends, neighbors, and citizens. The Shers make civic revitalization the condition for economic revitalization. Ron Sher insists he can "do well by doing good," and his business success vindicates his claims.[23]

Mashapee Commons on Cape Cod is another space built for commerce on the premise, however, that commerce can take place only where there are people, and that to draw people into markets requires that they are treated as multifaceted human beings with many different identities and interests. Crisscrossed with local streets that afford storefront parking, and built on a plan that permits street entry to individual stores that accommodate living quarters above, Mashapee is an attempt to create a town around a shopping center. In Willingboro, New Jersey, developer Robert Stang and architect Bice C. Wilson (Meridian Design Associates) are working with community officials to refurbish a closed mall (Willingboro Plaza) in a relatively poor central state area. Building around a community college, the group hopes to anchor its commercial venture with a newly created "neighborhood" (adjacent to a residential district) that includes public institutions, a theater, a post office, and retail space.

There are a variety of ordinary institutions that can be found in any urban neighborhood or rural town that could serve to diversify a shopping center: a school or post office or performance stage, like the ones at Crossroads or Mashapee or Willingboro; or a childcare center, a speakers' corner, a public library, a recreation area, a school or a college, a public-access cable studio, an Internet café, a teen club, an art gallery, a playground, an interdenominational prayer hall. The presence of such facilities would do more than introduce variety: it would turn private back into public space, and it would lace commercial behavior with a dose of civic activity, allowing customers to reconceive themselves as neighbors and citizens as well.

There are a number of points of leverage that might move both private developers and public officials in a civic direction. The development of an appropriate civic architecture that takes the mall as its starting place would offer realistic designs to committed developers. Public officials can utilize zoning laws, permits for curb cuts that allow developers access from the highway, and environmental and safety regulations as both carrots and sticks to modify developers' behavior. The courts can be used to argue the case that malls are public rather than private and must allow public and political activity. Currently, about a dozen states have taken a legal position or, like New Hampshire, are hearing cases, with New Jersey, California, and Colorado having ruled that free-speech rights are protected in enclosed malls, implying that they enclose public rather than private space. Finally, public transportation and road patterns can do much to determine whether malls become suburban neighborhoods or isolated, upscale retail megaplazas unrelated to their surrounding ecological and demographic territories.

## The Agora Coalition

In New Jersey, a group of architects, planners, social scientists, developers, vendors, and state government officials under the aegis of the Walt Whitman Center at Rutgers University are collaborating to create a coalition of forces that can pilot model designs, foster creative cooperation, and broker public-private partnerships around what might be called the establishing of "mall-town squares" in commercial spaces in the Northeast.

This coalition—the Agora Coalition, named for the ancient Greek marketplace that served as the public square for Athens—begins with the challenge of architecture, because in the spirit of Paul Goodman and Jane Jacobs, its founders are persuaded that we create our public and interactive lives in the first instance through the shaping of physical space. The logic of big-box malls commands anonymity, the layout of enclosed boutique store malls encourages permanent shopping around manufactured needs, the design of storefronts and their retail layout (following principles of "scientific marketing") lure customers deep into the interior to maximize shopping. Contesting such marketing designs and their consumer strategies, well-conceived public space invites loafing, public gatherings, playfulness, hanging out, communication, people watching, and spontaneous interaction. Such space requires ample seating with a pleasant sense of social proximity, multiple foci for casual entertainment, spontaneous opportunities for encountering friends and strangers, and activities that attract diverse demographic populations and allow them to interact around something more than shopping.[24] Where malls are currently designed to maximize retail circulation by minimizing the distractions of leisure spectatorship (hence, minimal seating and no leisure distractions that might impede the progress of ardent shoppers through retail venues), an ideal multiuse public plaza would do exactly the contrary. That is, it would increase risk a little, and perhaps induce visitors to do more than just shop, but would bring in far more people for longer periods of time and hence enhance business over the long run.

To address the problems of suburbanization is to address the underlying logic of the suburbs, a logic linked to the automobile, the decentering of community, the decoupling of residential and retail space, the elimination of sidewalks, the preference for automobiles over pedestrians, the default attitude that leaves culture to nearby cities, and the pervasiveness of commercial sprawl. The Agora Coalition starts with the mall, because it is symbol and spirit of suburbia's logic and because, most important, it is also where the people actually are. Moreover, it is some considerable trouble: duration of visits is down and vacancies are up; developers are looking for new approaches, which turn out to be old approaches rooted in the attraction of retail space that is rooted in residential communities and multiuse civic space. If the township has given way to mall, malls must be made more a town—call it "Mall-town Square."

The Agora Coalition proposes to create "Mall-town Square" both as a model and as a commercial reality. The coalition, sponsored by the Walt Whitman Center at Rutgers University (www.wwc.rutgers.edu), comprises a group of developers, architects, businesspeople, planners, and academics who are committed to pragmatic action aimed at creating public spaces that are both commercial and civic, both profitable and pluralistic, viable for vendors and consumers who also want to be neighbors and citizens.

The coalition begins with the premise that social planning cannot be defined by perfection, that its beliefs and norms have to be proven in the real world of citizens and businesspeople, in the public and the private sectors. Its guiding norm is democracy, understood as the vibrant life of the engaged, responsible community; but its anchor is commerce, understood as the satisfying of a community's needs in ways that benefit producers and consumers alike. In this sense, it supports business but by insisting that successful commerce demands a strong setting of community life. Commercial development necessarily seeks benefits for the community and profits for investors, and only a pragmatic and flexible approach to growth is likely to secure both.

The coalition has adopted defining principles rooted in three simple imperatives: that commerce must be anchored in community; that community must be anchored in place; and that place must be anchored in democracy. These imperatives yield principles that propose:

• the aim of development sensitive to community, place, and democracy should reflect the ideal of the ancient "agora"—the core public space of Greek free cities that acted at once as marketplace and civic space, a place where citizens traded and talked, did economic business and political business, bargained interests and discovered common ground; that, in other words, commerce and civic life are complementary activities that need and sustain one another;

• as the agora teaches, commerce draws people out of their homes into common areas, and that people create commerce simply by being there. A healthy public space is thus both commercial and civic. It has multipurpose uses that serve community, civic, and recreational interests, as well as commercial interests that reward investors and businesspeople. In short, a healthy commercial space is always anchored in community;

• a truly living place means a place animated by local citizens and neighbors reflecting the full gamut of their life interests and the natural, cultural, and historical features of their environment; that, in short, community is always anchored in a particular place, with its own ecology, demographics, and economy;

• a community representing truly human faces must be diversified, multicultural, and inclusive, reflecting the multihued tapestry that is America and encompassing different economic and cultural groups in a fashion that makes a site inviting to all and accessible to all; in sum, that place in a free society must always be anchored in democracy;

• anchoring commerce in community, community in place, and place in democracy requires that developers and consumers, investors and citizens, act as partners, working with and within the communities served, respecting and utilizing the resources already there and the natural and historical character of the places in which they build. The goal is not to impose abstract blueprints developed by designers, architects, and urban planners but to unearth, to bring out and polish what is already in place in potential;

• we begin not with a blank tablet (tabula rasa) but with a living reality and an existing fabric—whether it is a town fallen on hard times, an unsuccessful mall, or a centerless suburb. The aim is to bring out a spirit already there in potential, not to endow a place with a foreign soul.

• the ecology and natural history of the community served must therefore play a central role in any development plan so that weather, the seasons, the time of day, and the geographical and water resources of the region be given full play in design and planning elements. This suggests a "vocabulary of place" suited to the immediate environment rather than a single blueprint to be everywhere applied. This kind of pragmatic localism is not only good for community, it is good for business;

• the utilization of existing fabric and site resources means including the community to be served in the planning process and, wherever possible, to include local entrepreneurs and vendors among those participating in commercial and civic development;

• when the imperatives of community, place, and democracy are made integral principles of development, it is possible for developers and entrepreneurs to do good even as they do well by marrying profit to the full needs of the community and by assuring that the entrepreneurship of the developer will kindle and support entrepreneurship and citizenship in the community being served;

• and finally, that each of these beliefs be regarded as a practical guide to action, not applicable in every situation, but rules of thumb for people wanting to get things done in an environment conducive to business and community.

There are a number of specific tasks the Agora Coalition wishes to undertake. It can offer:

• a template for development rooted in design, planning, and architectural principles—with a focus on adaptability to place, site, and local resources;

• "best practices" and real-world exemplars drawn from actual experiences with civic redevelopment from across the country and around the world;

• "mentoring" in the form of counseling, guidance, and technical assistance from the interdisciplinary coalition;

• microfinancing for new entrepreneurs participating in civic development projects;

• venture capital access and assistance for developers interested in civic development projects;

• a "Coalition Civic Certificate" attesting that a project has met minimal specifications set forth by the coalition for a civic space;

• prize competitions for developers, designers, and individual entrepreneurs participating in site development;

• a support network (including a website) to help new civic developers and entrepreneurs weather early challenges and the loneliness of fighting the battle.

The Agora Coalition represents one approach to addressing the challenges of ubiquitous commercialism in suburban space defined by privatization, consumerism, civic alienation, and sprawl. Its principles, if not its practices, suggest a strategy for reform that makes partners of the commercial vendors and developers about whom it is implicitly critical, and offers a point of departure that starts with realities as they are on the ground. It was not the search for utopia but the circumstances of suburbanization and the pursuit of business that gave rise to the malling of our public spaces; it is not the search for utopia but the circumstances of pervasive sprawl and the pursuit of a balanced civic life that can become the occasion for (quite literally) the civilizing of our malls.

## Appendix

The Agora Coalition

Developing
Public Spaces, Living Places, Human Faces

public spaces—anchoring COMMERCE in COMMUNITY
because consumers are
also citizens and neighbors
and doing well and doing good
can go hand in hand

living places—anchoring COMMUNITY in PLACE
because the places where we
live, work, and shop are rooted in

time, nature, and history and remake
us even as we remake them

human faces—anchoring PLACE in DEMOCRACY
because we live in a world of
diversity where communities must
be just as well as prosperous and
inclusive as well as neighborly

## Notes

1. Manuel Castells, *The Information Age: Economy, Society and Culture,* Vol. 1: *The Rise of the Network Society* (London: Blackwells, 1996).

2. Benjamin R. Barber, *A Place for Us* (New York: Hill and Wang, 1998).

3. See Alan Ehrenhalt, "New Recruits in the War on Sprawl," *New York Times,* April 13, 1999, p. A23.

4. See Richard Sennett's diminutive classic *The Uses of Disorder* (New York: Knopf, 1970).

5. Herbert Marcuse, *One-Dimensional Man* (Boston: Beacon Press, 1964).

6. Tom Peters in his *Brand You* (New York: Knopf, 1999), cited in Paul Starr, "Strategic Narcissism," *American Prospect* (March–April, 1998): 96.

7. Many developers have agreements with municipal transportation systems *not* to permit stops near their malls. Trumbling (Conn.) Shopping Park fought a three-year battle with the Greater Bridgeport Transit District to stop buses from discharging passengers near the mall on Friday and Saturday nights and in 1996 was supported by an arbitrator who ruled the mall had the right to limit service! In Buffalo, in 1995, a black teenager was killed crossing a highway to get to a mall in a suburb that barred inner-city buses from entering its property (though buses from upscale suburbs were allowed in!). See Jane Fritch, "Hanging Out with the Mall," *New York Times,* November 25, 1997.

8. Robert Reich describes this strategy of secession by which middle-class Americans try to escape the trials and burdens of the city by seceding into gated suburbs in which they buy private services with the monies withheld from public expenditure as part of a (public) tax reduction policy, thereby starving the public sector of needed support and worsening the conditions that justify secession to begin with; see his *Work of Nations* (New York: Knopf, 1991).

9. There are a few welcome exceptions. At the Stamford Town Center, mall managers hired youth social workers both to control teenagers and help make them feel welcome. See Fritch, "Hanging Out with the Mall."

10. For a ruthless and somewhat hysterical critique of the Disney Company, see Peter and Rochelle Schweizer, *Disney: The Mouse Betrayed (Greed, Corruption, and Children at Risk)* (New York: Regnery Publishing, 1998).

11. For an account of the history of Celebration in its first two fateful years, see

Michael Pollan, "Disney Discovers Real Life: Town-Building Is No Mickey Mouse Operation," *New York Times Sunday Magazine,* December 14, 1997.

12. Cited from the Disney promotion packet on Celebration, as are all the other quoted passages in this section.

13. Witold Rybczynski, "Tomorrow Land," *New Yorker,* July 22, 1996.

14. Cited by Pollan, "Disney Discovers Real Life," 82.

15. An exemplary model can be found in the "Haekische Hoefe," a mixed-use apartment, gallery, light industry, and restaurant complex in a renovated complex set of "hofs" (literally, "courtyards"), the formerly Eastern section. These "hoefe" make a remarkable contrast with the new corporate park that is rising in Potsdammerplatz, where the wall once separated East and West Berlin.

16. For the story of Disney's relationship to Osceola County, see Tom Vanderbilt, "Mickey Goes to Town(s)," *Nation,* August 28–September 4, 1995.

17. For an uncritical account of the development of Celebration's schools, see Jo Anna Natale, "Education Goes Mickey Mouse," *Education Digest,* October 1995.

18. "Disney's Sinless City," editorial, *Boston Globe,* March 25, 1996, p. 66.

19. See Robert Venturi's self-styled "gentle manifesto," *Complexity and Contradiction* (New York: Museum of Modern Art, 1966). Venturi's more recent book is *Iconography and Electronics upon a Generic Architecture: A View from the Drafting Room* (Cambridge: MIT Press, 1997).

20. Martin Filler, "Fantasia," *New York Review of Books,* October 23, 1997, p. 12.

21. This can make sense in certain parts of the country like New England, where a strong tradition of small town self-governance persists, and where hostility to suburbanization has strong roots. But in New Jersey or Ohio or central California, it looks merely nostalgic or, worse, indulgently elitist. As Michael Sandel has shown, when Sears and Montgomery Ward first began their catalog marketing campaigns a century ago, small-town shopowners were miffed, but consumers were delighted (see Sandel, *Democracy's Discontent* [Cambridge: Harvard University Press, 1996]). Too often, planning and zoning boards merely reproduce the aesthetic concerns of the wealthy—something critics like Venturi and Steven Izenour rightly criticize.

22. That is the goal of another Walt Whitman project called "Civic Exchange," which, with the collaboration of the Yale Information Society Project, is exploring deliberative debate on the World Wide Web.

23. Ron Sher, a founding member of the Agora Coalition, recently took over Seattle's most successful (and troubled) bookstore and has made it a part of his effort to revitalize mall spaces.

24. See William H. Whyte's classic *The Social Life of Small Urban Spaces* (Washington, D.C.: Conservative Foundation, 1980) for a portrait of such principles.

# Conclusion

# Public Space, Virtual Space, and Democracy

## Marcel Hénaff and Tracy B. Strong

A common thread in the preceding essays is the recognition that the achievement of democracy cannot be separated from development of shared information and of free access to this information. Without this, public debate is not possible. The first form of democracy with which the West experimented, that of the Greek city, constituted itself around three essential qualities: transparency of decisions, publicity of debate, and a guarantee of information about public affairs to all citizens. In like manner, the great emergence of democracies that has occurred since the Enlightenment appears to merge with the affirmation of the importance of public opinion, most especially in the development of the press.

Today, we think it natural that the emergence of new sources and means of information would first of all contribute to the reinforcing of democratic institutions. After the triumph of the free press, starting in the nineteenth century, and the appearance of new media in this century—from radio to television to the Internet—we often tend to think that the extension of democratic means of information constitutes also a perfecting of the *practice* of democracy itself.

This is certainly a dangerous illusion for two reasons of which we are all aware, or at least should be. First, information is not in fact in itself democratic, that is, it is not always objective, honest, equally shared. That it can be partial, manipulative, or lying is hardly worth being reminded of. Second, in principle democracy is not and cannot be identified with the mere increase in information: democracy does not consist only in sharing information; it is instead the taking of decisions in terms of practices of justice that are communally accepted and sanctioned by the vote of citizens.

With the new media we do find an appearance of what some might call a new public space, *virtual public space*. There is a foreshadowing of the promise of *a new democracy*. This is not surprising, for it is clear that technological changes in the realm of information, as elsewhere, change the practice of democracy and require a redefinition of the rules of life in common at any time that this life is itself materially transformed. Such is the case with the contemporary communication revolution. All manners of communication networks have profoundly transformed the economy (business management, financial institutions, national and international administrative practices, banking and stock-market networks, and so forth). We find the same changes at the level of political institutions and of the organization of public life. If there is widespread talk of a virtual public space, we need to consider two questions:

- How may we define such a space more accurately?
- Is it the case that another opportunity is thus prepared for democracies in the twenty-first century?

## The New Virtual Public Space

With the development of the Internet and the other networks that continually develop from this system, it would seem that we have clearly entered the era of virtual communities. Is this in fact the case? What are the promises of such a technology? Can one really speak of important effects of the Internet on the democratic practices of contemporary societies? We know that it is with the development of this network that we have acquired the expression "virtual space." Has this space managed to become a public space? One would be tempted to think so because, as opposed to radio and television, it is a transitive system. No one is simply in a passive receptor position. One can answer, question, approve, and thus debate. It is a space given over to agonistic exchange. In this sense, there is a clearly decisive step toward a democratic norm. But at this point we must first understand what is meant by "virtual," for a critical understanding of this term may well be the key to the answer to both our questions.

The expression "virtual space" today designates a space that is not physically locatable, thus not perceptible, but which, thanks to the tools of communication, exists as a network of relations. There is a paradox here: these technologies make concrete and effective or active relations that were until now only virtual. But because they operate on a large scale and their density continues to increase, one attributes to them the status of "virtual," which, nevertheless, they continually make actual.

Thus, in a not-too-distant past, persons who lived a long ways from one another could know themselves to be attached and still only have a few times in which they actually communicated by mail or in a visit. These groups or communities were quite precisely in a "virtual space." One might even understand nations and religious communities in this light, but a more specific example will help.

Between the seventeenth and eighteenth centuries in Europe, the community of scientists and scholars constituted itself into a virtual "republic of letters."[1] They communicated by mail, in publications, or through the intermediary of "scholars" who wandered from city to city and ensured an oral transmission of information. These journeys continued under a new form, the *peregrinato academica* of the Middle Ages.[2] In England, the informal community even received the name of "invisible college." It was a community that owed its entire existence to the desire for intellectual communication, to the certainty of sharing common values and the necessity of promulgating a collective project for knowledge and liberty. This was truly a virtual public space. Thus, it is noteworthy that in the Latin translation of the *Discourse on Method,* Descartes renders "the public" (meaning the audience) as *Respublica litteraria.* Again: Leibniz, when attempting an account of the knowledge of his time, found it quite natural to entitle his essay "Account of the Present State of the Republic of Letters" (1675). "Letters" then meant all forms of written matter. When Pierre Bayle, the great Protestant thinker, having fled France where he had been condemned, launched from Holland the most prestigious scientific review of the period, he called it *Nouvelles de la République des Lettres.* And when the scientist and philosopher, D'Alembert, like Leibniz before him, gave in 1760 an account of the knowledge of his time, it was once again entitled "Reflections on the Present State of the Republic of Letters."

There are innumerable such usages. All the world knew that the "Republic of Letters" referred to a cultivated community of knowledge taken as a whole, a sort of autonomous intellectual "International." In 1752, Voltaire expressed its reality like this: "One has seen a literary republic establish itself imperceptibly all over Europe, despite wars and religions."[3] In 1729, a disciple of Bayle had already given the best definition, one that anticipates Rousseau's definition of a just polity: "It is a state that extends in all states, a republic where each member, in perfect independence, recognizes only the law as that he himself prescribes to himself." The citizens of this "Republic" never found themselves in one place, never organized a convention. But they all recognized a certain tone or style, an ethic to share knowledge, a will to political emancipation. The community was all the more virtual for the fact that the means of communication were very limited.

With the idea of "virtual," we are thus dealing with a very old story. If, however, today we take particular notice of these invisible communities, it is because technologies manage to make actual these relations that until now remained purely virtual. What is new is not the network of relations but the possibility of making them active, or reinforcing them, of extending them by the tools of communication and representation. What materializes with and as the Internet is, first of all, *existing* institutions and communities of exchange that were waiting for a means to become actual. *The Internet makes real the virtual, not the reverse.*

However, the materialization or technological realization of these virtual relations is so overwhelming that it has come to be seen as the actual birth of the virtual world. Such an understanding misses the point. We must rather recognize that, for human beings, the virtual begins with language and the imagination. Any work of fiction already expresses it. It is the same with the spaces that are called "virtual": synthetic images materialize and extend the possibilities of the imagination, just as the telephone and the radio delocalize voice and sound, as also does television with pictures. If one means by "virtual space" the common and invisible space in which relations occur, one must say again that we have in everyday life a constant experience of such virtuality. Thus an invisible, un-sited space arises between two persons who exchange letters or call each other on the telephone, a space that is not *of* either party. (One might say the same with a simple conversation.) Rather than a "between-two," it is a "half-place" or even a "nonplace," some place different from each place in which the participants speak. It is an intermediate, not-physical, space here where our messages cross. Michel Serres (who has given a remarkable analysis of this elliptical space in his *Atlas*) calls this elsewhere the *"hors-là"* ("outside there"); the *hors-là* is not added onto the experience of exchange we have with others but belongs to the very condition of being with partners or interlocutors.[4]

Contemporary communication technologies thus do not displace us from some more natural original and concrete manner of being in the world. Nor do they disrupt a supposedly parochial niche, for in language and in our ties to others, we live in the *elsewhere*. New communication technologies do not stop simply at extending our sensory and/or motor organs. They go further: they actualize and make real the world we had represented to ourselves; our imagination becomes images, our voice becomes messages, and the "outside-there" is transformed into a network of connected sites. What is happening today is that the virtual space we have known for a long time—and which was in fact *only* virtual—is realizing itself materially, that is, it is accomplishing itself by means of communication media and by the use of intellectual technologies for treating information.

Understood like this, virtual space is not simply space as space has been logically and traditionally understood. Virtual space stands in contradiction to the laws determining the occupancy of space, and it subverts the principle of the excluded middle. Each of us, in such a space, is at the same time *here* and *elsewhere*. These technologies make clear to us that this is not a new power but rather the revelation or realization—taken practically and not as an epiphany—of that which we have always been. Here something has changed in a profound and exciting manner. This allows us simultaneously to free ourselves from the old model of an abstract universal and from the understanding of ourselves as particular localities related to the global. In other words, even if it is the case that virtual space is not new, what is new is its realization in the tools of communication.

This is what produces a decisive change in the general model of public space. We have always implicitly understood public space—literally and metaphorically—as monumental, that is, as a way of attaching oneself to the global or universal. However, the practice of networked communication makes it possible to conceive totality not as pre-existing but as constituting itself in the sharing of singularities.

According to ancient tradition, the global was ultimately one with the universal. Universal was defined as an escape from contingency, from the unrepresentable singularity of a space. A formal definition has been with us since Aristotle: that for which there exists an always verifiable law is universal. The local—the paradigmatic form of the contingent—could in no way hope to become universal nor acquire the truth of a law unless it presented qualities that could be subsumed under law. Thus, traditionally it is the universal that confers on the local its status as a part of the whole. As such, the local or the singular remains the unapprehended. It is, at the most a kind, of exotic particularity: its choice is either to take its place in a totality that assigns it its place or to have only an unthinkable, insensible place.

The new thought of the global now reverses these terms. The global does not pre-exist the local but is the whole of their relations, a networking. As soon as one gives up the center/periphery model or relations, the center is everywhere and the circumference nowhere. At this point, local installations change status: each point is a center in the multiple intersections of the network; each place is in real or virtual communication with all of the others. Each local point implicates the global network, for it is nothing without the multiplicity of singular sites.[5]

What, however, do we mean by "network"? As with "virtual," the idea of a network has existed for a long time. Leibniz is certainly its most remarkable and profound exponent in the Western philosophical tradition. Recently, however, the idea of "network" has taken on an importance that corresponds exactly to the recent transformations in information and communication sciences. What is characteristic of a decentered network is that each entry is as good as any other because each node, being linked multiply to several others, finds itself in rapid succession in contact with all the others. The network transforms the relation of the local to the global in several ways. Here are three:

1. *Reserves.* The power of older civilizations (and ours is still of the old) was tied to the concentration in one place of all the instruments of domination, influence, and organization (arms, money, communication centers, bureaus, knowledge, production, and so forth). We might think of this as the "stock." Such an understanding was, famously, the basis for Weber's definition of the state as the "monopoly of the legitimate means of violence in a given territory." Who controlled a given stock—a monopolist, so to speak—controlled that world. However, the monumental conception of power has been, or is becoming, obsolete.[6] From now on, we might say, stock is flux. Flux goes through individual sites and raises them to the level of the global.

2. *Folds.* In addition to the simple dispersion of previously existing elements, there is most importantly their simultaneous miniaturization. Stock tends to lose in volume what it gains in information: a fold refers to the intensification of information in a similar or smaller space. This is the movement from hardware to software. An electronic chip is a tracery of folds, that is, a package of coded molecules. Each local point is, as it were, a molecule. A local point is not just a point but a center of information: this is what makes it a point of transit and relations. We must therefore be careful of overly simple images that depict the network as a kind of cloth made up out of connections, a sort of immense device composed of intersections. Such a standard picture en-

visages the network as a kind of set of paths or roads, as things going places. One must rather think of it as a neuronal system. In this latter view, connection points are above all points for the *redistribution and transformation* of information. Even more, each point can be a local center of organization, all the while being the place of a connection to the whole. Such a schema may apply to an individual, an institution, a geographic site, or an enterprise.

3. *Ubiquity.* Each site is virtually in every site: in this, the old dream of ubiquity acquires reality. More precisely, the dream is materializing itself, in various ways. There is the ubiquity of bodies that can now change continents in the space of a few hours, taking trips that used to require weeks or months. Even more, communication techniques permit us to intervene in real time and at the same moment at different places on the planet.

From all this one can conclude that if virtual space is not new, what is new is the mode of relations in this space. The network model that prevails in connected systems permits a previously impossible affirmation and acknowledgement of the local. It is here that we find a new public space, new not because it is virtual but because it permits an integration of individual spaces into a common one without thereby emptying them of their singularity. This opens, we think, a new chapter for democracy.

Are we to think of this as a direct democracy? We turn now to that question.

### Virtual Community and Direct Democracy

The public space of the ancient city was, at least in Greece, a real and in no ways metaphorical space. With its public spaces and buildings (assembly, council, temples, theaters, stadiums), the agora was the space in the democratic city where citizens could assemble, meet one another, enter into dialogue, disagree. The Greek Assembly, the *ekklèsia,* was a direct democracy and not a representative one. All citizens were statutory members. The five hundred members of the council, the *boulé,* were chosen by lot. Public political space was directly in the sight of citizens.[7] For a long time this criterion seemed so integral to the definition of a democracy that Montesquieu and Rousseau thought it indispensable. For Montesquieu, democracy was the ideal regime, but because contemporary states comprised millions of members, he concluded that a democratic regime was no longer possible in the modern world. Rousseau approached the problem from the other end. He urged that states be limited in size or even reduce themselves in size in order to make possible local democracies at the community level. At the level of what constitutes a political community as such, he thus refuses to countenance any form of representation: famously, the general will cannot be delegated.[8] To summarize a long story, Rousseau comes to an impasse: while there is no reason *in principle* that a state cannot be large and democratic, it is also the case *in fact* that the larger the state, the more powerful will have to be the institutions that can maintain its virtue and thus the greater the danger that they will become corrupt.

In contemporary societies public space, however, is no longer physically perceivable such that citizens would be present in person. Instead, such a space becomes metaphorical and designates not a physical meeting place but a nonvisible network of positions. Before radio, when a politician gave a speech to parliament (say, in England in the seventeenth century or in France during the Revolution), he was only heard by the representatives present. The rest of the nation learned of this speech in the press or by oral transmission. The political community was already virtual.

However, neither radio nor television makes citizens' presence more immediate. They rather enshrine a space that is public only as a network. In fact, democracy only functions as a virtual public space when it is no longer direct. Representation is thus necessary to a virtual public space. Even in Athens, three quarters of the citizens were absent from the Assembly; of the thirty thousand citizens recorded during the fifth and fourth centuries BCE, at most only several thousand attended even the most important meetings. Six thousand present is generally understood to be the (rarely attained) upward limit.[9]

Today, we confront a new situation: for the first time since the ancient city, direct democracy appears technically possible. One can, in fact, imagine that all citizens in a given state would be able to cast an electronic vote (with appropriate security mechanisms assured). It would thus seem possible to place public decisions before millions of voters on a regular basis. One might think, then, that voice had at last been returned to the citizenry and that a major step forward in the history of democracy had been taken. But is this the case?

Certain technical limitations are immediately apparent. It would be easy to vote but it would not be practically possible to hold a debate among several million people. As we have said, democracy is not, first and foremost, free and solitary voting by each individual but rather public and agonistic debate, argument in and between a community of citizens. There would, furthermore, be a question of who and how the agenda would be set, and of who and how the questions to be decided would be formulated. For this, one would have to set up committees, thereby immediately reintroducing the principle of representation.

These, however, are empirical difficulties and not fundamental ones. The real problem has to do with the question of political justice and the very nature of a democratic system. Any democratic system is essentially contractual, not only in the sense of a fundamental compact (Rousseauist, or other) but in a more restrained sense of an agreement on the procedures and practices of justice that each agrees to observe, of the rules of the game that one acknowledges as prima facie obligatory. We have in mind such practices as these:

- At regular intervals (say four or five years) citizens are called to chose representatives who have defined programs or values in a general framework shaped by political organizations that are recognized as parties.
- The victory of one group—a majority—leads to that group being entitled to control the workings of a legislature for a certain period.
- Unless such a government is unseated or a majority is lost by defection, it is accepted that this group will continue to so control matters until the end of its term.
- Laws passed by a majority are accepted as the law of the land and oblige all citizens to respect them.

And so forth. A democratic system can only work by means of such rules and practices, each of which have the quality of being publicly recognized and accepted forms of mediation.

Naïve discussion of electronic democracy neglects these ordering practices of justice. It is equally naïve to believe that the development of the media is an automatic guarantee of information and an assurance of public liberty. The media have become a source of danger for democracy not so much in that they provide means that might be exploited by totalitarian forces (and the twentieth century knows enough examples here) but by the daily confusion that they have brought about—even in the best democracies—between public and private space. This is a confusion between all that is new in this realm (and, indeed, all that is news) and *public debate* between citizens. It has become, all too frequently, a confusion of the public display of the private person of political figures with political information itself—a confusion of entertainment and political debate.

## Conclusion

Just as Rousseau raised questions about the geographical, climatic, and demographic preconditions for any "people that would constitute" itself,[10] so must we also ask ourselves about the technological conditions underlying a new political compact: How have the changes in means of communication and public debate changed the possibilities of democracy? It is the case that virtual public space only makes concrete actual networks that were before in fact real. This is, however, an important transformation for two reasons. First, in terms of the two dimensions of public space we discussed in the introduction, it radically alters a traditional intransitive relation into a transitive and interactive one; second, it raises unavoidably the possibility of recognition of singular communities in their singularity.

These developments in no way solve the question of public debate. However, they obligate us to rethink the foundations and formulations of the very nature of the political contract that will define democracy as we move into the twenty-first century. What is new is less the existence of invisible communities than the opportunity given to the local to be heard and articulated in all or localities. The new agora becomes the public network of singular sites: it is without any nostalgia we should say farewell to the old model of a monumental public space.

## Notes

1. Cf. Marcel Hénaff, "Les routes de Lumières ou le Naissance de la république des Lettres," *La Philosophie* (Paris, 1985); Deena Goodman, *The Republic of Letters* (Ithaca: Cornell University Press, 1994).

2. Cf. Helen Waddell, *The Wandering Scholars* (New York: Barnes and Nobles, 1958).

3. Voltaire, *Le Siècle de Louis XIV* (Paris: Garnier, 1929), chapter 34.

4. Michel Serres, *Atlas* (Paris: Bourrin, 1995).

5. We recognize a certain debt here to Gilles Deleuze, *Difference and Repetition* (New York: Columbia University Press, 1994), and, with Félix Guattari, *A Thousand Plateaus* (London: Athlone, 1988), where they discuss the idea of a rhizome.

6. Cf. again Serres, *Atlas,* 152–53: "Today, the relation of support structures to delivery structures is reversed. Delivery structures become essential. Of what importance are stockpiling centers when our networks connect them together; if one

wishes they can be dispersed as much as are the nodes that exchange information between themselves."

7. We are thus brought back to the consideration of vision raised by Sheldon Wolin in our introduction to this volume.

8. For a fuller discussion, see Tracy B. Strong, *Jean Jacques Rousseau and the Politics of the Ordinary* (Thousand Oaks, Calif.: Sage, 1994), chapter 3, and C. Nathan Dugan and Tracy B. Strong, "A Language More Vital Than Speech": Music, Politics and Representation in Rousseau," forthcoming in Patrick Riley, ed., *Cambridge Companion to Rousseau* (Cambridge: Cambridge University Press).

9. See Josh Ober, *Mass and Elite in Democratic Athens* (Princeton: Princeton University Press, 1989).

10. See Rousseau, *Social Contract,* Book II, chapters 8–10 in Donald Cress, ed. *The Political Writings of Rousseau* (Indianapolis: Hackett, 1984).

# Contributors

**Sylviane Agacinski** lectures at the Institut des Hautes Etudes en Sciences Sociales in France. She is the author of *Critique de l'égocentrisme, Politique des sexes,* and *Le Passeur de temps, modernité et nostalgie.*

**Benjamin R. Barber** is the Walt Whitman Professor of Political Science and director of the Walt Whitman Center for the Culture and Politics of Democracy at Rutgers University. He is the author of fifteen books, including *Strong Democracy, Jihad vs. McWorld,* and most recently *A Place for Us* and his collection of American essays, *A Passion for Democracy.*

**Marcel Detienne** is the Basil L. Gildersleeve Professor of Classics at The Johns Hopkins University. Among his many books are *The Gardens of Adonis, Cunning Intelligence in Greek Culture and Society* (with Jean-Pierre Vernant), *Dionysus Slain, The Creation of Mythology, Dionysus at Large, The Cuisine of Sacrifice among the Greeks* (with Jean-Pierre Vernant et al.), and *The Masters of Truth in Archaic Greece.*

**Paul Dumouchel** is professor of philosophy at the University of Québec in Montréal. He is the author of *Emotions* and coeditor of *Tolerance, Pluralisme et Histoire.*

**J. Peter Euben** is professor of politics at the University of California, Santa Cruz. He is the author of *Corrupting Youth* and *The Tragedy of Political Theory,* and coeditor of *Athenian Democracy and the Reconstruction of American Democracy.*

**Marcel Hénaff** is a philosopher and anthropology professor at the University of California, San Diego. He is the author of *Claude*

*Lévi-Strauss and the Making of Structural Anthropology* and *Sade: The Invention of the Libertine Body*, both published by the University of Minnesota Press. His *Le prix de la verité: le don, l'argent, la philosophie* (The price of truth: Gift, money, philosophy) will appear in 2001.

**Jacqueline Lichtenstein** is professor of philosophy at the University of Paris X. She is author of *The Eloquence of Color: Rhetoric and Painting in the French Classical Age*.

**Anne Norton** is professor of political science at the University of Pennsylvania. Among her publications are *Republic of Signs: Liberal Theory and American Popular Culture, Reflections on Political Identity*, and *Alternative Americas: A Reading of Antebellum Political Culture*.

**Tracy B. Strong** is professor of political science at the University of California, San Diego. He is the author of *Friedrich Nietzsche and the Politics of Transfiguration, Right in Her Soul: The Life of Anna Louise Strong* (with Helene Keyssar), *The Idea of Political Theory: Reflections on the Self in Political Time and Space*, and *Jean-Jacques Rousseau and the Politics of the Ordinary*. He was the editor of *Political Theory: An International Journal of Political Philosophy* from 1990 to 2000.

**Shigeki Tominaga** is a fellow of the Institute for Research in Humanities at Kyoto University. He is the author of *Toshi no Yûutsu* (Melancholy and the city).

**Dana R. Villa** is the author of *Socratic Citizenship, Arendt and Heidegger: The Fate of the Political*, and *Politics, Philosophy, Terror: Essays on the Thought of Hannah Arendt*. He is the editor of *The Cambridge Companion to Hannah Arendt*. He teaches political theory at the University of California, Santa Barbara.

**Samuel Weber** is professor of comparative literature and director of the Paris Program in Critical Theory at the University of California, Los Angeles. His books include *The Legend of Freud, Return to Freud: Jacques Lacan's Dislocation of Psychoanalysis*, and *Unwrapping Balzac*.

# Index

Abélès, Marc, 43ff
Adorno, Theodor, 109, 139
Advertising: and public space, 192
Agora, 1, 11f, 44–47
Agora Coalition, 214ff; principles of, 215ff
Alberti, Leon Battista, 18–20
Allarde, Pierre-Gibert, 79, 81
American Revolution, 49
Appearance, 21
Arendt, Hannah, 5, 110, 124, 132, 135, 138, chapter 7, passim; and action 155f; and common sense of the world, 150; against expressivism, 155ff; 166; on Lessing, 147f, 166; in *On Revolution,* 153; and the place of the other, 135; and public sphere, 145; and theatricality, 155
Aristophanes, chapter 5, passim; as political educator, 98ff; and Socrates, 101; and television comedy, 111; *The Clouds,* 103f; *The Frogs,* 98;
Aristotle, 5, 6–7, 132, 136f, 167, 172, 184
Artifactuality: as condition of public space, 5 ff, 22f
Audience: for Habermas, 160; in Nietzsche, 125, 178ff; in Sennett, 163f

Author: as artist and monarch, 74ff; as self-authoring, 76f; and theatricality, 38

Bayle, François, 223
Benda, Vaclav, 110
Benhabib, Seyla, 125, 145ff, 152, 154ff
Benjamin, Walter, 130, 178; *Origins of German Mourning Play,*181ff
Bloch, Marc, 13f
Bodin, Jean, 20
Bourdieu, Pierre, 108
Brasart, Patrick, 42
Brecht, Benjamin, 181f
Brissot, Jacques-Pierre, 84ff
Brunelleschi, Filippo, 18
Buzot, François-Nicolas-Léonard, 82, 90

Castells, Manuel, 201
Certeau, Michel de, 190
Cities: Greek, 51f; and graffiti, 126; and malls, 126; and philosophy, 10f; and the senses, 189; and sound, 189
Citizenship, 82ff
Civil society, 39
Cleisthenes, 41
Comedy: and politics in Athens, 98ff; and public space, 39–40